China and the Global Economy in the 21st Century

As China continues to ride out the global economic crisis while still retaining year-on-year remarkable GDP growth, it is increasingly important to understand how this 'new' economic giant, with its communist-capitalist political economic system, operates its economic and business environments. This book is designed to scientifically examine the contextual variables that foster sustainably dynamic economic growth in China. In particular, the contributors provide an incisive analysis of the contextual bases underlying such a dramatic rising economic power and the immense implications for enterprises and countries involved in dealing with China. Drawing on the latest studies and cutting edge research findings, this book analyses FDI, project management, internationalization, the continued role of state-owned enterprises and doing business in China.

As such it will be essential reading for all students of Chinese business and economics, as well as businesses seeking to develop a critical understanding of the driving global economic force which is China.

John Saee is the former Dean of the School of Business Administration and Faculty of Communication Studies at the International University in Germany and the Editor-in-Chief of the *Journal of Management Systems*.

Routledge Studies in the Growth Economies of Asia

China and the Global Economy in the 21st Century

John Saee

LONDON AND NEW YORK

First published 2011
by Routledge
2 Park Square, Milton Park, Abingdon, Oxon OX14 4RN

Simultaneously published in the USA and Canada
by Routledge
711 Third Avenue, New York, NY 10017

Routledge is an imprint of the Taylor & Francis Group, an informa business

British Library Cataloguing in Publication Data
A catalogue record for this book is available from the British Library

Library of Congress Cataloging in Publication Data
A catalog record for this book has been requested

ISBN 978–0–415–67051–7 (hbk)
ISBN 978–0–203–80638–8 (ebk)

Typeset in Times New Roman
by Book Now Ltd, London

This research book is dedicated to the memories of my beloved mum and dad

Contents

Illustrations

Tables

Figures

Contributors

John Saee has for the past twenty years or so held senior leadership/managerial and professorial appointments in industry and universities internationally, including Chair Professor and Academic Director at a leading French elite University in France, and Academic Leader/Head of School and Director of Doctoral programs at Australian universities. He is Chair Professor of International Economics and Human Resources, and former Dean of the School of Business Administration and Faculty of Communication Studies at the International University in Germany. Professor Saee is an international research award winning scholar who has authored more than 250 international research publications comprised of books and research articles published by leading international publishing houses and in major international journals, as well as in publications relating to refereed international conference proceedings; he is also Editor-in-Chief of the *Journal of Management Systems* and serves as Editor-in-Chief of nine other internationally refereed academic journals.

Donald Henry Ah Pak is at Xi'an Jiaotong-Liverpool University, Department of Business, Economics and Management, China.

Xiaoming Ding is at Xi'an Jiaotong-Liverpool University, Department of Business, Economics and Management, China.

Gaston Fornes is at the University of Bristol, UK and ESIC Business and Marketing School, Spain.

Yu Guocai is at the Institute of International Economics, Nankai University, China.

Yuanfei Kang is at the School of Management, Massey University, New Zealand.

Ramiro Mora is a lawyer with a postgraduate degree in International Business and he is also an Executive Assistant to the Leader, New Democratic Party of Ontario, Canada.

Li Ping is at the Business School, Shandong University of Technology, China.

Francis Schortgen is Assistant Professor in the Department of Political Science and International Studies, University of Mount Union, Ohio, USA.

Preface

China's spectacular rise in global economic power has been observed with considerable admiration in many quarters around the world. For the purposes of illustration, not only has China enjoyed a remarkable sustained economic growth since its open-door policy in 1979, but has also steadily improved its foreign exchange currency reserves, which have increased to about US$2.4 trillion in 2009, up by US$453 billion for the year. These stupendous figures – and the likelihood that the country's reserves will continue to rise in 2010 and beyond – render China a superpower in terms of a financial, economic and geopolitical reality globally (Samuelson, 2010).

With this in perspective, this research book is designed to scientifically analyse the contextual variables that have thus far fostered a sustained annual high economic growth rate in China while rendering it the number one world champion in terms of China's largest volumes of international trade globally in 2010.

Chapter 1 provides an incisive analysis of the contextual bases underlying such a dramatic rising economic power, with immense implications for enterprises and countries involved in dealing with China. The next seven chapters based on the latest studies and cutting edge research findings illuminate various dimensions of Chinese society and the Chinese economy in terms of foreign direct investment, cultural issues, and economic issues including, internationalization of Chinese firms and investment, research and development and internationalization of automotive industries and corporate governance and performance of state-owned enterprises in China, coupled with bilateral trade with Australia and other trading partners. A critical examination in this research book is also made of organizational issues such as the Chinese global mindset and Chinese business practices, as well as Chinese corporate governance related issues together with strategies for international project management in China. Finally, Chapter 9 analytically synthesizes and summarizes the key findings of the entire book, while providing a spectrum of strategic reflections on prospects and challenges confronting Chinese society in terms of their economic and social development sustainably, all of which give considerable insight to government policymakers and captains of industries globally, as well as to students specializing in international trade.

Acknowledgements

I wish to express my grateful appreciation to my family and friends, as well as to my students and colleagues from around the world, for their kind encouragement, support and inspirational feedback during the writing of this research book; these include Katrin Walz, Renate Renz, Erwin Renz, Heidrun Walz, Helmut Walz, Ryzagul Jon, Qamardeen Jon, Nuria Jon, Dennis Ottley, Frank Percy, Tom Kartel, Kiram Jon, Mohamed Baqaahi, Bruce Roberts, Pierre Steux, Parween Jon, Tsunehiko Nawano, Ameer Mohamed Jon, David Hayward, Ed Needle, Elian Chekroun, Stephanie Rogers, Barry Graham, Shirley Saunders, Terry Claque , Qiyaam Jon, Elias Hadzilias, Robert DePold, Julian Chang, Ilan Alon, Christoph Lattemann, John R.McIntyre, Marc Fetscherin, Danial Boyle, John Soccio, Ric Small, Qandighul Jon, Manuela Tvaronaviciene, Theodor Valentin Purcarea, Pascal Ameye, Henri Jolles, Claude Baco, Philippe Tesse, Wil Hamel, Liviu Voinea, Maureen Allen, Nadira Jon, Omar Jon and Carl Rower.

I also wish to record my profound gratitude to anonymous reviewers of this research book (as previously commissioned by Routledge/Taylor & Francis publishing group), along with the many anonymous reviewers who provided scholarly reviews of the research articles (which now form the chapters in this research book), prior to their presentations at Harvard International Conferences held in 2008 and 2009 at Harvard University, Boston, MA. I also wish to acknowledge Taylor & Francis for permission to publish an earlier version of Chapter 3 which has since been updated and revised with special reference to China.

1 International investment strategy in China

Opportunities, prospects and challenges confronting multinational corporations and global entrepreneurs

John Saee

Napoleon Bonaparte once referred to China as a 'sleeping giant', but I maintain that 'the sleeping giant' is awakened and is now pushing forward with full rigour the growth-engine for the global economy in the 21st century (John Saee, 2011).

Introduction

Generally speaking, the main players contributing to such a spectacular foreign direct investment (FDI) globally have been the multinational corporations (MNCs).

With that in mind, the production of goods and services by an estimated 79,000 MNCs and their 790,000 foreign affiliates continues to expand, and their FDI stock exceeded US$15 trillion in 2007. The United Nations Conference on Trade and Development (UNCTAD) estimates that total sales of MNCs amounted to US$31 trillion – a 21 per cent increase over 2006. The value added (gross product) of foreign affiliates worldwide represented an estimated 11 per cent of global gross domestic product (GDP) in 2007, and the number of employees rose to some 82 million of the Chinese national economy. On the whole, FDI flows to South, East and Southeast Asia including China rose to a new record level in 2007, reaching US$249 billion (UNCTAD, 2008).

Key variables contributing to this exponential growth in FDI included a favourable business sentiment about the region's economies, the significant rise in cross-border merger and acquisition (M&A) sales and progress towards further regional economic integration and country-specific attributes. While East Asia continued to represent the lion's share of FDI to the region, flows to South and Southeast Asia also increased significantly. China including Hong Kong remained the largest FDI recipients in the region (as well as in developing economies as a group) (see Table 1.1 showing the top five recipients of FDI inflows).

China as a host destination country for FDI

For much of the twentieth century, China's economy was closed to foreign competition. This changed in 1978 when the Chinese Government adopted its "open-door" policy (*kaifang zhence*), a strategy aimed at internationalizing the country's economy. This was followed quickly by the enactment of the Law of

Table 1.1 South, East and Southeast Asia: top five recipients of FDI inflows, 2006–2007 (billions of dollars)

Country	FDI inflows (billions of dollars)	
	2006	*2007*
China	**72.7**	**83.5**
Hong Kong	45.1	59.9
Singapore	24.7	24.1
India	19.7	23.0
Thailand	9.0	9.6

Source: adapted from UNCTAD (2008).

the People's Republic of China on Joint Ventures using Chinese and Foreign Investment (1979), which granted FDI legal status in China. This law, and its subsequent amendments, provides the basic legal framework for MNCs to invest in China. Following these developments, FDI in China grew exponentially; particularly in the 1990s. China's strategy for using FDI to promote economic development has three important dimensions. First, from the outset, Chinese authorities pursued the equity joint venture (EJV) as the primary mode for foreign investment, in order to accelerate the transfer of technology and both scientific and managerial know-how (Beamish, 1993). Second, the strategy of opening up the local economy to foreign investors proceeded in stages, targeting initially light manufacturing, followed by more technology-intensive industries and more gradually, the service sector. Third, foreign investors' access to the local economy has also changed gradually, through the creation of specially designated areas for foreign multinational enterprises' (MNEs') operations (Chadee *et al.*, 2003).

Consequently, China has been able to attract enormous FDI. For instance, annual utilized FDI in China (excluding the financial sector) grew from US$636 million in 1983 to US$75 billion in 2007. The cumulative level of FDI in China at the end of 2007 stood at nearly US$760 billion, making China one of the world's largest destinations of FDI.

Manufacturing was the largest sector for FDI flows to China in 2007, accounting for about 55 per cent of the total. The Chinese Government estimates that through June 2007, it had approved over 610,000 foreign funded companies and that 28 million people were employed by such firms, which is almost 10 per cent of all people employed in urban areas (Morrison, 2008).

Trade and foreign investment continues to play a major role in China's booming economy. From 2004 to 2007, the value of total Chinese merchandise trade nearly doubled. In 2007, China's exports (at US$1,218 billion) exceeded US exports (US$1,162 billion) for the first time. China's imports were US$956 billion and its trade surplus was US$262 billion (a historic high). Well over half of China's trade is conducted by foreign firms operating in China. The combination of large trade surpluses, FDI flows, and large-scale purchases of foreign currency have helped make China the world's largest holder of foreign exchange reserves at US$1.5 trillion at the end of 2007 (Morrison, 2008).

Foreign enterprises represent 28 per cent of China's industrial added value and one-fifth of taxation. They export about 57 per cent of the country's total goods and services account for 11 per cent of local employment. China's preferential foreign investment policies, inexpensive labour, increasing purchasing power and improving investment environment, especially after entry into the World Trade Organization (WTO) in 2001, have rendered the country a favourite destination for global investment (Yunshi and Jing, 2005).

The most prominent contribution of FDI has been expanding China's manufacturing exports (Zhang and Song, 2000). Increases in foreign-invested enterprises (FIEs) not only added to China's export volumes, but also enhanced its export structure. While China's exports were ranked 26 in the world in 1980, with a volume of US$18 billion and 47 per cent of its exports as manufactured goods, the corresponding numbers in 2003 were the fifth ranking, US$438 billion, and 92 per cent (National Bureau of Statistics, 1996). The value of exports by FIEs in 2003 (over 90 per cent of them as manufactured goods) was US$240 billion, comprising 55 per cent of China's total exports in that year. FDI has also enhanced China's economic growth through raising capital formation, increasing industrial output, generating employment, and adding tax revenue (Zhang, 2001). The share of FDI flows in China's gross fixed capital formation emerged from a negligible level in the 1980s to 7 per cent in 1992, and then to 12 per cent in 2003. The share of industrial output by FIEs in total industrial output grew from 6 per cent in 1992 to 33.4 per cent in 2002. FDI has also reduced China's unemployment pressure and contributed to government tax revenues. By the end of 2003, the contribution of FIEs is prominent in terms of employment of 23 million Chinese, comprising 11 per cent of the total non-agricultural labour force. Tax contributions from FIEs increased as a result of FDI flows, and their share in China's total tax revenues grew from 4 per cent in 1992 to 21 per cent in 2003 (Zhang, 2006).

Strategic modes of entry by MNCs

Multinational corporations (MNCs) penetrated the Chinese market in a variety of ways including as equity joint ventures (EJVs), contractual joint ventures (CJVs) and the establishment of wholly foreign owned enterprises (WFOEs). From the late 1970s, CJVs were the most important type. Since the late 1980s, EJVs and WFOEs became predominant and recent years have seen a proliferation of WFOEs. EJVs have been a popular entry mode for two reasons. First, the Chinese Government believes that EJVs best serve the Chinese objective of foreign capital, technology, and management experiences. Second, foreign investors hope that by engaging in joint ventures, they secure local partner's assistance within the domestic markets (Zhang, 2002). Deng (2001) observes that many foreign investors have chosen WFOEs as the preferred entry mode in recent years so as to avoid problems associated with EJVs. Multinationals have built more R&D centres in China.

According to UNCTAD (2001), by the end of 2000, MNCs had established more than 100 such centres in China. Most of them are located in Beijing,

Shanghai and Guangzhou. Intensifying market competition has driven the localization of the R&D capacities of MNCs. It can speed up the launch of new products on the domestic market, which is crucial for capturing market share. It can also help improve relations between MNCs and the host country, which often hopes MNCs can transfer more state-of-the-art technologies (Ali and Guo, 2005; Yunshi and Jing, 2005).

Key drivers behind exponential growth of FDI into China

China as a nation offers several specific advantages that are equally considered to be the main drivers underlying FDI. Swain and Wang (1995), Liu *et al.* (1997), Zhang (2000), Wei and Liu (2001), Zhang (2002) and others have argued the key variables of FDI inflows into China identified by FDI theories can be categorized into three classifications: micro, macro, and strategic determinants. Micro-factors concern firm-ownership-specific advantages such as product differentiation and the size of the firm. Macro-determinants of FDI emphasize the market size and the growth of the host country, which is measured by the GDP, GDP per capita, gross national product (GNP), or GNP per capita, as rapid economic development may bring about large domestic markets and businesses. Other macro-factors entail taxes, political risk, exchange rates, and so on. Strategic determinants represent those long-term factors such as to defend existing foreign markets, to diversify firms' activities, to gain or maintain a foothold in the host country, and to complement another kind of investment (Ali and Guo, 2005).

Costs factors are one of the determinants of FDI, among which labour costs have been extensively investigated in studies within this field. China has rich resources of labour and China has paid great attention to the education of its people; therefore, Chinese labourers are of relatively high quality and there are comparatively numerous technical personnel with average salaries at a low level (Andreosso-O'Callaghan and Wei, 2003). Swain and Wang (1995) discovered that there was a positive relationship between the relatively cheap labour in China and inward FDI.

Research showed that FDI in China has been motivated by several factors, including China's potential market size and growth. Another related motivation for FDI is to seek new markets. The larger the market size of a particular province, the more FDI the province should attract. Host countries with larger market size, faster economic growth and higher degree of economic development will attract more market-oriented FDI, as is the case with China (Ali and Guo, 2005).

Other trade costs are also seen to be the catalysts for attracting FDI. For instance, the availability of infrastructure, such as rail lines, is positively correlated with foreign entry, whereas high tariffs on imported inputs hamper entry. Provinces, which are more open to foreign trade, attract more foreign firms. In brief, barriers to trade whether in the form of tariffs on imported inputs, informal barriers to inter-provincial trade or underdeveloped infrastructure can hamper new foreign investors contemplating entry into China. Decreasing internal trade costs increases the extent of supplier and market access, and thus attracts the entry of new foreign firms (Amiti and Smarzynska Javorcik, 2008).

Challenges facing MNCs in China

There are some major challenges confronting MNCs in China. For instance, there is a cultural gap between the East and West, which was caused by societal differences in work attitudes, motivational structures, interpersonal norms, and negotiation patterns that cannot be eliminated in a short time (Luo and O'Connor, 1998; Yi, *et al.*, 2004).

While, China remains the top destination for FDI in the developing world, there are still a number of crucial impediments for foreigners wishing to do business within the country.

These shortcomings are underscored by our business environment ratings. A study by Business Monitor International (2010), as tabulated with a selected number of countries with respect to their respective ratings in Table 1.2, reveals that bureaucracy and the legal framework are the biggest drag on China's overall score of 52.5, while the country also remains uncompetitive with regards to its tax environment.

The Chinese Government is increasingly giving more protection and encouragement to the burgeoning private sector, which is now the most dynamic part of the economy and accounts for most of the country's job growth. However, the commanding nature of China's economy means that bureaucracy remains a key obstacle to doing business within the country and the legal framework is still weak despite two decades of reform (Business Monitor International, 2010).

Consequently, the rule of law is still a major challenge for MNCs operating in China, notwithstanding the fact that new regulatory organizations are being established, and researchers such as Eakeley (1997) claim that 'China is showing an interest in the rule of law' by virtually transforming its legal system. However, there is still considerable debate concerning how fast China is moving toward a

Table 1.2 Business environment rankings index for randomly selected countries

Country	Business environment	Rank
Singapore	83.8	1
Hong Kong	82.2	2
South Korea	73.4	3
Taiwan	65.2	4
Malaysia	61.5	5
Thailand	59.5	6
China	**52.5**	**7**
Philippines	45.0	8
India	39.8	12
Laos	35.2	16
North Korea	11.5	18
Global average	46.1	
Regional average	45.2	
Emerging markets average	42.3	

Source: adapted from Business Monitor International (2010).

Westernized emphasis on the rule of law. Some believe that global business forces will speed the transition as China's need for capital creates a demand for certainty and impartiality. Despite the introduction of the rule of law, traditional Chinese business practices and the Guanxi system still remains a major hurdle for conducting effective international transaction in a transparent and fair manner.

Chinese business practice requires an understanding of Guanxi and Chinese business networks; the two are intertwined and inextricably linked, and it is difficult to try and explain one without the other. Networks are a mechanism used by the Chinese to build trust and speed decision-making, provide customer satisfaction and provide competitive advantage; whereas, Guanxi is a Mandarin word for which there is no precise English translation. Guanxi is essential to business relationships. It has similarities to goodwill, and arises from trust, family relationships and friendship, philanthropy, status, doing favours, receiving favours and reciprocating; it can be earned but like respect it cannot be bought. (For a detailed discussion on these intertwined issues, refer to Chapter 6).

This type of mode of transaction based on Guanxi has produced unethical business practices in China. To illustrate this point, one needs to look at for example the case of McDonalds in China, where they signed a 20-year lease with the Beijing municipal government to open a restaurant in a prime location. But in 1994, the Beijing government told McDonalds to vacate, because a well-connected businessman, Li Ka-shing, wanted to build an office-shopping-residential complex on the same site. McDonalds, holding a valid lease, took the Beijing government to court, but ultimately lost the case. It is well known that Li Kashing has been a close friend of Chinese Communist Party leaders for a number of generations; thus, he was able to use his personal relationships with Chinese officials to influence the legal system in order to secure the site. In the end, McDonalds defeat was hardly a surprise (Hill, 2003). Bo (2000) argues that there is a prevalence of perceived corruption within Chinese society.

According to He Zengke, cited in Zhu (2008), four kinds of corruption are identified by the Chinese official terminology. These are: (a) crimes (especially economic crimes) committed by government officials while on duty; (b) a variety of malpractices in government agencies where officials use public power for private gains; (c) extravagant use of public funds; and (d) immoral conduct by Party and government officials such as gambling, etc. For instance, from 1993 to 1997 over 387,352 cases of corruption were investigated, of which 16,117 were Communist party members, 17,214 were government officials, 8,144 were public security personnel, and 13,330 economic management officials. Cases of corruption have been increasing with each passing year. In recent years, for example, the number of the cases handled by the discipline and supervision agencies at all levels increased by about 10,000 every year. The number of big and important cases such as those involving big sums of money rose by 10 per cent each year during the same period.

Statistics show that within the 10 years between October 1992 and September 2002, the discipline and supervision agencies at all levels handled over 1.6 million cases. Over 1.5 million cadres were disciplined, with over 47,000 at the section (*chu*) level, nearly 4,000 at the bureau level and almost 200 at the provincial/ministerial level. There seemed no sign of improvement in the subsequent years. Within one year between December 2002 and November 2003, the number of cases of corruption nearly reached 173,000. Approximately 175,000 cadres were disciplined, with more than 6,000 at the section level, over 400 at the bureau level, and 21 at the provincial/ministerial level. The year of 2004 witnessed over 166,000 cases with nearly 171,000 cadres being disciplined (Yiming, cited in Zhu, 2008).

It is worth noting that the amount of money involved in corruption cases has been enormous. Corrupt officials used their power to get huge profits by leasing land improperly, giving credit unlawfully, cheating in the stock exchange or engaging in smuggling. There were as many as 1,780 cases in 2003 that each involved more than 1 million yuan. Among them, 123 cases involved even more than 10 million each (Zhu, 2008).

A possible explanation provided by Bo (2000) is that economic reforms in China have produced the environment conducive to both motives and opportunities for corruption. On the one hand, the economic reforms in China have promoted money fetishism. 'Get rich is glorious' has been a popular slogan of the day. On the other hand, economic reforms have also fundamentally transformed the way in which money is made. Localities, enterprises, and individuals are encouraged to maximize their utilities in a constantly changing environment. Under such circumstances, some cadres used their public offices to increase their personal wealth.

In the same vein, Li (2005) maintains that there is an absence of checks and balances in a relation-based system – namely, Guanxi, in China – and the end result being that the Chinese political system tends to be dominated by a powerful ruler (the Chinese Communist Party); thus the policy tends to favour industry leaders and big business. Consequently, minority shareholders such as portfolio investors are being disadvantaged. This fact was further corroborated by the governance environment index (GEI) in which China was ranked the lowest of all 48 countries, as illustrated in Table 1.3.

Corporate governance in China is also perceived to be weak. Consequently, weak corporate governance can raise the cost of capital, lower the operating performance of industry, and impede the flow of investment. Furthermore, weak corporate governance breeds corruption (Wu, 2005).

A series of corporate scandals in China came to light in 2001, such as Lantian Co. Ltd, an agricultural company that overstated net profits up to US$60 million. Scandals such as Lantian helped to fuel the corporate governance reforms that resulted in the Code of Corporate Governance for Listed Companies in China (2001), issued by the China Securities Regulatory Commission (Mallin, 2004). Nevertheless, the Chinese corporate governance system still has many weaknesses (Braendle *et al.*, 2005; Lin, 2001; Tam, 2002).

A study by Pei (2007) found that the direct cost of corruption in 2003 was as much as US$86 billion; the indirect costs had been incalculable in China. Another related research study conducted in China also identified several obstacles when

Table 1.3 Estimated governance environment index
(GEI) for randomly selected countries

Country	GEI
Finland	6.80
Norway	6.68
Sweden	6.66
Australia	6.09
United Kingdom	5.87
United States	5.82
Germany	5.73
France	5.05
South Korea	3.97
India	3.19
Philippines	2.06
Russia	1.01
China	**0.47**

Source: adapted from Li and Filer (2004).

Notes: high = rule-based, low = relation-based, mean = 4.

The GEI consists of five dimensions: rule of law, political right, public trust, level of corruption, and free flow of information.

investing in China by international firms, including political instability, unsatisfactory foreign trade policy, lack of systematic enforcement of regulations, an unsatisfactory banking system, foreign capital limit, too cumbersome application processes and low productivity (Ali and Guo, 2005).

In recent times, however, Chinese local governments appear to be developing and enforcing the rule of law, which is predicated on an impartial, efficient and fair legal system. However, in practice, to successfully conclude a business transaction in China, one still has to some degree cultivate Guanxi with local government and thus the type of Guanxi that results in special favours from government officials is directly inconsistent with the existence of a just legal system based on the rule of law (Dunfee and Warren, 2001).

According to Zhu (2008) to combat corruption in China may take a lengthy while. The key to the success of combating corruption in China lies at the local levels. Local leading cadres and their behaviour set the tune for local anti-corruption efforts. The present institutional arrangement has enabled the local first-in-commands to use power at their will. Checks on these leaders are basically non-existent. Laws and regulations can do little when confronting them. For example, after Chen Liangyu was removed from his post, Han Zheng, the mayor of Shanghai who served as the city's acting Party chief, commented that institutional supervision over the first-in-command was almost good-for-nothing (People's Daily, 2005). It remains an unsolved problem how major Party and government leaders at and above the county and section level can be supervised, as a large number of them have in fact been involved in one way or another in cases of crime or violating the disciplines of the Party and the government. What has made things even worse is the fact that most people do not have the courage, ability, or even intention to confront those corrupt but still powerful officials (Shao Daosheng cited in Zhu, 2008). The weakened supervision system, therefore, leaves more room for Party and government officials to engage in corruption, either under the guise of boosting the local economy or directly seeking personal gain (Zhu, 2008).

Finally, another formidable hurdle facing MNCs in China, which may require their strategic response for China's continued economic prosperity, is the development of effective human resources, as this issue is identified by several surveys to be an enormous challenge (Weldon and Vanhonacker, 1999). This in turn calls for a systematic MNCs' human resource development, i.e. from recruiting/selecting local Chinese with potential to their training and development, as well as retention of competent personnel in China.

Concluding remarks

Since the initiation of economic reforms in 1979, China has become one of the world's fastest growing economies. This has resulted in China becoming increasingly a major global player in contemporary world economy with an unfettered potential for economic development and business opportunities for MNCs and international entrepreneurs alike.

Notwithstanding these enormous business opportunities and prospects for FDI, as expounded upon previously, there are still several major challenges facing MNCs that could potentially hamper their sustained foreign direct investment strategically. Consequently, it is in the best interest of Chinese society, let alone the MNCs, that the Chinese Government comprehensively addresses these perceived obstacles identified in research studies mentioned previously, including weak corporate governance, corruption, unsatisfactory foreign trade policy, lack of systematic enforcement of regulations, an unsatisfactory banking system and overly cumbersome application processes for FDI, while endeavouring to create and enforce systematic checks and balances based on the rule of law applicable to all in a transparent and impartial manner.

2 An empirical study strategically assessing the role of the state government in corporate governance, ownership and performance of SOEs

Donald Henry Ah Pak and Xiaoming Ding

Introduction

Over the last three decades, China has propelled itself to becoming an economic giant and the world stands in awe; without a doubt, China is a global player and will retain that position for an indefinite time. Foreign direct investment (FDI) is on the increase, the world looks to China for economies of scale, and the literature on 'doing business in China' fills the shelves and a Google search yields close to 100 million hits. This is astounding, a new Rising Dragon in our midst, its relationship to the world has become more maturing and sophisticated and at times, a challenge. It is within this context, that the authors investigate the rise of the state-owned enterprise (SOE) and its associated variables.

With the help of a "communist–capitalist model" China has surprised the world with gross domestic product (GDP) growth averaging 9 per cent for the last decade. It is in a new era and striving to make itself an economic and political force within the global environment.

Although the economy is moving ahead, with breakneck speed, amidst the global crisis, it still has not shed the SOE, and alongside it collective, private and foreign enterprises operate. According to Chang (2001), 'there are about 300,000 state-owned enterprises in China but the real problem lies with these very large enterprises that need ongoing subsidies to survive.' These SOEs employ in the region of over 75 million, so if one works out the economics politically it would not be viable to just close them down.

The problem is that the government cannot afford to constantly inject funds to maintain this ineffective mechanism, but it is doing so and this makes the SOEs less inclined to carry out major restructuring and much needed transformations.

Simultaneously, the central government will launch comprehensive monitoring of enterprises, in areas such as key decision-making and important business operations, making the operation of centrally administered SOEs more transparent.

The study seeks to understand the role of the Chinese Government in regard to the following areas: corporate governance, ownership and the overall role that the government takes in managing SOEs operating in China.

A strategic overview has been undertaken to evaluate the role of the Chinese Government and answer the question whether the government adds or subtracts value to the overall strategic management of the SOEs; a comparison is drawn to evaluate national SOEs in China.

To appreciate the contents is to understand the burden that Beijing has to carry and the reformation it has to incur.

State-owned enterprises in perspective

The current leadership is faced with an enormous burden created by an increasingly inefficient SOE sector. As other sectors of Chinese industry 'modernize,' the SOE sector falls further behind. The hope is that the dynamic effect of improving the overall efficiency of the industrial capitalist sector will allow China's economy to continue at the extraordinary pace of growth that has become expected since the post-1978 reforms began to bear fruit. Failure to meet these expectations, with the subsequent rise in unemployment and slowdown in material improvement in living conditions, could erode the legitimacy of the current regime, shatter the aforementioned relative docility of the populace, and spark increased social unrest.

The question remains on how deep the reform process will be? Will it try for some variant form with elements of capitalism? The leadership is still weighing the potential risks and rewards of different configurations of reform measures. And they are continuing to observe carefully the events unfolding in the rest of Asia and the world.

Openness and ownership

According to a McKinsey report on the assessment of China's SOEs: 'China's state-owned companies, like China itself, are diverse. Many of them would make better partners for multinationals than some of their private-sector counterparts.' Openness, not ownership, is the key. Although, Bruton *et al.* (2004) state that various government ministries were the actual shareholders and they controlled the SOEs, they managed the SOEs according to their own agendas, which may have differed from the best interests of the nation. To address these problems, the State diffused the ownership of most SOEs and transferred control to a board of directors, with the power to appoint the chief executive officer (CEO) and other top SOE managers.

For many years, the West has viewed China's state-owned enterprises in two ways. One opinion is that they are infiltrators to be viewed with suspicion. An example is the Aluminum Corporation of China's (Chinalco) recent multibillion-dollar purchase of a stake in Rio Tinto, which raised fears about China's agenda for the acquisition of Australia's resources. The other viewpoint sees state-owned companies as muscle-bound goons: without the brains of a private company but with plenty of brawn. In this characterization, they are relics of a failed economic experiment that still dominate the national economy, controlling natural resources, utilities, and many other vital sectors. Their power and influence – particularly their links to the ruling Communist Party and government – give partners and competitors pause for thought.

Both views, however, fail to recognize that as the Chinese economy evolves, it is no longer so easy or desirable to pigeonhole SOEs. Over the next five years, as the economy and business climate continue to shift, the ownership structure of state-owned companies will matter much less than the degree of openness they show in their business practices and management – that is, their transparency and receptiveness to new ideas.

A more current view would, for example, have them consider more favourably the value that certain state-owned companies might bring to a global partnership. A realistic multinational must also recognize that they will become more attractive to top talent and, probably, more innovative. Both developments will ratchet up the level of competition.

Many observers define a Chinese state-owned company as one of the 150 or so corporations that report directly to the central government. Thousands more fall into a grey area, including subsidiaries of these 150 corporations, companies owned by provincial and municipal governments, and companies that have been partially privatized yet retain the state as a majority or influential shareholder. State-owned companies of all kinds have gradually been losing some of the advantages once conferred by their relationship with the state. Since the 1980s, the Chinese Government and the ruling party have followed a policy of *zhengqi fenkai*, which formally separates government functions from business operations. The policy has been applied gradually, first to the consumer goods industry, then to high-technology and heavy manufacturing, and, more recently, to banking, as officials have attempted to strengthen domestic businesses and the economy to prepare them for unfettered global competition.

As a result, government favouritism toward state-owned companies is fading. Top officials have started holding them more accountable for their successes and failures. Their access to capital at below market rates has been severely limited. From 1994 to 2005, 3,658 state companies failed, according to official statistics. More such bankruptcies are likely.

As the distinction between a state-owned and private enterprise blurs, the challenges that both face are converging. Chinese companies, in the public or private sector, must gain approval from government officials for cross-border merger and acquisition (M&A) and other global activities. Even the top-tier state-owned companies – those reporting directly to the central government – struggle with many of the same problems confronting their private-sector counterparts as they move beyond China's borders.

A better way to judge a Chinese state-owned company (and a private-sector one as well) is to examine the openness of its organization. Experience in developed and developing markets alike shows that open companies, in either the public or the private sector, have a greater chance of prospering. An open company is institutionally more adept at understanding the context of its business and pushing through the necessary responses to change. One important indicator of a company's openness is its approach to talent: open companies are willing to bring in external managers, including foreigners, as needed. Other indicators of openness are the efforts that companies make to broaden their investor base, to adopt best-practice governance systems, and to embrace new ideas no matter what the source might be. Open companies are also more transparent and have a greater awareness of risk, particularly during overseas expansion, because they take part in a broader dialogue with their stakeholders and are more willing to challenge internal shibboleths. All told, open companies are more likely to understand and adapt to different environments; closed ones are much less flexible.

Further blurring the distinction, market forces unleashed by government reforms are pushing state-owned companies to become more open. The need for capital and the desire for new markets abroad are significant factors. International public offerings, even when they represent a small fraction of total shares, create more transparent reporting requirements. Evaluating Chinese companies by their degree of openness and not their ownership is more than an academic exercise. By accepting the idea that a state-owned Chinese company can be an open one (and that a private-sector Chinese company can be closed), competitors and potential partners alike can more accurately assess the threats and opportunities posed by state-owned companies entering global markets – and respond with knowledgeable rather than reactionary strategies. For multinationals, four areas will be significant.

Corporations outside China should increasingly see the country's open SOEs as partners in global markets rather than only as conduits into the Chinese market. Such companies, which have global aspirations and easier access to capital than their private-sector counterparts do, will help to propel a larger, more sustained wave of Chinese cross-border acquisitions than we have seen thus far. They should be accepted as peers capable of adding value to joint ventures around the world and as credible buyers of assets.

Global leaders – public and private – must recognize the importance of taking a nuanced view of China's state-owned companies. On closer inspection, many are quite different from the stereotypes. Multinationals that recognize this reality will be a step ahead of the game as Chinese state-owned companies pursue their global ambitions.

Policymakers in the developed world would also do well to understand these nuances. Rather than discouraging investment by an entire class of Chinese companies, they should consider the benefits of attracting well-run, open ones. The goal should be to draw quality global investment, no matter what its geographic origin or ownership. Arbitrary legislative barriers and economic disincentives will lead only to missed opportunities as open companies seek out more welcoming locations.

China's SOEs: board governance and the Communist Party

Huang and Orr (2007) state that as the state-owned sector attracts strategic investors, they find themselves befuddled by the role of an almost invisible power: the Communist Party.

As more and more major Chinese SOEs list in Hong Kong and on international exchanges, the governance of those companies has become an increasingly important issue. This trend has been reinforced by the fact that foreign strategic investors are now allowed – for the first time – to acquire a significant shareholding in SOEs listed on China's renminbi-denominated A-share exchanges, in Shanghai and Shenzhen.

Too often, however, investors and independent international directors remain unsure how governance really works in China's SOEs and how it is changing. Outside directors on boards may be frustrated or simply puzzled by the seemingly invisible forces that make important decisions about, for example, appointments of chief executives or major acquisitions. In China's SOEs, the board of directors often seems to have no more than the ability to rubber stamp the big decisions. Investors are rightly concerned about how key decisions are made in companies in which the majority shareholder is still the government and the Communist Party plays a powerful if shifting role. By better understanding that role in the governance of SOEs, foreign companies can learn to deal with them more effectively.

China has 70 million party members, and a typical SOE may have hundreds if not thousands of them on the staff. Consequently, as long as a company remains an SOE, the Communist Party committee plays a pivotal role in key decisions – for example, the nomination of top executives, executive evaluation and compensation, asset acquisitions and disposals, and annual budgets. Sometimes the party committee may even get involved in operational decisions, such as whether to take on a specific major supplier or to purchase housing for key employees.

True, the party recognizes that boosting the market value of SOEs is good for the economy and therefore in its own best interests. It also understands that conflict between the board and the party committee will hurt the valuation of an SOE because of the 'governance discount' that foreign investors apply. As a result, the party is paying greater attention to investor reactions and is increasingly willing to seek out and test solutions.

This is easier said than done, however. Although most academics, government and party officials, and company executives accept broad best-practice principles, few are putting much effort into designing the details necessary to implement good governance, because of the apparent domestic sensitivities and complexities involved. Foreign investors, in other words, should not expect China's SOEs to reach world-class standards of corporate governance anytime soon.

Which is hardly to say that there is not an evolving debate in the government about the party's role in decision-making: there is. Key questions that have arisen recently include just how many directors the party should appoint, which decisions it should influence, and how involved it should be in evaluating executives and determining which posts they should move to and when.

By following the current debate and trying to understand where the party committee draws the line, foreign investors will be able to focus their efforts more successfully. On some issues they will have little leverage: for instance, on appointments of top personnel, at least for the foreseeable future, outside directors can express their views, but the party committee will make the final decision. On issues concerning company strategy or major deals, however, the party values the views of strategic investors more highly. A seat on the strategy committee can be crucial because it exposes outside directors to issues and their associated data before they come before the full board. At one company, by the time investment decisions worth hundreds of millions of dollars came before the board, the role of that body was typically just to conduct a yes-or-no vote based on a one-page summary. By joining the strategy committee, one international board member was able to gain greater influence over decisions, to introduce international benchmarks on capital intensity, and to influence the timing of the company's investments.

Best practice is to obtain the SOE's organization chart showing both party committee members and senior executives. Then investors must ask themselves whether they have covered most of the real decision makers (including those who do not speak the investors' home language) and whether their influence is broad enough to get the party committee's attention.

Foreign strategic investors have a crucial role to play in upgrading the standards of corporate governance in China's SOEs. Unfortunately, we have seen far too many foreign investors fail to appreciate the importance of the Communist Party. They should actively participate in the ongoing governance debate in China, the better to safeguard their own investments and to help SOEs move closer to international best practice. While a confrontational push for a major change of direction will achieve little, constructive input on how to move forward step by step can create real momentum for change.

The process of reformation and corporate governance in China

As the Chinese Government grants these enterprises more commercial freedom and puts in place the legal and financial framework essential to a market economy, the SOEs themselves face a tremendous challenge in developing competitive strategies, renewing their organizations, restructuring their financing, and reacting to a fast-changing regulatory environment. Revitalizing the ownership structure, management, and operational performance of China's SOEs is an economic necessity: subsidies to SOEs topped US$90 billion in 1992 – an unsustainable 14 per cent of government revenue. It is also a philosophical necessity: the country's leaders now recognize that continued economic growth depends on the introduction of market and business discipline.

Corporate governance has received much attention in China in recent years. At the core of such attention is the debate on how China can develop an effective corporate governance system to improve its listed companies' performance and protect the minority shareholders (Liu, 2006: 415/6). He further states: 'Improving the level of the Chinese firms' corporate governance practice is an ongoing battle that calls for the participation of many parties, including regulators, market participants and academics.' Due to data availability, most studies so far have focused on listed firms and this study takes that approach too.

Lin (2001) investigated the economic transition in China's corporate governance and concluded that a major factor impacting on this is the relatively underdeveloped market and legal institutions and processes. Many of the shortcomings in the actual practice of corporate governance derive from peculiar cultural and political governance traditions. Tam (2002) concluded that in order for China to have the same mechanisms in place as the United States for example, but given the severe problems of many state firms, getting corporate governance is critical.

Most of the literature concentrates on the West and their 'best-practices model'. Fundamentally, the researchers argue that China is culturally different and, given the dramatic differences between the West and China, not only in terms of culture, but also its foundations of law, company formation and structures, China is a special case deserving an individual study (Wei and Geng, 2008).

To comprehend and fully appreciate the corporate governance of Chinese firms, one has to bear in mind that China is continuously changing and is going through phases as the central government slowly and carefully surveys the market and proceeds cautiously before implementing models or legislature in practice.

Chung *et al.* (2005) provide additional insight into Chinese corporate governance issues and the problems faced, and categorically state it is vital for Chinese companies to maintain competitiveness and efficiency, and to rely on domestic/foreign capital. Issues of corporate governance come from various sources. First, the separation of ownership and control within an organization gives rise to the agency cost. Second, the contract theory argues that it is difficult to specify complete terms of contracts for the company in which stockholders maintain residual control and managers receive ex post control rights. The implication is that closer attention should be given to the overall relationship among stakeholders like shareholders, managers, creditors, debtors, employees, suppliers and consumers (Wei, 2003).

Sound corporate governance needs to define more clearly the objective of the corporation in order for us to assess the performance of the corporation. Although value maximization for shareholders is an ultimate goal of a corporation among other objectives such as social responsibility and workers welfare, the achievement of the goal presumes an efficient and competitive capital market in which the corporation operates. To alleviate the agency problem, several mechanisms, such as the board of directors, an annual meeting of the shareholders and a supervisory board, have been put in place for checks and balances on the activities of the corporate agents. We need to understand better the forces behind the corporate governance structure of a company, such as individual ethics and corporate cultures, internal control, the incentive mechanism, the market and external monitoring mechanism, and the regulatory framework, in order to improve the corporate governance structure for China (Ho, 2003).

As China moves toward a market-oriented economy, much effort has been put into shaping China's own corporate governance structure. Policymakers have tried to build China's own model based on both the insider-based and outsider-based systems, but the prerequisites for the proper functioning of the models are not well developed in China. Absence of a liquid equity market results in the failure of a competitive financial market for corporate control in monitoring the management. The state still possesses substantial control in listed companies rendering the insider-based mechanism ineffective. The new regulation to transform non-tradable shares to tradable shares and the requirement of a simple majority vote for future projects are steps in the right direction. China should continue to enhance private ownership and improve the legal institution as a protection of individual property rights. This area appears to be promising as the new laws on protection of individual property will be enacted in accordance with the new Constitution adopted by China in 2004.

In addition to improving information disclosure requirements and board structure for better corporate governance structure of the Chinese companies, the Chinese Government also cannot ignore the development of a well-functioning capital market, which Chinese policymakers have an equally challenging task to accomplish. Continual efforts need to aim at improving the transparency, information flows, and trading mechanism of the capital market, which would give market participants important signals and, thus, in turn help discipline the corporate managers. Apparently, the immediate challenge to reform the stock market is ultimately for the smooth transition of all non-tradable shares to tradable ones.

The challenges faced by Chinese enterprises come from both internal and external competition. As China is going to be open to foreign competitors in light of World Trade Organization membership in the goods market and foreign investors in the financial market through qualified financial institutional investors programs, Chinese companies need a good governance structure for sustainable growth and competition. Sound governance practice is therefore indispensable in China as the economy makes these transitions. Li *et al.* (2006) investigate the antecedents and outcomes of market orientation during these transitional times and states, that institutional forces are affecting SOE behaviour and as the economic reforms has broadened, the SOE have evolved toward more autonomy in their operations, and the government has gradually streamlined its economic agencies/sections and changed their functions from a direct administrative role of monitoring subordinate enterprises to a more indirect role of formulating regulations and policies. Yet in an earlier study, Child and Tsai (2005) found that some of the key characteristics of the SOEs' institutional environment still existed: a high-level of control by government, strong bargaining power with government officials, easy access to political privileges, and soft budgets.

SOE role from a neo-classical economics to realistic policy

Lin (2003) asks the pertinent questions: 'What should the government of China do to guide China's economic system during this period of transition? In particular, what should be done with China's state-owned enterprises (SOE)?'

An implicit assumption in neo-classical economics is that 'in an open, competitive market, a firm is expected to earn a socially acceptable profit without any external subsidy or protection, if the firm has a normal management' (Lin, 2003). Firms that are not profitable – in other words, firms that are not viable – will (and according to neo-classical theory, should) fail. This assumption may be suitable for market economies but it may not be for transition economies; with the sale of the SOEs this adds up to a lot of potential investment targets for private and foreign buyers and this has led China to grow in experience and test the waters in the form of green-field Sino-foreign joint ventures, and domestic and offshore

IPOs, and to be able to achieve liquidity of government investments through the public stock markets.

The other key trend in the sale of state-owned assets is M&A activity, both domestic and cross-border, with share acquisitions now more popular than the old-style asset deal.

Its transition process has exhibited two important qualities. It is locally chaotic and unpredictable, but globally stable (Gleick, 1987). The transition process essentially has been the breakdown of old rules. As a result, the Chinese economy has sustained steady growth. Furthermore, the sustained economic growth has made its economy resistant to exogenous social, political, and economic shocks. These qualities would indicate that the Chinese economy has operated in a sort of punctuated equilibrium (Brown and Eisenhardt, 1997).

The economic reform has been a major driving force behind the transition and has been the source of tremendous energy for the Chinese transitional economy. The successful firm faces up to the pressures of a turbulent environment by importing the energy required to sustain the viability of the organizational system.

As time goes by, the scale and scope of the economy also increase, featuring more complex modes of transactions involving more transaction parties. Organizational adaptation over time requires managers to alter the state of their organizations as the environment changes. For example, as competitive pressure escalates, it will become increasingly important that organizations make quick responses to the changing competitive landscape. Thus, it is imperative that managers recognize the strategic and organizational implications of (or requirements for) competing in changing environmental contexts (Slevin and Covin, 1997).

Increased globalization and technological innovation have reshaped the competitive landscape SOEs face. Entry barriers have collapsed due to gradual reform, and customers have become increasingly demanding as the shortage economy typical of a command economy became history. Top management and corporate executives are often elected by the employees, the board, etc. They have greater autonomy and are therefore more responsive to market demands than to policymakers.

Faced with unrelenting uncertainty and turbulence, the firms have no choice but to develop new strategies and new ways of organizing to deal with this exceedingly complicated landscape. As a result, they have become more willing to be innovative and proactive and assume more risks than their predecessors.

This has led to the emergence of new opportunities and a new generation of entrepreneurs grown out of the old state planning system. In terms of real changes in resources and capabilities, many existing organizations may not actively initiate strategic transformation; instead, because of organizational inertia, they may only react to the crisis of the day as it occurs, hoping to 'muddle through' the transitions with minimal changes (McCarthy and Puffer, 1995; Newman, 2000; Whitley and Czaban, 1998).

These firms can 1) significantly improve efficiency and utilize China's low cost labour to compete in low and medium quality markets, and eventually build the position of global low cost leader, 2) maintain strategic flexibility and position themselves as outsourcers and strategic alliance partners for multinational enterprises, and 3) totally revitalize themselves, develop new sets of strategic competencies and competitive advantage, and eventually grow into leadership positions in certain niches. These strategic alternatives require a new generation of corporate leaders who have appropriate vision and who are not imbedded in the old system.

Research methodology

Resource-based view

More recent theoretical contributions focus on the resource-based view (RBV) of the firm and were largely introduced to the field of strategic management in the 1980s and became a dominant framework in the 1990s. Armstrong and Shimuzu (2007: 960) define RBV as 'assets, capabilities, organizational processes, firm attributes, information, knowledge, etc. controlled by the firm' (Barney, 1991: 101). The RBV helps to explain the conditions under which a firm's resources will provide it with a competitive advantage.

The field of strategic management is eclectic in nature, but with the recent development of the resource-based view (RBV) of the firm (e.g. Barney, 1991; Wernerfelt, 1984), it has, once again, increased emphasis on firms' internal strengths and weaknesses relative to their external opportunities and threats. Calls for the use of qualitative methods to identify a firm's resources are increasing as each firm is considered to have a distinctive bundle of resources.

This approach often uses single case studies as used in instruction and by early strategy scholars (e.g. Learned *et al.*, 1965) to study particular firm strategies or industry structure. Another line of research that has also drawn increasing attention is competitor action–reaction studies (see Grimm and Smith, 1997, for a review of this work).

A series of studies using detailed data on competitive moves (Chen and MacMillan, 1992; Chen and Miller, 1994; Smith *et al.*, 1989), studied the dynamics of how firms compete with one another; how they make use of strategies to build competitive advantages over competitors has also been examined (Grimm and Smith, 1997; Smith *et al.*, 1992). Two factors characterize this line of research.

First, a variety of theoretical frameworks have been employed. For instance, Smith *et al.* (1991) used an organizational information processing model to explain the type of action to which a firm is responding and the capabilities of the responding firm. Second, Chen and MacMillan (1992) employed a game theoretic framework to study the effects of competitor dependence and action irreversibility on the characteristics of a firm's response to competitive moves.

Recently, popularity of the RBV of the firm has returned, as can be seen by the focus on the inside of the black box of the firm. The RBV emerged as 'an important new conceptualization in the field of strategic management' and is 'one of the most important redirections of the [content of] strategy research in this decade' (Zajac, 1995: 169).

Theoretically, the central premise of RBV addresses the fundamental questions of why firms are different and how firms achieve and sustain competitive advantage.

Research sub-streams also focus on specific types of resources inside a firm, such as strategic leadership and tacit knowledge. Methodologically, the RBV also has helped the field reintroduce inductive, case-based methods focused on a single or just a few firms into the research to complement deductive, large-sample methods and it is in this essence we intend using the methodology.

The greatest challenge, and at the same time the most interesting aspect, of strategic management as a scholarly discipline is the ever-evolving nature of its research. The fluidity of many strategic issues requires strategy researchers to keep advancing the extant body of knowledge.

As we have entered the new millennium and a new competitive landscape, constituted by rapid technological changes and increasing globalization, financial crises will continue to pose different research questions for strategic management researchers (Bettis and Hitt, 1995). This is reiterated by recent events brought about to extend the RBV theoretically.

One, the 'dynamic resource-based view' of the firm (Helfat, 2000; Helfat and Peteraf, 2003), focuses on the resource side of the firm. This dynamic RBV incorporates the notion central to dynamic capabilities that resources and capabilities are continually adapted, integrated, and/or reconfigured into other resources and capabilities (Eisenhardt and Martin, 2000; Teece *et al.*, 1997). In line with this dynamic view, more attention has been paid to the relationship between resources and strategy implementation (Hitt *et al.*, 2001; Newbert, 2007).

Strategic researchers will be increasingly challenged to respond to frequent, discontinuous changes and provide answers to new problems. In fact, the results of strategic management research will become increasingly important for current executives and in educating future executives (e.g. MBA programs).

As such, the quality of this research and its ability to provide answers to critical strategy questions takes on a new urgency with the highly dynamic competitive landscape (Hitt *et al.*, 1995). Because the nature of strategy problems cannot easily be framed within a fixed paradigm, strategic management is necessarily a multi-paradigmatic discipline, requiring varied theoretical perspectives and methodologies.

Furthermore, as Rumelt *et al.* contended, 'Strategic management as a field of inquiry is firmly grounded in practice and exists because of the importance of its subject' (1994: 9). As a result, because of the practical nature of the field, strategic management is likely to continue to flourish by using a wide variety of theoretical perspectives and methodologies in order to help explain firm performance and as this study wants to research from a strategic perspective the state's role in SOE.

Ferdinand *et al.* (2005) provide a summary; RVB of the firm required further theorization to address competitive advantage in a dynamic fashion, as well as corporate-level concerns, even with its own parameters and underpinning assumptions.

Data analysis

The ordinary least square (OLS) company performance model is used in this study. The model can be expressed as: $Z_{it} = A_{it} + BX_{it} + HY_{it} + \varepsilon_{it}$, where Z is the profitability index, in this study, return on assets or Tobin's q; X is the array of control variables, including five firm-specific variables; and Y is the array of six corporate governance and ownership variables. (See Tables 2.1 and 2.2.)

Table 2.1 List of variables

Profitability	Annual return on asset
TOBIN_Q	Dividing the market value of a company by the replacement value of the book equity
SME	Small to medium enterprise, dummy variable
LOG(TOTAL_ASSETS)	Log value of total assets
LIQUIDITY_RATIO	Measured by near cash or quick divided by current liabilities
DEBT_RATIO	Debt to equity ratio
CAPITALIZATION_RATIO	Ratio measuring the debt capitalization
ULTIMATE_OWNER	Dummy variable measuring the ultimate owner of the company, 1 for state-owned businesses
AGM_ATTENDANCE	Percentage attendance of annual general meeting
CHAIRMAN_CHANGE	Dummy variable measuring the change of board chair, 1 for change
CEO_CHANGE	Dummy variable measuring the change of CEO, 1 for change
INSIDER_HOLDING_PERCENTA	Percentage of insider holding
LOG(NUMBER_OF_SHAREHOLDERS)	Log number of shareholders
HERFINDAHL_5	Sum of the squared percentage of top five shareholders

Source: Ah Pak, D. and Ding, X.M. List of variables researched (2010).

Table 2.2 Sample distribution

Year	Number of observations
1999	822
2000	874
2001	1070
2002	1094
2003	1095
2004	1226
2005	1301
2006	1277
2007	1361
Total	10120

Source: Ah Pak, D. and Ding, X.M. List of data sample distribution: CCER (Centre of China Economic Research), 2010.

Note: The data set was extracted step by step. First, the financial data of the Chinese listed companies was acquired from CCER (Centre of China Economic Research) for all available Chinese listed companies. 14,178 companies-year records were found. At the same time, another data set containing 12,158 company-year of corporate governance information was also established for the same batch of companies from the same source. Then these two datasets were merged. After screening for the availability of the variables, a final dataset containing 10,120 company-year records was established.

Conclusion

Satya (1998) puts the situation in perspective:

> It is clear that the current administration, though cautious about the pace of these reforms, is intent on implementing a more 'free market' version of capitalism, but they are not unaware of the risks involved. Indeed, in many ways the Chinese leadership seems more willing to reform than the leaders of other nations in the region with longer histories of capitalist enterprise, such as Indonesia. And the Chinese leadership confronts a relatively more docile, even if not completely cooperative, population than is the case in many of these other nations.

As time goes by, the scale and scope of the economy also increase, featuring more complex modes of transactions involving more transaction parties.

Organizational adaptation over time requires managers to alter their organizations' states as the environment changes. For example, as competitive pressure escalates, it will become increasingly important that organizations make quick responses to the changing competitive landscape. Thus, it is imperative that managers recognize the strategic and organizational implications of (or requirements for) competing in changing environmental contexts (Slevin and Covin, 1997).

In China's case, the transformation of the economy was not an action but a result of the reform. The transition has essentially opened the economy to the entrance and emergence of new business participants and opportunities. As a result, despite the turbulence and chaos in the environment, with sufficient time, firms have gradually transformed themselves and adopted a new set of strategic orientations.

The co-existence, competition and struggle between two competing systems have led to a transition process with unique 'Chinese characteristics'. And the economy continues to grow. With the reforms underway this also means that no organization will be given preferential treatment and that all will be treated the same under the national regulations.

3 Strategies for best practice in international project management with some reference to China

John Saee

Introduction

Project management provides an organization with powerful tools that improve the organization's ability to plan, organize, implement, and control its activities and the way it uses its people and resources. The need for project management arose as a result of a number of emerging environmental forces in modern society. Of the many emerging environmental forces involved, three feature more prominently:

- the growing demand for complex, sophisticated, customized goods and services;
- the exponential expansion of human knowledge; and
- intense competition among firms for profit maximization and provision of quality service fostered by globalization of the contemporary market economy.

This has in turn put extreme pressure on modern organizations to make their complex, customized outputs available as quickly as possible. Responses must be made faster, decisions must be made sooner and results must occur more quickly (Meredith and Mantel, 2006).

Project management, including international project management, is not simply regarded as an interesting application of previously expounded theory, it is regarded as very much the future of management (Jackson, 1993; Saee, 2007).

Meanwhile it is argued that international project teams are where most of the boundary spanning work in international enterprise goes on, making them a key factor in organizational success and an important catalyst for individual and organizational development. In particular, the ability to learn in and through international project teams is seen as a key developer of a more international outlook. Project teams also help the organization share information, knowledge and resources across boundaries, transmit and recreate corporate culture, and provide examples of best practice (Iles and Paromjit, 1997).

In today's highly competitive and global business environment, project managers face challenges very different from those of the recent past. Historically, project management has its roots in the aerospace and construction industries.

A project is a temporary endeavour undertaken to create a unique product, service, or result (Project Management Body of Knowledge (PMBOK) cited in

Thom, 2009). A more extensive representation of projects is offered by Roberts (2007) who states that: A project is a one-off, temporary activity with a clear start and a clear end; it has full or part-time resources clearly assigned to it; it has a temporary management hierarchy that takes precedence over the company hierarchy; and it sets out to deliver something: an IT system, a new product, etc. This definition considers a project as 'any undertaking with a defined starting point and defined objectives by which completion is identified,' and 'in practice, most projects depend on finite or limited resources by which objectives are to be accomplished' (Yasin, 2000).

Project management serves a number of functions. The functions can be identified in three categories:

1   The general project management processes: project integration, strategic planning, and resource allocation.
2   Basic project management functions: scope management, quality management, time management, and cost management.
3   Integrated project management functions: risk management, HR management, contract management and communication management.

(Dinsmore, 1993; Slack et al., 2001)

The fundamentals of project management

The primary objective of project management is designed to meet and exceed the expectations of the sponsors of the project. These expectations can be categorized in three different ways:

- *Quality* – the project produces desired outcomes with minimum defects.
- *Cost* – the project produces desired outcome for the anticipated cost.
- *Schedule* – the project produces the desired outcome within the anticipated time frame.

(Kahn, 1993)

With that in view, the question arises as to what constitutes the factors underlying project management. A review of the literature (Dinsmore, 1993) points to ten factors that form the foundation for project management, which managers have to carefully consider and implement in their overall project management so as to ensure its success:

1   *Concentrate on interfacing.* This involves both defining frontiers and making efforts at bridge building amongst various areas that have interdependent relationships with the project in question.
2   *Organize the project team.* This calls for selecting qualified team members for the project as well as sound management practices in so far as to ensure high-level motivation of project team members through the appropriate incentive programs coupled with the increased delegation of responsibility for the team members.

3 *Plan strategically and technically.* Use a top-down planning approach whilst breaking the project down into component parts using a work break down structure or other project logic.

4 *Remember 'Murphy's law'.* According to Murphy, 'If anything can go wrong, it will.' Thus, strategies, plans and systems should be tested to ensure fail-safe implementation.

5 *Identify project stakeholders.* Identify who has a stake and influence regarding project outcome, such as clients, users, managers, financiers, suppliers of technology and higher management, and create systems for involving and satisfying their needs and expectations.

6 *Be prepared to manage conflicts.* Apply conflict management techniques: negotiate when interests clash, promote collaboration when talents and capabilities are complementary, force the issue when important principals are at stake, and finally set off conflict, if necessary, to realize project goals.

7 *Expect the unexpected.* Reducing the unexpected helps keep projects on track. In project environments, surprises can be minimized by participative planning, contingency allowances, use of expert opinion, and statistical comparisons with similar prior projects.

8 *Listen to intuition as part of project decision-making.* Intuition reflects the gut feeling formed by the experiences logged over the years.

9 *Apply behavioural skills.* This involves application of sound interpersonal skills on the part of project managers to influence their team members in a positive manner.

10 *Follow up and take remedial action.* Create a system for measuring progress, then estimate that progress against initial plans and take remedial action.

The distinction between line and project management

Research by Jackson (1993) shows that many of the competencies required of project managers are similar in many ways to those required of line managers; there are nonetheless some differences. Whilst it is a truism that project managers like line managers do indeed work to tight schedules and for specific objectives, line management practice is predicated on a 'business as usual' approach, whereas project managers have a 'one off' finite deadline.

Overall, project managers are expected to:

- convert business objectives to project objectives;
- obtain value for money through planning and controlling both physical and human resources over a set period of time;
- integrate complex effort and multi-professional growth of people, often across cultural divides;
- communicate with all levels of management, upward and across;
- react to continual change;
- accelerate innovation and change;

- restructure new teams and develop attitudes and facilitate working relationships, often in a very short space of time;
- work with and satisfy the needs of a client.

(Jackson, 1993; Saee, 2007)

Meanwhile, research by Weiss and Wysocki (1992) shows that for a project manager to be effective, they need to possess five demonstrable attributes and qualifications:

1   background and experience relevant to the project;
2   leadership and strategic expertise;
3   technical expertise in the area of the project in order to make sound technical decisions;
4   interpersonal competence and the people skills to take on such roles as project champion, motivator, communicator, facilitator and politician; and finally
5   proven managerial competencies in relation to a track record of getting things done.

The distinction between project strategy and tactics

There is a major difference between strategy and tactics in project management. Project strategy defines, in a generalized rather than a specific way, how the organization is going to achieve its project objectives and meet the related measures of performance. It accomplishes this in two distinct ways (Saee, 2007). It defines the phases of the project. Phases break the project down into time-based sections; the project strategy sets milestones that are important events during the project's life at which specific reviews of time, cost and quality are made (Slack *et al.*, 2001). Tactics on the other hand refers to client consultation, personnel recruitment and training, identification of tasks, gaining client acceptance, monitoring and feedback, communication and trouble-shooting.

Projects are often typified by a weakness in either strategy or tactics, and this may lead to different types of errors:

- type 1: failing to take an action when one should be taken;
- type 2: taking an action when one should not have been taken;
- type 3: taking the wrong action or solving the wrong problem; and
- type 4: solving the right problem but the solution is not used.

(Jackson, 1993)

Best practice in project management

Research by Pfeiffer (1994) shows that other things being equal, utilization of best practice can lead to competitive advantage for a firm and/or project management. Best practice means adopting managerial practices of the most successful organizations and/or through benchmarking.

Given increasing application of projects worldwide, it becomes necessary to understand the project management system and consider its unique attributes within the international setting. It is within this framework that the best practices for international project management are required to be developed (Smith and Haar, 1993). Thus, the important factors, critical for success and, therefore, needed to be considered for adopting the best practice in project management, are described below.

Conceptualization and initiation

This stage involves identifying the business needs for setting of goals and specific objectives, and gaining support for the project from the key stakeholders by identifying and communicating the benefits of the project (Jackson, 1992).

Planning

Planning is broadly defined as determining what needs to be done, by whom and when, in order to accomplish one's assigned responsibility. It is a process involving the assessment of the environment for opportunities, threats, strengths and weaknesses (Saee, 2006, 2007).

The components of planning normally include objective, program, schedule, budget, forecast, organization, policy, procedure and standards. However, in an attempt to plan the work of a project management team, Johns (1999a,b) has further simplified the process of planning to include only five fundamental management tools, namely:

- *Determination of clear and measurable project objectives.*
- *Work-breakdown structure* – this component of planning enables personnel and clients to get a general overview of the project as a whole entity.
- *Project organization* – the organization of the project requires the accountability and ownership of tasks to be clearly defined and placed on key personnel. 'The participation of workers in objective setting is fundamental to all current management ideologies as well as classic management ideologies' (Johns, 1999a,b).
- *Project schedule* – scheduling of project accomplishments is a necessary tool for the success of the program, and for this to be successful the schedule must be communicated in a simple and comprehensible form, so that all may easily acknowledge the direction in which the project is heading towards.
- *Budget* – an effective method in which managers can control financing and task duration, is through the determination of resource requirements used by each personnel in each task, and the interdependence of each product onto others used in those individual tasks.

Furthermore, it is argued the extent to and rigor with which these tools are used must be allowed to differ in a company, because the sizes and natures of projects differ, the natural styles and cultures of the people involved differ, and the business situations differ (Johns, 1999a,b).

Meanwhile, Pinto and Slevin (1987) consider project plan, as one of the key factors for success of a project, as it involves scheduling of all the activities along with the resources required. They suggest that at plan stage, it should be perceived that the plan is workable; the amount of time, people and money allocated is sufficient; the organization is ready to carry through the plan and the funds are guaranteed.

Project management within an international dimension

International project management plans are subject to the same threats and opportunities as domestic ones. However, there are a number of additional constraints that shape objectives, goals and strategies. Factors such as political instability and risk, currency instability, competition, pressures from national government and nationalism can all interfere with project management planning (Smith and Haar, 1993). Strategy development therefore requires that the company:

- evaluates opportunities, threats, problems and risks;
- assesses the strengths and weaknesses of its personnel to carry out the job;
- defines the scope of its global business involvement;
- formulates its global corporate objectives;
- develops specific corporate strategies in the organization as a whole.

(Saee, 2007)

Overall, the project manager needs to develop a thorough understanding of the environmental factors that will impinge upon the individual project for example, in a particular country including:

- Knowledge of geography about the country in question.
- Finance.
- Local politics that have a bearing on the successful completion of a project.
- National culture. Developing an understanding of the host culture is crucial and obviously has a major impact on the way a project is conducted.
- Local laws can vary considerably and influence the resources needed for a project. For instance, in Francophone African countries, local labour law allows employees to take three days leave of absence when a close relative dies. With large families this can cause serious disruption to staff availability (Saee, 2007).
- Basic to any project management system, is a control subsystem, comprised of standards, comparisons and corrective actions. Control and its associated problems in international projects are much more complex than in domestic ones as a result of differing political, cultural, economic and legal environments. Geographic distance, language barriers, communication habits, culture and differing frames of reference all influence the control subsystems (Saee, 2005).
- Criticism and how it is expressed can seriously affect managerial control; detailed reporting and tight control are not accepted in some cultures. For

example, in Japanese culture, maintaining group cohesiveness is more important than reporting a problem to a supervisor; supervisors tend to solve the problems at the group level before referring them to upper management (Clutterbuck, 1989).

Communication

The critical importance of communication in organizations, in particular its influence on the acceptance of something new, is well documented (Timm, 1989), as is the critical importance of intercultural communication competence in an organization/project based on cultural diversity (Saee, 2005).

Lack of communication has been cited as the biggest reason for the failure of many change projects to meet their expectations (Pardu, 1996). Successful communication needs to be focused and the timing is of crucial importance. Used effectively it can reduce non-productive effort, avoid duplication, and help eliminate mistakes (Saee, 2005). Time, cost and performance vary considerably within the international areas. Time is a communication system just like words and language. For example, Western culture views time as a resource; 'time is money.' Eastern and Middle Eastern cultures view time quite differently, as do most Mediterranean people. Consequently, concepts such as schedules and deadlines, which are essential to project management, are not held in the same regard and therefore are not followed as conscientiously as in Western cultures. Another communication factor to be considered is directness. In the USA, one is direct and gets straight to the point. In other cultures, the direct route is avoided and even disliked. Arabs, some Europeans and Asians do not go straight to a point (Saee, 2005).

Control systems

This is an important project managerial function. Moder (1988) conceives controlling as the process of making events conform to schedules by coordinating the action of all parts of the organization according to the plan established for attaining the objective. It is for this reason that control is essential to any project managers, especially for those that are dealing within an international context (Saee, 2007).

The process of project control involves three sets of decisions. These include monitoring/measuring, evaluating and action. Through the use of an agreed metric toward the accomplishment of established objectives, a measurement of actual project progress is compared to that of planned directions. Evaluating relates to the process of determining causes and their solutions to notable variations in performance within the project. The course of acting often involves a manager briefing appropriate individuals of progress in the project, taking corrective action in light of unfavourable situations, and exploiting opportunities to benefit from, and take advantage of it. These control processes are a necessity for any international project management. However, without the presence of project execution plans; procedures for analyzing, reporting and reviewing performance against baselines; and the disciplined process for considering, approving and implementing change, the project will certainly lose control (Johns, 1999a,b; Peters, 1994).

International project management within the Chinese context

China is the world's largest emerging economy and the most preferred destination of foreign direct investment (FDI) in recent years, China plays an important role in the international strategies of many multinational corporations (MNCs). Most leading MNCs are increasingly setting up R&D operations in China (von Zedtwitz, 2006).

Although there is scant published research literature available on how successful MNCs are in managing projects in China, there has been a recent phenomenological study (Briggs and Dyke, 2006) of a wide range of industries including education, computers and software, human resources, management consulting, telecommunications, and energy, who were surveyed in terms of their experiences while managing projects in China.

The study presented the following phenomenological data:

- 57 per cent of represented companies are headquartered in the United States;
- 83 per cent of those companies adhere to a project management methodology based on Western management theory;
- 82 per cent of those companies currently have operations in China;
- nearly 90 per cent have managed or are currently managing a project in China.

The respondents acknowledged certain difficulties while managing projects in China based on the Western concept of project management and hence they had to make changes to their respective Western style of project management. For example, they all cited the following reasons for their decision for changing their management strategy and practice:

- language differences;
- cultural differences;
- financial institutions;
- government intervention;
- logistical infrastructure; and
- intellectual property protection.

The respondents made further comments as to why they had to make changes with respect to their Western project management style: execution plans based on Western templates appeared to be unworkable, which impacted wide-range tasks: from engineering to contract and hence and overall project management.

Finally, confronting team members directly, as in the West, was less successful than encouraging other team members to influence the behaviour of their peers in

China. Even when a team leader was assigned, decision-making and its implementation unlike in the West was still group-based, which in turn reflects Chinese collectivist culture (Briggs and Dodyk, 2006).

A separate study of construction joint ventures dealing with project management in China (Shen *et al.*, 2001) identified four main risk factors: management risk, policy risk, technical risk and market risk, all of which can amongst other things result in: improper project feasibility study; forecasting marketing demand; increased project cost; design changes and hence project delays.

Generally speaking, project managers who follow the Western style of project management in China still find their projects being delayed, resulting in cost over-run and problematic managerial and quality-related issues. Few Western managers in China realized the fact that project management is in fact a management culture, a culture that must be embedded into the project, delivering models in order to maximize the management knowledge in practice, and hence make project management workable (Vaughan, 2008). Thus, understanding the cultural dimension with reference to China by Western project managers is a must in order to ensure that they incorporate cross-cultural dimensions into their respective project management. (For a full discussion on Chinese culture, see Chapter 6.)

Key determinants of successful international project management

Project management has provided a sound foundation for change management in recent decades – for example, in the integration and reorganization of major businesses and in developing new initiatives between company, its customers, suppliers and partners. Even so, there are opportunities for making it a more effective tool. Many organizations will admit to having problems or issues that limit their use of project management for managing change (Clarke, 1999; Kahn, 1993). By understanding these issues and working to eliminate them, it may be possible to improve the effectiveness of project management.

As with many managerial responsibilities, the management of an international project involves planning, organization and control of a large number of complex factors, activities and their interrelations. Managing them simultaneously and giving them all equal attention is virtually impossible. However, adapting the Pareto rule of separating out the important few from the trivial many helps to focus attention on the key factors which are critical for achieving success (Morris, 1996).

There is ample evidence in the literature to support the existence of critical or key success factors for project management. Baker *et al.* (1983) postulated that the perceived project success or failure is not a function of time and cost. While Kerzner (1998) identified six critical success factors for successful projects:

- corporate understanding of project management;
- executive commitment to project management;

- organizational adaptability;
- sound project manager selection criteria;
- project manager's leadership style; and
- commitment to planning and control.

Similarly, project managers' understanding of cross-cultural dimensions is critical when managing international projects.

Meanwhile, additional research by Pinto and Slevin (1987) identified the following factors as being critical to the success of the projects:

1   *Project mission.* This involves determination of clearly defined goals for the project by management, with clear indications that the project is necessary and the reasons why.
2   *Competent project manager.* A skilled project leader who possesses the essential interpersonal/intercultural, technical and administrative competencies is essential.
3   *Top management support.* No project is likely to succeed unless it enjoys the full support of the senior management within the organization. Thus acquiring support for the project whilst communicating top management support for the project to every employee within the organization is critical.
4   *Project plan.* All activities surrounding the project have to be meticulously planned for and the necessary resources required to carry out the project have to be fully allocated. As well, there have to be ways of monitoring its progress in terms of the specific stage deadlines. Managers have to consider: if the plan is workable; if the amount of time and money, and people allocated is sufficient; if the funds are guaranteed; if the organization will carry through the project; and if there is flexibility in the plans allowing for over-running the schedule.
5   *Client consultation.* A detailed understanding of the client requirement is a must for a project manager, and thus regular meetings between client and the project manager are deemed necessary at all stages of the project.
6   *Competent project team.* Recruitment and selection of competent staff backed by their training is critical in order to ensure the success of the project.
7   *Technical skills.* Technical skills have to be matched with the right people in terms of qualifications and expertise.
8   *Client acceptance.* Gaining acceptance from one's client for any given project is critical. Thus a project manager needs to develop a sound selling strategy at an early phase of the project in order to sell the project to the client. Developing good interpersonal relationship with client is deemed necessary so that the project manager can negotiate with the client where appropriate (Jackson, 1992).
9   *Monitoring and feedback.* Obtaining feedback throughout the project from key individuals is necessary to ensure quality outcome for the project. This obviously involves establishing sound monitoring procedures to capture a systematic feedback on all aspects of the project.

10 *Communication.* The concept of communication in project management refers to the spoken and written documentation, plans, and drawings used in the processes of an international project. Thus, it is critical in managing an international project that project managers develop intercultural communication competence, based on a sound understanding of cross-cultural dimensions.

11 *Trouble-shooting mechanisms.* A system or set of procedures capable of tackling problems when they arise, tracing them back to their root cause and resolving them is essential. All team members should act as 'look-outs' for the project, and all team members should monitor the project. When a problem is identified by a team member, action needs to be taken at once to remedy the problem (Jackson, 1992).

Rosenau (1984) suggested that the essence of successful project management consisted of satisfying the triple constraints of time, cost and performance.

One of the most important findings arising from the preliminary literature survey is that the factors expounded could not explain the reasons why the project could be considered as successful by one party and at the same time be considered a failure by another. However, it is argued that there are two possible viewpoints of project success: The macro viewpoint, which takes care of the question 'does the original concept tick?' The users and stakeholders are usually the ones looking at project success from the macro viewpoint. The micro viewpoint usually concerns the implementation parties (Lim and Mohamed, 1999).

Essentially the project manager must be able to negotiate a successful balance between project control imperatives and the reality of the cultural diversity milieu in which the project operates. This calls for an effective intercultural communication competence on the part of the international project manager.

Organizational designs across cultural frontiers

Authority, responsibility and accountability vary by project, culture and a company's priorities and preferences. For example, technically and security sensitive projects tend to be more centralized and more tightly controlled. Group decision-making seems to work well in Japan. But it is not prevalent in other societies. French companies show more autocratic behaviour, while large and experienced companies in the USA and most of Western Europe exhibit the highest level of management delegation (Saee, 2007). These findings are germane to project success, for while there are many reasons for the failure of projects in the international environment the most significant is the inability to get maximum performance out of people. Each culture has different expectations of the superior-subordinate relationships.

Position, rank, authority and respect are supported in many foreign countries by informal and formal codes of dress, behaviour and attitudes. While delegation and participative management are practiced and supported in the Scandinavian countries, this is not the case in many other countries. Clearly these organizational and operational patterns significantly affect project management (Saee, 2005).

Organizational support

Johns (1999a) maintains that as companies experiment with project-based organizations, what executive managers frequently find missing is instinctive knowledge pertaining to how to create an organizational management culture. The questions and challenges facing executives are how to:

- create explicit senior management goals that support and encourage cross-functional project teams;
- work with one another as a senior management team and how to mutually support cross-functional project teams;
- establish clearly communicated priorities for work done by cross-functional project teams in relation to other work.

The main steps senior management must take in creating a project-based organizational culture are to:

- write a clear policy stating the support of the project team's responsibility and authority to accomplish their missions, goals and objectives;
- continually repeat the messages that the project teams are empowered to act as long as their actions are in the best interest of the organization.

In a recent and ongoing survey of senior managers from international companies being conducted at the Management Centre in Europe, it was found that all of these companies use cross-functional project teams as a primary way of conducting their business. These companies have also exhibited organizational support for project management in the areas of frequent use of management committees for reviewing project teams` performance, establishment of priorities between projects, periodic review of project team members' performance and the existence of planning and control processes. Weak organizational support was exhibited by these companies in areas such as resource planning and re-planning project management training for project team members and an absence of management support of the project (Saee, 2007).

Johns (1999b) holds the view that a prerequisite for effective organizational support is the existence of a specific management form where the project team can openly and regularly discuss problems they are encountering so that appropriate strategies can be developed to address these perceived problems at all levels.

People as subsystems

Human subsystems in international project management are by their very nature far more complex and complicated than in the management of domestic projects. For example in the case of motivation, with little job security, American workers are motivated to work hard in order to earn money. But motivation varies widely by country and culture. To the French, quality of life is what matters most. In Japan, society and companies come first, and workers are motivated by permanent or lifetime employment, bonuses and fringe benefits based on the company's performance as a whole (Saee, 2005).

Another aspect in human subsystems is negotiations, which within the international context are made all the more difficult by differences in culture, trade customs and legal order. Language barriers can complicate negotiations. Interpreters can slow the pace of negotiations and/or take the unwanted active roles. However, the successful negotiator in international project management sees and understands the world as others do; manages stress and copes with ambiguity; sells the merits of the proposal in meaningful terms that express ideas clearly; and demonstrates cultural sensitivity and flexibility (Saee, 2005).

Smith and Haar (1993) advocated that no prescription can demonstrably be iron clad. Moreover, the human dimension in project management is of utmost importance in international projects. Many projects that are technically, financially and organizationally strong have failed as a result of cross-cultural factors, i.e. the inability of managers and supervisors to comprehend and respond to foreign environments.

Guidelines for international project managers

Research by Kerzner (1998) identified the following guidelines for international executives involved in initiation, planning and implementation of projects:

- be aware of the environment of the host country;
- study the host company's developing plans and develop a long range plans for future cooperation;
- survey the financial institutions involved in the project and study the investment laws if applicable;
- before undertaking a project, study its feasibility from the technical, economic and operational point of view; also study the contribution of the project to the development of the host country;
- develop relationships with governmental and business leaders and develop a special relationship with project's local 'Godfather';
- choose the right project manager for managing and implementation of the project and assign him to the project at an early stage;
- communicate with the client and learn how to deal with the counterpart effectively;
- study the different stages and phases of the project: preparation and initiation, implementation and operation;
- study the decision-making process and the different organizations responsible for project implementation and operation.

Project personnel management

Within the operations of an international project management team, there are often a wide variety of positions held by personnel from different nations around the globe. It is for this reason that the manager should explore the conditions and benefits, then define clear standards which outline the working conditions before recruiting personnel. International projects vary in working conditions, which relate uniquely to each individual work site involved, and the duration of the working week is also contingent upon the work nature and/or location of the project.

With these factors of international project management in mind, selected personnel, including project managers, must meet certain criteria in ensuring that the most suitable individuals are employed for work overseas in different cultures:

- technical and managerial skills and abilities;
- cultural empathy;
- adaptability and flexibility;
- diplomatic skills;
- family factors;
- emotional stability and maturity;
- motivation and aspiration.

(Saee, 2007)

As regards to employment strategy, it is highly unlikely that the availability of qualified and experienced local nationals will obviate the need for expatriate managers in foreign subsidiaries. According to Robinson (1978), it may be that some of the well-established multinational and transnational corporations actually plan on recruiting and maintaining between 5 per cent and 10 per cent expatriates or third-country nationals in local subsidiary management. The reason behind this managerial strategy is based on the assumption that there are benefits that can arise from this international human resource management practice, such as providing multinational experience and intensifying corporate socialization process for all parties involved in the project (Saee, 2005).

Client consultation and acceptance

As previously discussed, the client should be clearly identified, usually as the one who will be 'using' the completed project. Close consultation with the client is necessary for outside projects. Client acceptance is usually the 'bottom-line' which should be backed up with perceived and tangible benefits, and involves good communication. Hence, the following points are important to consider:

- know the client and what he or she requires;
- schedule regular meetings with the client;
- ascertain whether the client is accepting or resisting;
- develop a sound interpersonal relationship with the client so that you can negotiate with them where necessary.

(Jackson, 1993).

Training and education

Inadequate training and education for the international setting results in a group of managers who do not understand and, therefore, cannot master adequately the technical aspects of project management. Successful project management requires extensive and intensive training in techniques and methodologies of project operations (Snell *et al.*, 1993).

The training strategy, as identified by research (Kerzner, 1998) should include:

- training based on trans-cultural management in the context of the specifics of the job;
- an educational approach to training that enables managers to analyse case studies;
- training based on the host national's perceptions;
- training that sensitizes a manager to awareness of his or her impact on the host national workforce; and
- training for the purpose of acquiring technical knowledge for performing the job.

The use of scheduling, costing, modelling and programming techniques and methodologies should be much the same in large international projects. However, because of variation in education and availability of hardware and software, adjustment must be made in the project management systems.

Breaking the project into bite-size chunks

Breaking large projects down into subprojects or work packages is regarded as one of the most important tasks in the development of projects (Lewis, 1996). It ensures greater ownership by all those owning a 'chunk' of the project, spreading responsibility and accountability across a greater number of people. Furthermore, it is easier to manage in a number of ways: delegating responsibilities to the project team, monitoring against the objectives, communicating progress of the project, identifying problems up-front and making modifications of the project (Saee, 2007).

Product perspective

The ultimate outcome of a project is an artefact with technological complexities and many years of operational life. In addition, it is the result of a distributed collaboration not only during the engineering phase but also during the production and assembly phases. Thus, the product perspective emphasizes the role of configuration management that essentially concerns the control of specification changes and the work/information/data flow during the engineering and manufacturing process (Stark, 1992). Further, the role of product data management will become even more important in project management areas. The reason is that technological complexity of the products is continuously increasing; the duration of projects tends to be lengthening all the time; the number of geographically distributed collaborators is increasing due to diversity of skills needed; the economic benefits of outsourcing are growing exponentially; the needed investments are increasing; and the economic environment requires expeditious and flexible performance. Hence, ensuring the consistency of the product configuration is of utmost importance in order to succeed in international project management (Hameri, 1997).

Risk management

Given the many differences, complexities and uncertainties that distinguish international project management from domestic project management, a number of risk factors are worth noting in order to ensure success in international project management. The risks can emerge from the political, economic, social, technological and regulatory environments of the project (Saee, 2007).

According to Kerzner (1998), it is important that risk management strategy is established early in a project and that risk is continually addressed throughout the project life cycle.

In summary

In this chapter, it has been established that as a result of increasing competition in rapidly changing and financially challenging international environments, firms are adopting flexible strategies and structures, such as project management methods, in order to speed improved quality products and services to their market segments and to provide quality customer service (Johns, 1999b). Project management across professional, national and cultural frontiers is highly complex. The project manager's responsibility is to manage across these systems in order to meet specific business objectives within a finite timeline. The need to identify, distinguish and respond effectively to a distinct set of managerial requirements thus becomes the foremost challenge facing international project managers.

Consequently, in this chapter, various factors that are crucial in the context of project management across cultures were identified and must be considered in order to develop appropriate strategies to follow the best practice in international project management. The conclusion that may be drawn in this chapter is that in order for firms to excel in international project management, they have to carefully consider and implement appropriate strategies relating to the following critical factors: conceptualization and initiation; project plan; communication; organization; organizational support; human subsystems; breaking the project into bite-size chunks; client consultation and acceptance; education and training; and the product perspective.

Finally, most international projects often are identified by a weakness in either strategy or tactics that leads to different types of errors. Thus, the major challenge facing an international project manager is to ensure that the tactics pursued in an international project are entirely complementary to the overall project management strategy. Furthermore, the international project manager will greatly benefit by developing high-level intercultural communication competence, deemed an essential ingredient in managing successfully a culturally diverse project management team.

4 China's automotive companies shift gears

Manifestations and implications of global ambitions

Francis Schortgen and John Saee

Introduction

The reversal of fortunes in the global automobile industry in recent years has been nothing short of consequential for the sustainability of competitiveness, indeed viability, of established Western automobile giants (Ingrassia, 2010). The unfolding crisis, at least in part, appears to have been the inevitable by-product of hitherto unbridled corporate arrogance, ill-advised complacency, crippling legacy costs, flawed market intelligence, ill-fated consumer preference gambles, and a steadily eroding market position. Add to that the debilitating effect of the global economic crisis and aggressive inroads by foreign rivals, and the industry was bound to experience a near-perfect storm.

At a time when many industry players have been forced into the 'slow' lane, the Chinese automobile industry is generating significant buzz. In 2009, China, for the first time, surpassed the USA to take the global lead in car sales. Owing in large measure to anaemic sales growth in much of the developed world and targeted stimulus measures introduced in January 2009, China's automobile industry appears to have reached a critical milestone in its development and growth. Domestic industry dynamics notwithstanding, China's leading automobile companies have made little secret of their *outward* internationalization ambitions in recent years. In fact, the onset of the global economic and financial crisis may well have presented them with a unique opportunity to improve their overall competitiveness through critical technology acquisition and intellectual property transfer (Morrison, 2009: 9).

Outward internationalization is also being championed by the Chinese Government as a central pillar of a comprehensive and ambitious new automotive strategy. While confidence in successful near-term global expansion may well be premature, China's medium- to long-term impact on the global automobile industry will be as inevitable as it will be transformational. In light of this, it remains all the more puzzling that studies on the international aspirations of China's leading car manufacturers remain few and far between.[1]

Table 4.1 China's top ten automobile companies in 2009

Company	Volume	Share (%)
Shanghai Automotive Industry Corporation (SAIC)	2,594,956	20
Chang'an Automobile Group Co.	1,786,782	14
First Automobile Works (FAW)	1,755,640	14
Dongfeng Motor Corporation (DFM)	1,733,756	13
Beijing Automobile Works Co.	1,147,387	9
Guangzhou Automobile Industry Group Co.	612,218	5
Chery Automobile	500,303	4
BYD	445,097	3
Brilliance China Automotive Holdings Limited	348,308	3
Geely Automobile Holdings Group Limited	329,250	3

Source: J.D. Power and Associates (2010).

Chinese cars are coming!

The global economy in the early twenty-first century is experiencing a tectonic shift of heretofore unprecedented and unsettling proportion. Just as an irresistible and irreversible shift in the global distribution of wealth and power is reshaping socio-economic realities (Mahbubani, 2008; Prestowitz, 2005; Simpfendorfer, 2009; Zakaria, 2008), so too is it poised to induce a sweeping transformation of global competition (Khanna, 2009; Sheth and Sisodia, 2006; Zeng and Williamson, 2007). In the wake of the 2008–2009 global economic and financial crisis, the global automotive industry is presently in the process of navigating the stormy waters of industrial restructuring. The gradual coming of age and nascent global ambitions of China's automobile industry is but the latest trend, adding a peculiar sense of urgency to embracing a reinvigorated industrial paradigm reflecting the competitive dynamics of the twenty-first century.

In 2009, China hit a new milestone, having surpassed the United States to become the top global automotive market. According to the China Association of Automobile Manufacturers (CAAM), the total sales volume in 2009 reached 13.6 million units, compared to 10.4 million units for the USA. Of these, China's top ten automobile companies accounted for roughly 87 per cent of total sales (Table 4.1). For many established global automotive companies, exports to and sales in the Chinese domestic market represents one of the very few bright spots for an industry that is reeling from a global economic down-turn (Figure 4.1).

A forecast study of the Chinese automobile industry, conducted in 2005, sug-gested that brand management and customer retention rather than production strategies would come to determine domestic and foreign automotive companies' growth potential and market share prospects in China by 2010 (Mercer Management Consulting, 2005). Of the top brands in China's domestic market to date, Chinese brands dominate the commercial vehicle market segment, yet hold only a minority share in what is emerging as the world's largest and fastest grow-ing car market (Table 4.2). Amid accelerating surplus capacity and an impending

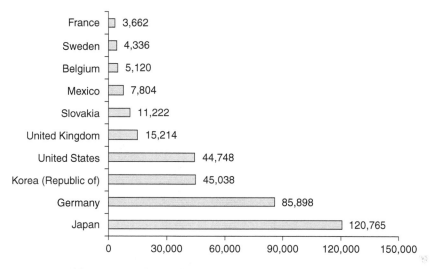

Figure 4.1 Chinese automotive market imports in 2009 (by country of origin).

Source: J.D. Power and Associates (2010).

industry consolidation push, China's leading automobile companies are presently in the early stages of transitioning from an exclusively *inward* internationalization strategy to a simultaneous *inward–outward* orientation.

Over the last few years, Chinese automobile companies have begun to express deepening aspirations of complementing their developing market penetration with forays into developed markets. The prospects of their determined and aggressive expansion into first-tier markets triggering a wave of heightened 'Sinophobia' approximating, if not exceeding, the Japan-bashing of the 1980s are hardly far-fetched; all the more so, considering the timing of the Chinese industry's international ambitions.

Though fears of Chinese automobile companies fielding competitive challenges with the potential of shaking up the pedestal of enterprise competitiveness in the near-term future seem comfortably misplaced, their medium- to long-term potential to emerge as a viable force appears much more realistic (Baker, 2007). Starting from a position of relative weakness – whether in the areas of brand power, quality control, technological sophistication, or comfort and safety – ever-rising Chinese consumer demands and pressures will be a major contributing factor to the domestic and international fortunes of the Chinese automobile industry (Perkowski, 2006; Sun, 2006).

Globalization of the Chinese automotive industry is indubitably on the rise, as can be evidenced by the fact that much of the content in cars sold in the US and elsewhere around the world today already originates from China. Because a significant percentage of the total cost of a car is in the manufactured components, there has already been a significant shift of the production of supplied parts to

Table 4.2 Leading brands in China's automobile market in 2009

	Brand	Sales (YTD)	Growth (%)	Share(YTD) (%)
Passenger cars				
1	Volkswagen	1,140,220	37	13.1
2	Toyota	650,478	14	7.5
3	Hyundai	593,345	87	6.8
4	Honda	576,436	23	6.6
5	Nissan	527,537	46	6.0
6	Buick	445,289	59	5.1
7	BYD	445,097	161	5.1
8	Chery	439,635	31	5.0
9	Chevrolet	331,954	57	3.8
10	Kia	254,545	69	2.9
11	Geely	249,650	36	2.9
12	Suzuki	243,673	23	2.8
13	Ford	230,928	48	2.6
14	Mazda	182,402	43	2.1
15	FAW	168,486	61	1.9
16	Citroen	160,579	57	1.8
17	Audi	160,414	34	1.8
18	Great Wall	155,225	114	1.8
19	Xiali	139,922	16	1.6
20	Skoda	128,597	113	1.5
Commercial vehicles				
1	Wuling	1,005,051	65	23.7
2	Chana	706,454	84	16.7
3	Foton	499,824	47	11.8
4	Dongfeng	399,292	51	9.4
5	Hafei	210,590	45	5.0
6	Jinbei	168,635	18	4.0
7	FAW	166,262	63	3.9
8	JAC	146,673	24	3.5
9	Kaima	96,780	49	2.3
10	JMC	78,651	20	1.9

Source: J.D. Power and Associates (2010).

China. A considerable number of the components incorporated in cars now either are or can quickly be manufactured in China. This is purely driven by the efficiencies gained from sourcing in China (Russo, 2009).

Furthermore, the reasons and motivations for *outward* internationalization are numerous, including seeking greater market share, pursuing higher returns on investment, leveraging location advantages, achieving economies of scale, acquiring critical knowledge. In a recent study of China's outward internationalization push, Child and Rodrigues (2005) suggested that the primary motivational basis for Chinese enterprise internationalization could well represent a desire to overcome competitive disadvantages rather than to leverage competitive advantages.

A surge in proposed and/or completed international merger and acquisition activities in the global automobile industry, combined with stated aspirations for organic expansion, present compelling evidence to that effect.

The pressing question, then, is: Will China's emergence as an ambitious player present a threat or an opportunity to the global automobile industry? In the short term, the prospects for Chinese companies wresting control of the commanding heights of the global automobile industry away from established Western counterparts remain rather bleak. The Chinese automotive industry's ascent thus far has been as dramatic as it has been erratic (*Corporate Financing Week*, 2009). Even so, and irrespective of the longer-term prospects of breaking into international first-tier markets, China has already emerged as the undisputed catalyst behind a much-needed – and arguably long overdue – restructuring of the global automotive industry. In fact, its global automotive aspirations reinforce the realization that China's competitive advantage is no longer exclusively centred on labour-intensive manufacturing. As Zeng and Williamson (2007) highlight, the newly emerging Chinese competitive challenge involves 'cost innovation' – the ability to offer an impressive line-up of products, incorporate high-technology at low cost, and produce products at volume prices. Combined with the downward pressure exerted by a host of externalities that have battered the global automobile industry in recent years, the impending Chinese 'economic tsunami' merely stresses the importance of *continuous* as opposed to *occasional* improvement by established players. Commenting on the expected Chinese challenge in the automobile industry, Ulrich Walker, chairman and CEO of Daimler Northeast Asia, aptly noted: 'It will come. The question is how long it will take.... The question is ... and it depends on the car maker ... how seriously they take this challenge' (Associated Press, 2009).

The remainder of this chapter applies a contextual framework to assess the potential and implications of the Chinese automobile industry's commitments to shifting gears and expand its international exposure. We will shed a clarifying light on a set of specific questions. First, how and to what extent, if at all, can Chinese automobile companies leverage their relative market penetration success in second- and third-tier markets for their quest to establish solid beachheads into developed economies? Second, has China internalized the lessons and initial setbacks experienced by Japanese and South Korean automobile companies in their respective targeting of first-tier markets in the 1970s and 1980s? Is such a comparison warranted in the first place? Third, what are the peculiar internalities and externalities behind China's expansion into the global automobile market? What is the likelihood of Chinese automobile companies successfully navigating the myriad of speed bumps ahead?

Next stop: developed markets?

With car ownership being the latest status symbol of China's emerging urban middle class (Farrell *et al.*, 2006), the domestic automobile industry, in conjunction and competition with foreign companies, has moved aggressively to service this new

Table 4.3 Chinese car manufacturers – export volume (2003–2008)

2003	2004	2005	2006	2007	2008	2009
43,000	78,000	173,000	340,000	612,700	680,700	285,533[a]

Sources: adapted from *China Daily* (2009); *Business Week* (2007); 上海国际海事信息与文献网 (2007).

Note:
a   Export volume for the first 11 months of 2009 (J. D. Power and Associates, 2010).

market segment through increased production capacity. The phenomenal pace at which the industry has expanded in recent years, however, has contributed to rising overcapacity, triggering a commitment by the government to push for industry consolidation. At the same time, it is unlikely that demand generated by the emerging middle class will be able to absorb the increased production output. By year-end 2009, the Chinese Government announced a gradual scaling back of the stimulus measures that fuelled an explosive growth in China's domestic automobile market in 2009.[2] Billed as a way of shifting into stable growth, this decision has also prompted speculation that the Chinese automobile industry's high growth period may already have ended. To address the demand–supply gap that has been gradually accumulating over the years, and encouraged by the Chinese Government's 'Go out' (zou chu qu) strategy (Accenture, 2005), China's leading automobile manufacturers are likely to pursue export aspirations with renewed vigour (Baker 2007).

Over the 2003–2008 period, exports of Chinese vehicles have grown over 1.480 per cent, rising from 43,000 units in 2003 to 680,700 in 2008 (Table 4.3). It is important to note, however, that passenger car exports continue to lag significantly behind those of commercial vehicles, including trucks and buses. Seen from the perspective that in their initial stage Chinese vehicle exports have predominately been targeting developing economies engaged in large-scale infrastructure development projects, this is hardly surprising. As Chinese vehicle manufacturers expand their export aspirations and begin to gradually take aim at first-tier markets in developed economies, exports of passenger cars are widely expected to gradually top export aspirations (Dunne, 2007).

Over the years, Chinese vehicle manufacturers have made substantial inroads into second- and third-tier markets in Africa, the Middle East, Eastern Europe, Russia, Southeast and Central Asia, Central and South America, and the Caribbean (Figure 4.2). FAW Haima Automobile Co., which made its debut on the international scene at the Dubai International Motor Show in November 2007, teamed up with Abu Dhabi-based First Motors in 2009 to target the mid-income market segment of the United Arab Emirates (UAE). Having first entered the South African market in 2006, Chang'an Automobile Group Co. (ChangAn), China's fourth-largest automobile manufacturer, announced plans to invest US$80 million over 5 years in 2009, including an assembly plant with an annual production capacity of 50,000 units, to take advantage of South Africa's growing market potential (*South Africa Good News*, 2009).

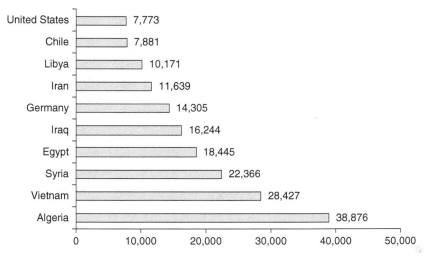

Figure 4.2 Top ten export destinations of Chinese vehicles in 2009 (by volume).
Source: J.D. Power and Associates.

On the African continent, in particular, China has already acquired a reputation as 'Africa's new car dealer' (Miller, 2007). Much of the initial market penetration success in developing economies can be attributed to favourable performance–price ratios of Chinese cars, comparatively less stringent safety and emissions standards, and negligible competitive pressures from established global players.

As Chinese companies expand their presence throughout the developing economy market, including the Middle East and North Africa (MENA) markets, their competitive challenge to established European, Japanese and South Korean brands is becoming readily apparent (Xinhua, 2007a, 2007b). The value of Chinese car exports to Senegal increased by a staggering 1,680 per cent to US$8 million between 2001 and 2006. Over the same period, car imports from Europe declined by 76 per cent to 2,272 units in 2006 (Miller, 2007).

The demonstrated ability of Chinese vehicle manufacturers to exert competitive pressures on established Western, Japanese, and South Korean car companies in second- and third-tier markets for low-priced cars may yet prove to be the beginning of a more unsettling dynamic as they begin to set their sights on first-tier markets. Among the most prominent Chinese car companies nurturing hopes of breaking into the European and US markets are Chery Automobile, Geely Automobile Holdings Group, Great Wall Motors, Brilliance Jinbei Automotive, and Nanjing Automobile Group (Alon *et al.*, 2008; de Oliveira *et al.*, 2006). Great Wall Motors ended up spearheading Chinese car manufacturers' initial push into mature markets in September 2006, exporting 500 Hover cross-over utility vehicles (CUVs) to Italy. In November of that year, Brilliance China Automotive Holdings, under the largest single export deal secured by any Chinese car manufacturer yet, expressed its intention to export 158,000 cars to

European markets over a five-year period (*China Daily*, 2007). By all indications, Chinese car manufacturers are fighting a major uphill battle in trying to break into first-tier markets of Western Europe. Within the first nine months of 2009, China's five leading car manufacturers currently exporting to the European Union – Brilliance Auto, Chana Auto Co. Ltd, Great Wall Motors, Landwind and the Lifan Group – sold only 745 units to the EU, with Great Wall Motors accounting for roughly 91 per cent of the export total (*China Daily*, 2009a). By comparison, the Russian and Eastern European markets have proved easier to penetrate. As observed in *Automotive Business Review* (2006):

> Russia's fast-growing car market seems like the best place for Chinese carmakers to start global expansion, as the country's increasing liberalization and development of consumer credit is enabling more and more households to buy their first car, which will likely cost below US$10,000. Moreover Russians are more forgiving towards patchy quality, as long as their car looks and feels more '21st century' than the home-made Ladas.

Undeterred by missed expectations and sales setbacks in second-tier markets like Russia where export volumes of Chery, BYD (Build Your Dreams) and Great Wall Motors in the first ten months of 2009 have dropped between 70 and 75 per cent year-on-year, China's leading automobile companies are showing no real signs of swerving off the road yet (China Daily, 2009a). In fact, of late, some of them have begun to set their sights on establishing a foothold in promising niche markets, notably the energy-efficient and environmentally friendly market segments. In 2009, BYD announced its plans to introduce an all-electric battery car into the US market within one year, establishing a beachhead in the Los Angeles market with its advanced five-seat e6 model (Shirouzu, 2009a, 2009b).

Are these expanding first-tier market aspirations indicative of a shift in the Chinese automobile industry's strategic orientation with regard to internationalization? Seen from an international business strategy perspective, does it represent a logical progression along the stage-like process of business internationalization (Johanson and Vahlne, 1977; Johanson and Wiedersheim-Paul, 1975) or does it imply the adoption of a competitive 'survival strategy' (Child and Rodrigues, 2005; Darwar and Frost, 1999).[3] In either case, it begets the question as to whether the decision by Chinese car companies to enter first-tier markets is advisable or premature. Are Chinese car companies ready to go global? What strategies do they adopt? What are the likely bumps (and possible setbacks) along the road to global prominence? What lessons can and should they internalize from Japanese and South Korean car companies' earlier forays into first-tier markets?

Fools rush in? Car-building and brand-building

As the latest manifestation of outward internationalization, Chinese automobile companies' export aspirations have caused widespread consternation in the global automotive industry at a time of large-scale shake-up and restructuring. By the same token, this latest development should not be all too surprising either. As Ernst & Young's Clive Saunderson aptly remarked:

> If 10 years ago, you asked whether Toyota was going to be as successful in the U.S. as it is today, many people would have been sceptical ... U.S. car companies are today under threat in their own backyards from the likes of Toyota. Why shouldn't Chinese car companies be able to do the same thing?
>
> (China Daily, 2005)

Aspirations and strategic considerations notwithstanding, the global road map for China's car manufacturers will not be an easy one to navigate. If recent overseas investment and expansion plans by a diverse selection of Chinese companies serve as predictive indicators, Chinese car manufacturers are likely to encounter major roadblocks in their pursuit of export opportunities in first-tier markets. These may include technology certification, intellectual property and protectionist trade barriers, as well as competitive disadvantages derived from negligible profit margins and a lack of extensive overseas sales networks and targeted sales strategies (Xinhua, 2009).

In particular, regarding intellectual property theft in the automobile industry, the practice of 'subtle pick-off' has been a sticking point for a number of Chinese car manufacturers and is likely to further complicate any overseas ambitions (AutoWeb, 2006). This technique has proved a particularly appealing alternative to sizeable R&D risks, costs and challenges (Gan, 2008). By the same token, however, it severely constrains and delays the development of independent innovation and technological capabilities (Xie *et al.*, 2008). If Chinese car manufacturers are determined to step onto and succeed on the global stage, the ability and willingness to embrace 'dynamic capabilities' (Winter, 2003), that is moving from duplicate innovation and creative imitation capabilities to exploitative innovation and explorative innovation capabilities (Helfat and Peteraf, 2003; Ma *et al.*, 2006) is a necessary component of competitive evolution.

Above all else, however, the combination of poor quality control, safety concerns and brand power weakness breathes reality into China's high-flying car export aspirations. Judging by the initial developed-market penetration of Japanese and South Korean car manufacturers in the 1970s and 1980s, respectively, the impact on the overseas fortunes of Chinese car manufacturers could well prove far-reaching. In the short term, Chinese car manufacturers would be running the risk of 'nurturing' negative customer perceptions from which it may be difficult to recover, if at all, thus potentially constraining overseas market prospects in the medium to long term.

Poor quality control, including the use of sub-standard components and hazardous ingredients in the manufacture of both soft and hard products, has been a long-standing problem for Chinese manufacturing (Midler, 2009). One major rationale behind this has been the fragmentation of the China automotive industry resulting from the highly fragmented landscape of licensed car manufacturers. The fact that that there are over 150 registered manufacturers is an outgrowth of a start-up phase for China's auto sector that also renders it very problematic in terms of focusing and allocating resources to the development of critical technologies associated with safety and fuel economy. This is an area of particular weakness for Chinese original equipment manufacturers (OEMs) who have relied on their foreign partners to lead the development of key component technologies (Russo, 2009). However, as China is increasingly shifting into production of higher-end products, including domestic car manufacturers eyeing first-tier export markets, strict product quality and safety controls are paramount. A series of crash tests conducted by various European agencies highlighted major safety concerns with Chinese cars. In a EuroNCAP (European New Car Assessment Program) crash test conducted by Germany's ADAC in 2009, Brilliance's BS4 sedan failed to earn any ratings whatsoever. This follows a dismal 2006 crash test performance of its BS6 sedan, conducted by Germany's TÜV Nord, and a miserable performance of Chery's Amulet in a crash test organized by Russian auto magazine *AvtoRevu* in 2007 (Bolduc, 2006; Osborn, 2007).

Lack of brand image is a second major liability for Chinese car manufacturers. In the words of an industry analyst:

> We cannot find a sweet spot for Chinese automakers, except 'high performance/price ratio' ... that is also how Americans and Europeans perceive 'Made in China'. However, we believe that it's hard to justify profitability if (the brand is) only targeting budget buyers.

Compared to second- and third-tier overseas markets where Chinese companies have successfully managed to do so, leveraging a low cost/high performance image will not be a viable long-term strategy for more mature markets that put a premium on quality, safety, environmental friendliness and overall product appeal. South Korea's Hyundai Motor tried a similar strategy in 1986, marketing a US$5,000 compact car in the US market. The combination of premature developed-market expansion and poor quality control had a long-lasting effect on the company's brand image (Kiley, 2007; Taylor, 2010).

In light of the inherent challenges of building a brand from the bottom up, some companies have adopted a set of strategic approaches to help mitigate the competitive limitations of their global aspirations. The strategy of bridging competitive disadvantages through merger and acquisition (M&A) activities, in particular, has received a new impetus, given the reverberations and restructuring pressures in the global automotive arena. Such acquisitions, if strategically planned and carried out, fulfil strategic asset-seeking goals (Rui and Yip, 2007; Wu and Ding, 2009), including extending a company's global reach by leveraging a target company's global sales networks, enhancing technological capabilities and production processes through technology transfer and leapfrogging, and strengthening brand power through incorporation of established global brand names.

Chinese car companies are rapidly expanding their M&A activities in an effort to strengthen their competitive basis and global viability. By acquiring Sweden's

Volvo car unit from Ford Motor Co., Geely Automobile aims to leverage the Swedish car company's manufacturing and safety reputation and overall brand recognition to break into the global market. Rather than blindly driving down the global M&A highway, however, Chinese companies will need to carefully weigh strategic aspirations against internal capabilities and carry out due diligence of the target company so as to minimize potentially costly missteps. While irrational and oversized ambitions eventually doomed the prospects of Beijing Auto acquiring General Motors' (GM) Opel unit by mid-2009 (Gupta and Wang, 2009), Nanjing Automobile appeared to have overreached financially in its acquisition of the United Kingdom's bankrupt MG Rover in 2005, while Shanghai Automotive Industry Corp.'s (SAIC) acquisition of South Korea's Ssangyong Motors in 2004 eventually ended in failure in 2009 following lengthy South Korean labour union strikes and accusations on insufficient financial backing.

An alternative to overt acquisition-driven resource integration would be a 'stealth' penetration of developed markets. Under this scenario, Chinese car companies engage in a cooperative venture with an established foreign car manufacturer to develop, build, and distribute Chinese-built cars into developed markets under the guise of foreign partner brand names. In July 2007, US-based Chrysler Group and Chery Automobile laid the foundation for a low-cost production venture to export China-made cars under the Dodge brand name to markets in Eastern Europe and Latin America by 2008, followed by Western Europe and the United States by late 2009. By 2008, however, a combination of corporate internalities and business externalities led to export plans for Western Europe and the United States being called off.

A new competitive threat? Not just yet

The Chinese automotive sector has been characterized by deep market fragmentation and cut-throat competition between state-owned and private automotive concerns, owing largely to a combination of bureaucratic means and market mechanisms on the one hand and de facto decentralization[4] on the other hand (Richet and Ruet, 2008). By pushing for the consolidation of smaller car companies (Shirouzu, 2009c), the Chinese Government hopes to simultaneously pre-empt overcapacity risks and nurture the development and growth of a small number of 'national champion' manufacturers with a strong potential to compete in the international arena.

At the same time, however, it has also acknowledged short-to medium-term competitive liabilities and disadvantages relative to global safety, quality control and emissions standards, and has been putting on the brakes by tightening export rules at a time when many of them appear poised to floor it (*China Daily*, 2007). In particular, the Chinese Government appears to have internalized the dangers of irrational market expansion, including ill-advised and counterproductive M&A deals (*China Daily*, 2009b; Xinhua 2009)[5] and potential costs and setback related to premature exports to the European and the US car markets, as evidenced by Japanese and South Korean car manufacturers' initial forays in the 1970s and

1980s, respectively. According to an industry analyst, much of the hype surrounding nascent international ambitions of Chinese car makers appears at best premature, as '[T]hese export aspirations are a marketing tactic, not a real solid opportunity. But it's certainly a possibility in the future' (Associated Press, 2009).

In the near term, the most immediately plausible impact of China on the global automotive industry will be in the form of foreign companies using the country as a lower-cost production base to serve the global car market. General Motors is said to have already expressed its intention to import cars from China to the USA, beginning in 2011.[4] Hence, even if a Chinese 'economic tsunami' in the global automotive arena does not appear to be imminent, the question is not one of *whether* it will reach the shores of developed markets, but rather *when* it will do so. And once it does, the prospects of Chinese car manufacturers sweeping away Western car companies, or at the very least engendering a fundamental restructuring of the global automotive industry, will be all too real indeed.

Notes

1 In similar fashion, Yongnian Zhang (2003: 222), is puzzled as to

> ... why and how such a distinctive and sustained outward orientation of the transitional Chinese economy and such a creative response to economic globalisation by China have received so little attention. It is particularly surprising when other aspects of China's foreign economic relations – China's bid for WTO membership, the impact of its accession and FDI in China in particular – have received, and continue to attract, unremitting attention in the study of China's economic transformation. China's outward FDI is therefore a 'novel dimension' of China's integration into the global economy ... only in so far as it has been just recently and belatedly brought to our attention.

2 In 2009, the Chinese Government cut the sales tax on small-engine cars from 10 per cent to 5 per cent, significantly spurring sales in that car segment. Though not phasing out these preferential tax policies in 2010, the suggested adjustments – including raising the sales tax on small-engine cars from 5 per cent to 7.5 per cent starting January 1, 2010 – are likely to dampen car sales. Forecasts for 2010–2015 have the Chinese automobile market growing at a more stable rate of 19 per cent to 20 per cent, with a significant downward growth adjustment expected in 2010 – 5 per cent to 6 per cent compared to 50 per cent expansion in 2009. For details on the 2010–2015 forecast, see 'Investment and Forecast Report on China Automotive Industry, 2010–2015' (年中国汽车行业投资分析及前景预测报告), available at http://www.ocn.com.cn/reports/2006 132qiche.htm.

3 Based on the competitive pressures for globalization prevailing in an industry (from 'low' to 'high') and a company's competitive assets (either from 'customized for home market' to 'transferable abroad'), Darwar and Frost (1999) identify four positioning strategies – dodger; defender; extender; and contender. The most prominent example of the 'contender' positioning adopted by a Chinese company to date is Haier Group's 'first difficult, then easy' (Haier Model) approach to competitive internationalization and survival.

4 For details on the dynamics in the political economy space of China, see: Yongnian Zheng (2007); Lin *et al.* (2006); Lin, Y. (2001).

5 Reacting to Sichuan Tengzhong Heavy Industry Machinery's announcement that it intended to acquire GM's Hummer brand, Vice Minister of Commerce Chen Jian observed, 'It's not in coordination with our nation's industrial policy'(Simpkins, 2009), especially considering the Chinese Government's open support for and encouragement of the development of more energy-efficient vehicles, as spelled out in China's auto industry revitalization plan.' The complete text of the auto industry revitalization plan can be accessed at http://www.gov.cn/zwgk/2009-03/20/content_1264324.htm.

6 Under the tentative plan, the total import volume would steadily increase, going from 17,335 vehicles in 2011, to 38,351 in 2012, to 53,302 in 2013, and 51,546 in 2014.

5 FDI location choice of Chinese firms

Traditional economic factors and institutional perspective

Yuanfei Kang

Introduction

The popularity of foreign direct investment (FDI) into China has been followed by the phenomenal growth of China's outward FDI in recent years. The volume of China's FDI outflow recorded an average annual growth of almost 55 per cent during the period of 2002–2007 (UNCTAD, 2008). China has now become the eighth largest contributor of the world's FDI and the largest among developing economies (Yang *et al.*, 2009). The dramatic growth and development in recent years and the anticipated future prospects of China's outward FDI have attracted great attention from international business scholars. A number of studies have examined a series of issues regarding China's outward FDI, including the trend and driving forces of China's outward FDI (Liu *et al.*, 2005; Morck *et al.*, 2008), the determinants and motivations of the involvement by Chinese firms in overseas investment activities (Buckley *et al.*, 2007; Child and Rodrigues, 2005; Deng, 2004, 2007; Liu and Li, 2002; Rui and Yip, 2008), and FDI entry mode decisions of Chinese multinational enterprises (MNEs) (Cui and Jiang, 2009). However, another important issue, namely, FDI location choice of Chinese firms, has not yet been empirically examined in the literature. This research was designed to address this theoretical gap and aims to make two major contributions. First, it developed an integrated theoretical framework that incorporates the institutional perspective (Scott, 2001) along with the traditional economic factors (Buckley *et al.*, 2008; Dunning, 1993) so as to provide a more comprehensive framework for empirical investigation on the issue of FDI location choice. Second, with empirical evidence, this study provided explicit insights explaining the factors influencing FDI location choice of Chinese firms and revealing the different patterns of location choice for different economy groups over different time periods.

The FDI activities of MNEs in developed countries have generated a rich body of literature examining the strategic choice by investing firms on the location of foreign operations (see Pajunen, 2008). Most of these studies have principally focused on the impacts of the traditional economic factors, such as market size, relative labour cost, resource endowments, inflation, and exchange rate, on FDI location choice (e.g. Buckley *et al.*, 2007; Liu *et al.*, 2005). Although these economic factors are important determinants for FDI location choice by MNEs (Cheng and Kwan, 2000; Grosse and Trevino, 1996), they only partially explain decision-making by MNEs on FDI location choice, especially in the context of FDI conducted by developing countries' MNEs. Investing firms require both economic efficiency and institutional legitimacy to survive and succeed in a challenging foreign environment (Kostova and Zaheer, 1999). Researchers have therefore called for more attention to be paid to the influence of institutional forces on FDI decisions and activities (Disdier and Mayer, 2004; Dunning and Lundan, 2008; Grosse and Trevino, 2005; Pajunen, 2008; Trevino *et al.*, 2008). It has even been argued that the need to integrate institutional factors into FDI theory can hardly be over-emphasized (Sethi *et al.*, 2002).

So far, international business research on the institutional influence on foreign direct investment of MNEs has focused mainly on regulative dimensions (e.g. Grosse and Trevino, 2005; Meyer *et al.*, 2009), while institutions influence organizational decision-making through multiple dimensions, including regulative, normative and cognitive pillars (Scott, 2001). Therefore, we believe that the location choice by MNEs is likely to be the result of joint influences from both traditional economic factors and institutional forces, and in the context of Chinese firms' FDI location decisions, the institutional forces may have an even greater impact than the traditional economic factors. In responding to the need to develop a more comprehensive understanding regarding factors and forces influencing FDI location choice of MNEs, this study developed a conceptual framework by integrating the traditional economic factors derived from Dunning's eclectic paradigm (1993, 1998, and 2001) and all three 'pillars' of institutional perspective (Scott, 2001) to empirically test the relevance of Chinese MNEs' FDI location choice in the Asian region during the period of 1995–2007.

The rationale for an Asian focus is twofold. First, geographically China's FDI has mainly flowed to the Asian region. As demonstrated in the literature (e.g. Cheng and Stough, 2007; Hong and Sun, 2006), in terms of both investment projects and capital value, more than half of FDI stock invested by Chinese firms is located in Asian economies. A calculation based on Chinese official data source of outward FDI (MOFCOM, 2004–2008) demonstrates that by the end of 2007, 67 per cent of Chinese FDI stock was located in the Asian region, and 93 per cent of this went to eight Asian economies: Hong Kong, Korea, Japan, Indonesia, Malaysia, Philippines, Singapore and Thailand. Second, international business theory suggests that the internationalization of firms is an incremental process achieved mainly through regional expansion rather than global expansion (Johanson and Vahlne, 1977) and most existing MNEs are regional rather than global players (Qian *et al.*, 2008; Rugman, 2005). In the case of China, Chinese MNEs have few firm-specific advantages, and base their international expansion primarily on country-specific advantages such as scale economy and low labour cost (Child and Rodrigues, 2005). It is even argued that a lack of firm-specific advantages will lead to a trend that FDI from Chinese firms flows mainly intra-regionally rather than globally in the foreseeable future (Rugman and Li, 2007). We therefore argue that the FDI flows into the Asian region from Chinese firms, especially to the eight economies mentioned above, deserve special research attention.

Theories and hypothesis development

Traditional economic factors

It has long been understood that firms entering a new market must adapt their overall strategies to environmental conditions in the foreign market (Kindleberger, 1969). The eclectic paradigm developed by Dunning (1993) provides a holistic approach to explain the level and pattern of FDI activities by MNEs. This approach proposes that both ownership and internalization advantages are examined by firm-specific factors, while location advantages can be investigated through host country-specific variables. These location-specific advantages arise from the business environment associated with a particular geographical location. Location factors, which define the degree of attraction of host countries with respect to the investment decisions carried out by MNEs, are one of the basic determinants that should be taken into account. These location advantages can be broadly categorized into two types. The first is the Ricardian type of endowments, which mainly consists of natural resources, pools of skilled or unskilled labour force, and proximity to target markets. The second type is associated with a range of environmental variables that act as a function of economic, infrastructure and policy factors in the host countries. The perspective of the eclectic paradigm focuses on the economic rationale of FDI behaviour and suggests that foreign firms are motivated to exploit location-specific advantages provided by the host country through internalizing their firm-specific advantages. Firms with different strategic motivations choose locations with different sets of location advantages. As Dunning (1998) encapsulated in his eclectic paradigm, the mainstream theory on location aspect identified four primary motivations for FDI, namely marketing-seeking, nature resource-seeking, efficiency-seeking, and strategic asset-seeking. These motivations are also relevant to the FDI location choice of Chinese MNEs (Buckley *et al.*, 2008). Derived from the eclectic paradigm, the first set of determinants in this study captures the economic location advantages offered by the host country and also accommodates the strategic motivations of investing firms in order to demonstrate the influence of macro-economic factors.

Market seeking   Factors related to the host country market are the most widely tested variables in influencing FDI location decisions. Empirical research has revealed a strong positive relationship between market size of the host country and FDI inflows (Barrell and Pain, 1997; Bevan and Estrin, 2004; Braunerhjelm and Svenson, 1996; Culem, 1988). Market-seeking investors are attracted by a large market size and high market potential in the host country. A larger market size offers increased opportunities for investors to reach cost effectiveness and to realize economies of scale through location production (Venables, 1999). Thus, the larger the market size, the more attractive the host country is. Moreover, a rapidly growing economy provides relatively better opportunities for profit-making than those that are slowly growing or stagnant. Rapid economic growth in the host economy leads to a high level of aggregate demand for products and stimulates greater demand for FDI inflows. Facing high market potential, market-seeking FDI is able to obtain economies of scale and to establish a long-term market presence. Thus, the higher the economic growth rates, the more FDI that is attracted to the host country. In the case of China's outward FDI, recent studies suggest that market-seeking is one of the major driving forces for Chinese MNEs (Buckley *et al.*, 2007, 2008; Deng, 2004). When a Chinese firm resorts to FDI as a motivation to pursue and penetrate new markets, it will take an interest in the market size and economic growth of the host market. Thus:

Hypothesis 1a: The choice of a Chinese firm's FDI location is positively associated with the market size of the host economy.
Hypothesis 1b: The choice of a Chinese firm's FDI location is positively associated with the market growth of the host economy.

Resource seeking Acquiring and securing a continual supply of natural resources is one of the major motives for FDI activity (Dunning, 1993) and the central cause for backward vertical FDI. FDI induced by the need to gain access to foreign natural resources is common to both developed and developing countries. The objective for resource-seeking FDI is to provide inputs into investing firms' downstream operations in the home country. Internalization theory emphasizes the importance of equity-based control in the exploitation of scarce natural resources (Buckley and Casson, 1976). In the case of China, as per capita availability of natural resources is quite low, particularly in the areas of minerals, petroleum, timber and fisheries, resource-seeking has been regarded as one of the key strategic considerations for Chinese outward FDI. This consideration has been highlighted by a number of high-profile resource-based Chinese acquisitions in the world (Cheng and Stough, 2007; Deng, 2004; Hong and Sun, 2006).

Hypothesis 2: The choice of a Chinese firm's FDI location is positively associated with the richness of the natural resource endowment of the host economy.

Efficiency seeking Vernon (1966) points out that the availability of cheap inputs in a foreign country is an essential determinant for moving production capacity abroad. Following this argument, it is logical that foreign investors display sensitivity to inter-country variation in labour costs when making location decisions for FDI. Thus, a negative relationship between labour cost and FDI flows to a host country can be suggested. Efficiency-seeking investors are attracted by a low level of labour costs, which results in a shift of production capabilities to developing countries. It is suggested that there are changing trends in the world economy in terms of location distribution of FDI activities during the past three decades with a shift of FDI flows from European- and American-developed to Asian-developing countries, caused by increasing exploitation of lower labour costs in

Asia's developing countries (Sethi *et al.*, 2002, 2003). However, empirical research has also suggested that a positive relationship between labour cost and FDI inflows also exists at the country level (Coughlin *et al.*, 1991; Culem, 1988; Dunning, 1998). The major reason for this pattern is that higher labour costs imply greater labour skills, and thus higher productivity. The Chinese domestic market provides a rich pool of low-cost labour, and thus it is unlikely that greater efficiency is currently a major motivating force for Chinese firms investing overseas. However, the focus of this study addresses the location choice among overseas destinations with different locational characteristics. Variations in labour cost in potential overseas markets are expected to have an impact on the flow of Chinese FDI into those locations.

Hypothesis 3: The choice of a Chinese firm's FDI location is negatively associated with the labour cost in the host economy.

Strategic asset-seeking   It is suggested that one of the major driving forces for FDI from firms in emerging markets is to compensate their competitive disadvantages in terms of proprietary technology, management know-how and product brands when competing with multinationals from developed countries (Child and Rodrigues, 2005; Luo and Tung, 2007; Rugman and Li, 2007; Svetličič, 2003). By resorting to outward FDI, firms from emerging markets proactively acquire or buy strategic assets from mature multinationals to compensate for their competitive weaknesses. In the case of China, it is reported that when investing in developed economies, Chinese firms are motivated primarily by the quest for strategic assets and capabilities. The underlying rationale for such asset-seeking FDI is the strategic need to compete at a global level (Cheng and Stough, 2007; Deng, 2004, 2007, 2009).

Hypothesis 4: Chinese FDI to an economy is positively associated with availability of strategic assets in the economy.

Institutional perspectives

It is well known that complex institutional structures impose constraints on social agents and reduce the uncertainty of social interaction (North, 1990). Following this argument, it has been suggested that more attention should be paid to the influence of institutions on FDI activities, as institutional infrastructure should be central to any study of the determinants of international business activity (e.g. Daude and Stein, 2007; Dunning, 2006; Grosse and Trevino, 2005; Meyer *et al.*, 2009; Pajunen, 2008; Sethi *et al.*, 2002).

The central premise of institutional theory is that organizations are embedded in, and must adapt to, their institutional environment to attain legitimacy (Suchman, 1995; Zukin and DiMaggio, 1990). From this perspective, location choice by MNEs can be viewed as a means of conforming to the institutional environment of a host country and to the organizational practice routines.

Although some institutional factors such as government policy, legal framework, political stability, and corruption have been included in the conceptual framework of the eclectic paradigm as determinants for location choice (e.g. Grosse and Trevino, 1996; Sethi *et al.*, 2002; Stoian and Filippaios, 2008), there are two central differences between the eclectic paradigm and the institutional approach in the adaptation of institutional variables. First is the primary criterion of location choice. By incorporating the transactional cost approach into an analysis of FDI activity, the eclectic paradigm focuses on economic efficiency as the ultimate determinant of location choice. From this perspective, the intersection of MNE investment strategy and the institutional environment is to analyse the ability of institutions to reduce the transaction costs associated with FDI that result from an uncertain environment, as suggested by Hoskisson *et al.* (2000). On the contrary, the institutional approach regards institutional legitimacy as the primary criterion. From the perspective of institutional theory, organizations are motivated to enhance their legitimacy by becoming isomorphic with their environment, even in the absence of evidence that such actions increase efficiency (Scott, 2001; Yiu and Makino, 2002).

Second is the issue of which institutional dimensions should be included in the conceptual framework of location determinants. Most existing studies examined only the regulative dimension of institutions, leaving the other two institutional dimensions untouched (Trevino *et al.*, 2008). Regulative, normative and cognitive systems are identified as three pillars of institutional environment, and each of them provides a basis for legitimacy, although from different institutional perspectives (Scott, 2001). The regulative pillar involves the capacity to establish rules, to ensure conformity to the rules, and to manipulate sanctions for influencing future behaviour; the normative system imposes constraints on social behaviour through prescriptive and obligatory values and norms; the cognitive pillar refers to the established structures in society that are taken for granted (Scott, 2001). Relating the broad theoretical framework of institutional theory to the issue of FDI location choice, it can be suggested that multinational enterprises tend to select a location for FDI activities where they are able to conform to the institutional environment in the host country and thus to attain legitimacy. Based on the argument of three institutional pillars, several determinants are identified to capture the influence of institutional forces on the FDI location choice of Chinese firms.

The second set of determinants in this study captures the institutional dimensions of the host environment. Some recent attempts have been made to incorporate the institutional environment into conventional approaches to FDI location choice, such as the eclectic paradigm and transaction cost approaches (e.g. Bevan *et al.*, 2004; Grosse and Trevino, 2005; Sethi *et al.*, 2002; Stoian and Filippaios, 2008). However, in these studies, the complex institutional environment is examined only on the regulative dimension and with a clear focus of economic efficiency. The other two dimensions of the institutional environment (normative and cognitive pillars) have not yet been incorporated into the conceptual framework of FDI location choice. Built on the framework of three institutional pillars

(Scott, 2001), this study aims to examine several institutional variables to demonstrate how the regulative, normative and cognitive dimensions of institutional environment, jointly with economic factors, influence location choice of MNEs.

Regulative institutions   The regulative dimension of the institutional environment establishes the rules of the game (including laws, rules and unwritten codes of conduct) that structure interactions as well as ensure stability and order in societies, and bound organizational actions (North, 1990). In comparison to local firms, MNEs are unfamiliar with the local rules of the game in business transactions and are likely to be under discriminative institutional pressure from the native government when entering a foreign market (Yiu and Makino, 2002). When deciding whether or not to enter a particular foreign market, the most appealing concern for an investing firm is if it is able to gain market legitimacy by establishing the right to do business in the local market. Through emphasizing conformity to rules, regulative institutions provide one of the bases of legitimacy to organizations: legitimate organizations are those established by and operating in accordance with relevant legal and quasi-legal requirements (Scott, 2001). Therefore, from the perspective of the regulative institutions, location choice for MNEs is a decision to determine favourable locations where regulative institutional constraints are less repressive to FDI activity so that MNEs can more readily conform to the regulative constituents of host countries. Empirical studies have confirmed that political and legal institutions in host countries have a strong influence on FDI inflows (Bevan *et al.*, 2004; Grosse & Trevino, 2005; Pajunen, 2008; Dunning, 2006), although findings are inconsistent as to which types of regulative institutions are more important.

Similarly, the institutional environment in the home country is also a major shaping force for firms' FDI behaviour. It has been suggested that the institutional environment facing Chinese firms in their home country is significantly different to their Western counterparts (Meyer *et al.*, 2009; Peng *et al.*, 2008; Yang *et al.*, 2009). A distinctive and highly dynamic home country institutional environment also contributes to the uniqueness of Chinese outward FDI. The Chinese Government maintains strong influence on the outward FDI of Chinese firms (Deng, 2004; Morck *et al.*, 2008; Peng and Delios, 2006). Until 2004, all outward FDI projects were subject to government approval, and annual reporting of overseas operational matters was also mandatory. Through the approval system and financial policies, the Chinese Government may favour or discourage certain types of outward FDI based on its short- and long-term economic development agenda (Liu *et al.*, 2005). Accordingly, Chinese firms have to adjust their FDI decisions and activities to comply with their home country institutions (Cui and Jiang, 2009), while also having to conform to the institutional requirements in host countries (Rui and Yip, 2008). These double requirements impose a challenge for Chinese firms to gain legitimacy for their FDI activities. It is easier to adapt to a new institutional environment where the institutional differences between home and host economies are smaller. Therefore, it can be suggested that Chinese firms are more likely to locate their FDI in economies where the differences between regulative institutions in the home and host countries are smaller.

Hypothesis 5: The choice of a Chinese firm's FDI location is negatively associated with differences of regulative institutions between China and the host economy.

Normative institutions   The normative dimension of institutions emphasizes the stabilizing influence of social values and norms, which imposes constraints on interpersonal and inter-organizational behaviour. As argued by Stinchcombe (1997: 18): 'The guts of institutions is that somebody somewhere really cares to hold an organization to the standards.' Organizations are embedded in the institutional environment of social values and norms that define socially acceptable organizational behaviour. While operating in foreign countries, MNEs need to establish social legitimacy, as in comparison to their local counterparts they are more vulnerable to attacks from local interest groups and face more stereotypes and different standards (Kostova and Zaheer, 1999). The establishment of social legitimacy can also be more difficult than the case for regulative legitimacy, as normative controls stress a deeper moral base and are much more likely to be internalized than regulative controls (Scott, 2001). Cultural distance is identified as a major barrier for MNEs gaining normative legitimacy in host countries (Yiu and Makino, 2002). It has been suggested that differences in national culture has a strong influence on location choice of FDI (Bhardwaj *et al.*, 2007). The bigger the cultural distance between the host and home countries, the more difficult it is for MNEs to gain normative legitimacy in the host country. Empirical evidence has also confirmed the tendency that, traditionally, MNEs would invest in those countries where cultural proximity exists with the home country (Sethi *et al.*, 2002). Thus, Chinese firms are more likely to locate their FDI in economies where cultural differences between China and the host economy are smaller.

Hypothesis 6: The choice of a Chinese firm's FDI location is negatively associated with the cultural distance between China and the host economy.

Cognitive institutions   The cognitive dimension of institutions is promoted from the perspective of anthropology. This dimension recognizes that internal interpretive processes are shaped by external stimuli, as mediating between the external world of stimuli and the response of the individual organism is a collection of internalized symbolic representations of the world (D'Andrade, 1984). Based on cognitive institutional theory, compliance occurs in many circumstances because other types of behaviour are inconceivable and routines are followed because they are taken for granted (Scott, 2001). Cognitive institutions affect the location choice of MNEs, as the mindset of MNE decision makers is influenced by intraorganizational imprinting, which is a process of institutionalization. Two cognitive barriers can be identified as factors influencing Chinese investing firms' FDI location choice. The first is the liability of foreignness and it is especially the case for those from emerging markets such as China (He and Lyles, 2008). This liability is derived from the major sources of unfamiliarity of the MNE with the local market, spatial distance between the host and home countries, and particular characteristics of the business environment in the host country (Zaheer, 1995). The second is the inherent characteristic of the Chinese culture in uncertainty avoidance. Uncertainty avoidance is defined as 'the extent to which the members of a culture feel threatened by uncertain or unknown situations' (Hofstede, 2001: 161) and it is identified as a major cultural factor influencing the FDI location choice of investing firms (Bhardwai *et al.*, 2007). Chinese culture scores highly on uncertainty avoidance (Hofstede, 2005).

Adaptation of an orthodox practice while facing the liability of foreignness and uncertain situations is a way to seek the legitimacy that comes from cognitive consistency, as cognitive legitimacy is gained through a mimetic mechanism (Scott, 2001). When facing uncertainty in a new foreign market, experiences of other organizations in comparable circumstances are taken as guidance or reference for an organization's decision-making. If a particular type of practice is frequently repeated by many organizations, it would be routinized as a behavioural stereotype and accepted as a cognitive structure. This behaviour pattern is named mimetic isomorphism (DiMaggio and Powell, 1983). Although a mimetic behavioural pattern does not provide a guarantee of reaching the expected high efficiency, it does help organizations to gain cognitive legitimacy. In the case of FDI location choice, empirical evidence suggests a bandwagon effect results from a follow-the-leader approach of decision-making (Sethi *et al.*, 2002). Frequency in business dealings by host and home country firms is reflected by the intensity of economic relations between the two countries, which can be proxied by exports to the host country. A large volume of exports represents a high frequency of business transactions conducted by firms of the home economy in a host economy. This repetitive pattern of business dealings in trade relations can become habitualized and objectified. By imitating this location pattern in trade relations, investing firms may expand the business transaction pattern to another similar area – FDI, especially for those motivated by market seeking. Furthermore, a high frequency of business dealings resulting from trade relations can also influence FDI location choice through a cognitive mechanism called external legitimacy spillover (Kostova and Zaheer, 1999). Local constituents make sense of new investors by referring to past patterns. When local constituents evaluate a particular foreign investment case, they may refer to the legitimacy of others in the same cognitive category. If firms in the home country export a high volume of goods to the host country, a good reputation for exporting firms may spill over to investing firms, thus facilitating attainment of legitimacy.

Hypothesis 7: The choice of a Chinese firm's FDI location is positively associated with the intensity of business transactions between firms of the host and home economies.

Research method and data

Dependent variable

FDI stock   FDI stock from Chinese firms in each of the eight host Asian economies, rather than FDI flows to these economies, is used as the dependent variable, as the stock variable can more accurately measure locational distribution of FDI. Data for the dependent variable were obtained from official Chinese data source MOFCOM, *Almanac of China's Foreign Economic Relations and Trade* (Vols 1996 to 2008), which was renamed the China Commercial Yearbook in 2004.

Independent variables from the eclectic paradigm

GDP per capita (GDPP) This variable captures the market size of a host economy and is measured by annual GDP per capita of the economy. Data for this variable were taken from the database *World Development Indicator 2008 (WDI)* published by the World Bank (2008).

GDP growth (GDPG) This variable captures the market potential of a host economy and is measured by the annual growth rate of the economy. Data for this variable were obtained from *WDI 2008*.

Resource (RESO) This variable is measured as the ratio of ore and metal exports to merchandise exports in the host economy and it captures the resource-seeking motive of the investing firms. Data for this variable were obtained from *WDI 2008*.

Unit labour cost (ULC) This variable is measured by the average wage in the manufacturing industry in the host economy and captures investing firms' efficiency-seeking motive. Data for this variable were taken from the *Labour Statistics Database 2008* published by the Bureau of Statistics, International Labour Organization (2008).

Patent (PATENT) Patent applications in the host economy are used as a proxy for the development level for technology and management know-how to accommodate the strategic assets-seeking motivation of the investing firms. This variable measures the availability of intellectual capital in the host economy. Data for this variable were taken from the database *Statistics on Patents* published by the World Intellectual Property Organization (2008).

Independent variables from the institutional approach

Three variables – economic freedom (EFREE), political influence (POLITIC) and FDI restriction (RESTR) – are used to represent the regulative pillar of institutions and to measure the extent to which regulative forces influence FDI activities in the host country.

Economic freedom (EFREE) Economic freedom is used as the variable representing economic regulative forces in the broad institutional environment of a host country. In order to conceptualize this variable, five component items in the domain of economic regulative institutions were used: 1) business freedom; 2) monetary freedom; 3) financial freedom; 4) property rights; and 5) freedom from corruption. These five items were derived from the annual *Index of Economic Freedom, 1995–2007* developed by the Heritage Foundation (2008), which provides time series data for most countries and economies in the world. In the original data source, economic freedom was measured by ten categories. The five items were selected based on two criteria. First is the theoretical relevancy of the item to FDI activities in the host country, and the second was the practical configuration of the composite variable. The five items were found to be highly correlated for the eight economies under study covering the period from 1995 to 2007, with all but one correlation coefficients greater than 0.60. Thus, the five component items were merged into a composite variable acting as a proxy for economic freedom. As suggested in hypothesis 5, relative differences of regulative institutions between China and the host economy, rather than the regulative institutions of the host economy, are to be investigated as the potential variable influencing FDI location choice of Chinese firms. Using score data taken from the *Economic Freedom Index*, the variable of difference in economic freedom between China and the eight host economies was measured by the five selected composite items.

Political influence (POLITIC)   Political influence is used as the variable representing the political and legal regulative forces in the institutional environment of both the home and host economies. Six component items were adopted to configure this variable: 1) the political system (the extent to which the political system adapts to current economic challenges); 2) bureaucracy (the extent to which bureaucracy does not hinders business activity and development); 3) the legal and regulative framework (the extent to which the legal and regulative framework encourages competitiveness of enterprises); 4) government economic policies (the extent to which the government adapts its policies to new economic realities effectively); 5) corporate tax (the extent to which the corporate tax regime encourages entrepreneurial activity); and 6) protectionism (the extent to which national protectionism does not prevents foreign products and services being imported). Data for these six component items were obtained from the *World Competitiveness Yearbooks 1995–2007 (WCY)*, a data collection of annual surveys published by IMD International and the World Economic Forum. The *WCY* data are considered a relatively accurate reflection of the subjective opinions from potential investors (Yiu and Markino, 2002), as the data are compiled from annual surveys which directly address corporate executives. As pointed out by researchers (e.g. Meyer *et al.*, 2009), a major problem with this source for research based on time series data is the availability of consistent data for the same component items, since definitions for survey items may change over time. However, a close check with the six component items used for this variable indicates that the definitions for these adopted component items have been relatively stable and unchanged for the duration of this study. A correlation test revealed that scores for the eight economies under study in terms of the six selected component items for the period 1995–2007 were highly correlated, with all correlation coefficients greater than 0.60. Thus, the six component items were merged into a composite variable acting as a proxy for regulative institutions and the mean scores of the six items are used to measure the degree of political influence. Following the method used in measuring the variable of difference in economic freedom, the variable of difference in political influence between China and the eight host economies is measured by using the score data for the selected six items from the *WCY*.

FDI restriction (RESTR) FDI restriction is used as the variable representing the institutional regime directly regulating FDI activities. It measures the extent to which foreign firms have difficulties in acquiring control over a domestic firm in a host country. Data for this variable were obtained from *WCY 1995–2007*. As one of the variables representing regulative institutions, FDI restriction is measured by the relative difference between China and the host economy by using the score data taken from *WCY*, following the same method used for the two variables of economic freedom and political influence.

Cultural distance (CULTR) Cultural distance is a variable representing the normative dimension of institutions and it measures the extent to which normative forces influence FDI activities. In this study, cultural distance is defined as the difference between the national culture of the home country (China) and those of the eight host economies. It is measured through the four dimensions of cultural difference in terms power distance, uncertainty avoidance, individualism, and masculinity identified by Hofstede (1983). Using the score data for individual countries provided by Hofstede (2005) and following the method developed by Kogut and Singh (1988), culture distance between China and the eight host economies was measured by using a composite variable consisting of the four dimensions of culture.

Chinese exports to the host country (CEXPO) The variable of Chinese exports to a host economy is used to measure the influence of cognitive institutions on FDI flows from Chinese firms to the host economy. The variable of exports is traditionally used as an economic variable and reflects the trade intensity between host and home countries. From the perspective of economics theory, the relationship between trade and FDI is not a straightforward one. On the one hand, Mundell (1957) suggests a substitute relationship between trade and FDI, as capital mobility (FDI) created by differences in factor prices between countries would lead to elimination of price differentials in both goods and factor markets, thus removing the basis for trade. On the other hand, Markusen (1983) demonstrates that factor movement and trade can be complementary to one another, provided the basis of trade is not different in relative factor endowment. The alternative bases for trade include external economies of scale, imperfect competition, distortion in product for factor markets and different production technologies. From the perspective of institutional approach, the variable of exports indicates a choice of exporting destinations by firms from the home country and reflects the intensity of transactional dealings for firms between host and home countries. If a particular destination choice for exports is repeated with high frequency over time so that it is institutionalized in managers' mindsets, expanding export destination choice to FDI location choice will be a way to gain legitimacy. Thus, the variable of exports from home country to host country was used as a proxy for the mimic pattern of location choice. Data for this variable were sourced from the *China Statistical Yearbook 1996–2008* by the State Statistical Bureau of China (SSBC).

Control variables

Two control variables were included in model testing to reveal the impacts of the main variables.

Market openness (OPEN)   When the economic orientation in a host country fits more easily into the patterns of global production and trade, the country is more attractive to foreign investors (Vernon, 1966). This variable is measured as ratio of an economy's exports over its total foreign trade, reflecting competitiveness and export orientation of the economy. It is used as a control variable in model testing, accommodating the market-seeking motive of investing firms. A positive relationship between the openness of the host economy and location choice of Chinese FDI is expected. Data for this variable were obtained from *WDI 2008*.

Inflation (INFL)   Inflation implies instability and uncertainty of the economy, and imposes a higher risk to firms operating in the economy. If foreign investors have a risk-averse orientation, a higher rate of inflation would lead to a reduction in FDI inflows. Thus, a negative relationship between inflation in the host economy and location choice of Chinese FDI is expected. This variable is measured by the annual inflation rate in the host economy and data were taken from *WDI 2008*.

Table 5.1 provides a summary for the hypotheses developed in this study, their theoretical justification, the proxies used to measure the relevant variables, and the data sources for empirical testing. It is expected that the distinctive features of the location choice nature of foreign investment from Chinese firms will be captured by the collective significance in the independent variables derived from the eclectic paradigm and the institutional perspective.

Estimation method

The panel data estimation method was adopted, as this analytical method combines information on the variation of individual units with information taking place over time. In this study, the use of the panel data model pooled together cross-sectional data of eight Asian economies over the period of thirteen years

Table 5.1 Description of hypotheses and variables

Hypothesis	Variable	Theoretical justification	Variable types	Data source
	Stock of Chinese FDI in host country		Dependent variable	*Almanac of China's Foreign Economic Relations and Trade* (1996–2003); *China Commercial Yearbook* (2004–2008)
H1a: Market size	GDPP: GDP per capita	Market-seeking	Independent variable	*World Development Indicator*, World Bank (2008)
H1b: Market potential	GDPG: GDP growth	Market-seeking	Independent variable	*World Development Indicator*, World Bank (2008)
H2: Nature-source incentives	RESO: Resource endowment	Resource-seeking	Independent variable	*World Development Indicator*, World Bank (2008)
H3: Production cost/ efficiency	ULC: Unit labour cost	Efficiency-seeking	Independent variable	Labour Statistics Database, International Labour Organization(2008)
H4: availability of strategic assets	*PATENT*: Patent applications	Strategic assets seeking	Independent variable	Statistics on Patents, World Intellectual Property Organization (2008)
H5: Regulative institutions	EFREE: Economic freedom	Regulative pillar	Independent variable	*Index of Economic Freedom*, Heritage Foundation (1995–2007)
H5: Regulative institutions	POLITIC: Political freedom	Regulative pillar	Independent variable	*World Competitiveness Yearbooks*, IMD International and the World Economic Forum (1995–2007)
H5: Regulative institutions	RESTR: FDI restriction	Regulative pillar	Independent variable	*World Competitiveness Yearbooks*, IMD International and the World Economic Forum (1995–2007)
H6: Normative institutions	CULTR: Cultural distance	Normative pillar	Independent variable	Hofstede (2005)
H7: Cognitive institutions	CEXPO: Chinese exports to host country	Cognitive pillar	Independent variable	*China Statistical Yearbook*, State Statistical Bureau of China (1996–2008)
	OPEN: Ratio of exports to total foreign trade	Market Openness	Control variable	*World Development Indicator*, World Bank (2008)
	INFL: Annual inflation rate	Macroeconomic stability	Control variable	*World Development Indicator*, World Bank (2008)

from 1995 to 2007. According Hsiao (2003), the advantage of the panel data estimation technique is that it allows idiosyncrasies (heterogeneity) existing among units (individual economies in this study) to be considered and controlled, thus avoiding problems of misspecification under other circumstances.

To account for unobservable country effects in the panel data, an error component model (ECM) is adopted, as suggested by Baltagi (2005):

$$y_{it} = \alpha + \beta x_{it} + \delta_i + u_{it} \qquad i = 1, \ldots, N; t = 1, \ldots, T \tag{1}$$

The dependent variable y_{it} is represented by Chinese FDI stock observed for individual unit i at time t. The symbol α represents the intercept term, β is the vector of coefficients, and x_{it} is a vector of regressors. The symbol δ_i indicates the individual country effect and u_{it} is a stochastic disturbance. The subscript i denotes an individual country and the subscript t denotes a time period. Equation (1) allows for a systematic tendency of the residual term u_{it} to vary across the N individual countries (individual country effects) as well as across the T time periods (time effects).

As discussed in the variable description in the current study, we have:

$$Y_{it} = (GDPP, GDPG, RESO, ULC, PATENT, EFREE, POLITIC, \\ RESTR, CULTR, CEXPO, OPEN, INFL) \tag{2}$$

Thus, the regression model is more precisely formulated as follows:

$$OFDI_{it} = \alpha_{it} + \beta_1 GDPP_{it} + \beta_2 GDPG_{it} + \beta_3 OPEN_{it} + \beta_4 RESO_{it} \\ + \beta_5 ULC_{it} + \beta_6 PATENT_{it} + \beta_7 EFREE_{it} + \beta_8 POLITIC_{it} \\ + \beta_9 RESTR_{it} + \beta_{10} CULTR_{it} + \beta_{11} TRADE_{it} + \beta_{12} INFL_{it} + \iota \tag{3}$$

where $i = 1, \ldots, 8$ represents host country i and $t = 1995, \ldots, 2007$ indicates the time period.

Model (3) was adopted for the empirical estimation of FDI location choice by Chinese firms. Panel data for the eight Asian host economies covering the period 1995–2007 were used and the random-effects (RE) model was selected as the model specification. A Lagrangian multiplier test was conducted to select the statistical model for empirical estimation. The result suggested that the RE model was more suitable for our data than the ordinary least squares (OLS) model, and thus the RE model was selected as the model specification. Table 5.2 provides the descriptive statistics and correlation matrix of the variables in the study. The correlation matrix shows that correlation coefficients for most explanatory variables are below 0.60; however, there are a number of correlation coefficients that are well above 0.60. A coefficient above 0.60 is considered to be rather high (Churchill, 1991). In estimating the empirical model, the issue of multicollinearity was taken into account. An introduction of closely related independent variables

Table 5.2 Descriptive statistics and correlations for independent variables

Variables	Mean	S.D.	1	2	3	4	5	6	7	8	9	10	11
1 GDPP	16260.130	12753.790	1.000										
2 GDPG	2.788	3.968	0.095	1.000									
3 RESO	2.192	1.866	-0.338	0.062	1.000								
4 ULC	940.579	999.217	0.793	-0.064	-0.257	1.000							
5 EFREE	2.426	1.933	0.766	-0.005	-0.296	0.626	1.000						
6 POLITIC	1.570	1.468	0.457	0.073	-0.077	0.345	0.620	1.000					
7 RESTR	2.548	2.948	0.642	0.103	-0.103	0.347	0.590	0.390	1.000				
8 CULTR	1.421	1.400	0.152	0.027	-0.287	0.113	-0.080	-0.356	-0.251	1.000			
9 CEXPO	2203140.420	3292454.480	0.627	0.094	-0.020	0.544	0.440	0.053	0.513	0.140	1.000		
10 OPEN	0.180	0.479	0.451	-0.010	0.037	0.358	0.641	0.374	0.665	-0.378	0.559	1.000	
11 INFL	3.854	6.562	-0.432	-0.415	0.402	-0.392	-0.337	-0.160	-0.292	-0.176	0.266	-0.156	1.000

Table 5.3 Variance inflation factors (VIF) test

Variable	VIF	1/VIF	Eigenvalue	Condition index
GDPP	9.58253	0.10436	4.38298	1.00000
GDPG	1.57913	0.63326	1.90964	1.51499
RESO	1.62776	0.61434	1.31170	1.82797
ULC	4.43981	0.22524	1.18333	1.92456
EFREE	4.21211	0.23741	0.66305	2.57105
POLITIC	2.52294	0.39636	0.47735	3.03017
RESTR	4.30329	0.23238	0.35443	3.51658
CULTR	2.61182	0.38288	0.27697	3.97802
CEXPO	3.21562	0.31098	0.24244	4.25192
OPEN	3.64646	0.27424	0.13541	5.68936
INFL	2.10983	0.47397	0.06271	8.36039
Mean VIF	3.62285			

simultaneously may generate a serious problem of multicollinearity in model estimation and this influences the estimation results. In detecting multicollinearity, a multiple regression analysis was conducted to examine the variance inflation factors (VIF). According to Bowerman *et al.*, (2005), multicollinearity is severe if the largest VIF value is greater than 10, which means that R_j^2 is greater than 0.9. As shown in Table 5.3, all VIF values for individual explanatory variables were under 10, leading to a reduction of multicollinearity concerns.

A structural break method was used to investigate heterogeneity within the data. After the full sample was estimated, data for the eight economies across the whole period 1995–2007 were split into different subsamples, following two data breaking lines. First, the full sample was separated into two groups of developed (Hong Kong, Japan, Korea and Singapore) and developing (Indonesia, Malaysia, Philippines and Thailand) economies, examining the different combinations of location choice variables for these two types of economies. Second, the full sample were split into two time periods (1995–2000 and 2001–2007), investigating the dynamic changes in character of FDI location choice by Chinese firms in different time periods. The dividing line is around the year 2001, which marked a milestone in Chine FDI outflows. In that year the encouragement to FDI outflows by the Chinese Government was formalized through the 'go global' policy outlined in its five-year plan, and by China's admission to WTO membership in the same year. Since then, FDI outflows from China have soared. The two-way split of the full sample into four subsamples was statistically supported by Chow tests, with results showing that the subsamples along the two breaking lines are statistically similar.

Modelling results and discussion

In the preliminary model testing, variable patent (*PATENT*) never attained significance. The statistical insignificance of this variable may reflect the fact that Chinese firms tended to invest in the USA, Canada, Australia, and to a less extent in European Union countries, not in Asian economies, when driven by strategic asset-seeking motivation (Buckley *et al.*, 2008). Moreover, preliminary correlation tests indicated that the variable patent is highly correlated with several independent variables such as GDP per capita, unit labour cost and cultural distance. Therefore, the variable patent was not included in the final model specification. Table 5.4 provides the summary of estimation results of five modelling specifications from RE model testing. The fitness of the models looks good, as the regression models explained over 65 per cent (except for model 4) of the variation in geographical distribution of Chinese FDI flows to the eight Asian economies covering the period 1995–2007.

Results from full sample testing

Turning to hypotheses testing, we first discuss the results for the full sample. The results provided limited support to the hypotheses for traditional economic

Table 5.4 Estimation results

	Full model (1)	*Developed economies* (2)	*Developing countries* (3)	*Period 1 (1995–2000)* (4)	*Period 2 (2001–2007)* (5)
GDPP	−0.0291	0.0518	−0.8299†	−0.0995	−0.0135
	(0.2077)	(0.1785)	(0.4553)	(0.2913)	(0.4725)
GDPG	0.0794	−0.0456	−0.1041	−0.0404	0.0788
	(0.0730)	(0.0690)	(0.1301)	(0.0479)	(0.0527)
RESO	−0.0856	0.1571	0.7631***	0.1161	−0.2979†
	(0.1414)	(0.1286)	(0.2147)	(0.1073)	(0.1526)
ULC	−0.5258***	−0.4714	0.6233	−0.0725	−1.5988***
	(0.1747)	(0.3414)	(0.4198)	(0.2456)	(0.5623)
EFREE	0.3323***	0.2710*	−0.1653	0.1459	−0.3190†
	(0.1063)	(0.1124)	(0.1195)	(0.1084)	(0.1666)
POLITIC	−0.1697*	−0.1322	0.0942	−0.0521	−0.0495
	(0.0653)	(0.0909)	(0.1488)	(0.0715)	(0.0688)
RESTR	0.0414	0.0795	0.0670	0.2802***	0.2157
	(0.1117)	(0.1341)	(0.1104)	(0.0679)	(0.1590)
CULTR	−0.2296†	0.9705	0.5992***	−0.3643	−0.0288
	(0.1243)	(0.8071)	(0.1107)	(0.2928)	(0.5926)
CEXPO	1.0053***	0.7731***	0.9516***	0.4207†	0.9636***
	(0.1072)	(0.1802)	(0.2090)	(0.2238)	(0.1624)
OPEN	−0.0076	1.4023***	0.0403	−0.0523	0.6169***
	(0.1036)	(0.2932)	(0.1151)	(0.1119)	(0.2052)
INFL	0.0561	0.0935	−0.1097	−0.0213	0.0008
	(0.0573)	(0.0745)	(0.1182)	(0.0524)	(0.1101)
N	104	52	52	48	56
Adjusted R-square	0.6703	0.8419	0.7784	0.4048	0.7972

Note: † $p<0.10$; * $p<0.05$; ** $p<0.01$; *** $p<0.001$. Standard errors are in parentheses.

variables. Among the four variables taken from a macro-economic perspective, only the variable unit labour cost (ULC) was significant. It was expected and found that the variable ULC had a negative impact on location choice. Thus, hypothesis 3 is supported, indicating that higher labour costs in the host Asian economies served as a deterrent for Chinese FDI. Given the fact that China has the largest pool of cheap labour in the world, this result is predictable. This result suggests that FDI activities conducted by Chinese firms are becoming more conscious of profit-maximizing, rather than being driven by political considerations and connections between China and host developing countries.

Results from full sample modelling demonstrate that institutional variables had strong influences on the FDI location choice of Chinese firms among the Asian economies. It was predicted and confirmed that all three institutional dimensions (regulative, normative and cognitive) had an influence on the location choice of Chinese FDI. Among the three variables based on regulative institutions, two (economic freedom and political influence) had a significant impact on location choice by Chinese firms but the impact of other regulative variable (FDI restriction) was not significant. Thus, hypothesis 5 has been supported to a large extent.

A major finding regarding the two variables representing regulative institutions was that their influencing directions were in opposite directions. The variable economic freedom (EFREE) had a significant and positive effect, suggesting that the bigger the difference in economic freedom between China and the host country in Asia, the more likely Chinese firms would locate their FDI there. On the other hand, the variable political influence (POLITIC) had a significant but negative effect, suggesting that the smaller the difference in political and legal framework between China and the host country, the more likely Chinese firms would locate their FDI there. The contrasting results for these two regulative variables call for discussion. It is understandable that Chinese firms would prefer FDI locations where there is a big difference in the levels of economic freedom between the home and host economies, as this result suggests that Chinese FDI preferred a host economy with higher orientation towards a market economy regime. In spite of the three-decade market-oriented economic reform, the Chinese economy is still heavily regulated with a much lower mean score in the economic freedom index than those of the host economies under study, as demonstrated in the *Index of Economic Freedom 1995–2007* from the Heritage Foundation. A higher level of difference in economic freedom between China and a host economy means that the economic regime in the host economy is less repressive and more friendly towards FDI activity. Thus, the investing Chinese firms could more readily conform to the economic regulative constituents of the host economy.

For the variable of political influence, as indicated in the definitions for its component items, a higher score value means that the regulative regime of the political and legal dimension in an economy is more stable, less risky and less centralized control, and vice versa. Data from the *World Competitiveness Yearbook* suggest that the Chinese economy scored relatively low on this variable. The distinctive and highly dynamic home country institutional environment (Meyer *et al.*, 2009; Peng *et al.*, 2008) may contribute to the uniqueness of FDI location choice by Chinese firms in terms of political influence. Several causes may contribute to the tendency that Chinese firms would locate their FDI flows in economies where there is a smaller difference in political and legal influence between China and the host economy. First, operating in a politically unstable and risky environment in the home country, Chinese firms may find that they can more readily gain institutional legitimacy in a similar political environment when involved in FDI activity, as the political embeddedness in a home country could provide them with an advantage in adapting to such an institutional environment. Second, the Chinese Government maintained a strong influence on FDI outflows conducted by Chinese firms (Deng, 2004; Morck *et al.*, 2008; Peng and Delios, 2006). All outward FDI projects were subject to government approval, and annual reporting of overseas operational matters was also mandatory. Through the approval system and financial policies, the Chinese Government may encourage or even direct FDI outflows to particular locations based on its short- and long-term economic development agenda, and also political and ideological heritage (Liu *et al.*, 2005). Third, as pointed out in the literature (Buckley *et al.*, 2007; Morck *et al.*, 2008), as a developing country itself, FDI outflows from China have been attracted mainly to developing countries. The similarity between China and other developing economies in terms of political and legal institutions may facilitate the establishment of regulatory legitimacy in the host economy by investing Chinese firms. Overall, a smaller difference in political influence between China and the host economy would act as an attracting factor for Chinese FDI.

Hypothesis 6 regarding normative institutions gained support to some extent from the full sample results, as a negative influence from the variable cultural distance is predicted and confirmed with a marginal significance level at 10 per cent, suggesting Chinese firms tended to locate FDI operations in economies with which China had a smaller cultural difference. Full sample testing provided supportive empirical results for hypothesis 7. Consistent with this hypothesis, variable CEXPO has positive and highly significant impact on Chinese FDI, suggesting that frequent trade transactions of exports by Chinese firms indeed have an impact on the mindset of Chinese managers when making decisions regarding FDI location choice.

Results of two economy groups

It is suggested that the FDI location choice of MNEs is affected by regional economic grouping, as neighbouring countries tend to have similar political, economic systems and economic development levels (Sethi *et al.*, 2002, 2003). Following this argument, it can be argued that Chinese FDI may have distinctive locational patterns in different economy groups that are shaped by different combinations of determinants for different types of economy groups.

Testing results justified the initial intent to split the full sample into two economy groups. Empirical results for the economy groups were sharply different to those generated from the full sample testing and there was also a difference between the two groups, especially for variables drawn from the institutional approach. Individual variables had different impacts on location choice for each group of economies, suggesting that different economy groups had idiosyncratic features in terms of location-specific economic and institutional advantages attracting FDI flows, and that FDI from Chinese firms followed different location patterns when flowing to different economy groups.

For the group of developed economies, one control variable – openness (OPEN) – and two institutional variables – economic freedom (EFREE) and Chinese exports (CEXPO) – were significant and all of them carried the predicted signs. The positive and highly significant impact of the variable OPEN suggests that a strong exporting orientation in the host economy facilitated Chinese FDI for the Asian industrialized economies. This result may help provide an explanation for the non-significance of conventional market-seeking variables. While seeking market expansion in Asian developed economies through FDI, Chinese firms may aim to serve broader foreign markets rather than the domestic market in the host economy. Similar to the case in full sample testing, the variable economic freedom was significant and had a positive sign, suggesting a big difference between China and developed Asian economies in terms of broad economic institutional environment acted as an institutional attraction to Chinese FDI. This result reflected the fact that the Chinese economy was still behind the developed Asian economies in terms of market orientation and that Chinese firms preferred a FDI location that had a stronger market orientation. Consistent with the results from the full sample, variable exports (CEXPO) had a strong positive relationship with Chinese FDI for developed Asian economies, suggesting China's trade pattern had a profound impact on the FDI location choice of Chinese firms.

For the group of developing economies, two of the four traditional economic variables were statistically significant, including GDP per capita (GDPP) and resource (RESO). The result for variable GDPP was marginally significant at the 10 per cent level but carried a negative sign, suggesting that Chinese firms were not motivated to invest in Asian developing economies by absolute market size and that the economic development level in these developing economies measured by GDP per capita acted as a deterrent to FDI flows from Chinese firms. The variable resource (RESO) gained strong significance for the developing economy group and carried a positive sign as expected, suggesting that FDI flows from Chinese firms were attracted to natural resources in these Asian developing economies. Turning to the institutional variables, the two variables of cultural distance (CULTR) and exports (CEXPO) were significant, but a different picture appeared in comparing the results with the full sample. Different to the results from both the full sample and developed economy group, economic freedom (EFREE) lost significance, suggesting that Chinese firms did not consider the broad economic regulative institutions in the host economy important when investing in the Asian developing economies. The result for the variable cultural distance was statistically significant, but surprisingly this variable carried a positive sign for the developing economy group, suggesting that Chinese FDI was flowing to the Asian developing economies that were culturally distant from China. The result for the variable CEXPO is consistent with the case in full sample testing, being positive and highly significant.

Results for two time periods

Modelling results changed when the full sample was split along the time dimension, indicating the dynamic nature of FDI location choice by Chinese firms for different time periods. For the first period, i.e. 1995–2000, two variables – FDI restriction (RESTR) and exports (CEXPO) – were statistically significant, both having a positive sign. The highly significant and positive influence of the variable RESTR suggests a difference between China and the host economy in the FDI regulating regime acted as a strong attraction for FDI flows from Chinese firms. Considering that China had a rather rigid regime in restricting foreign ownership for this period, this result may demonstrate that Chinese firms did prefer a friendly regulative regime directly linked to FDI activity, while not paying much attention to the broad regulative environment in a host economy. As was the case for the full sample and the two economy groups, the result for the variable CEXPO is positive and significant, although significance dropped to a marginal level (10 per cent).

For the second period covering the more recent years between 2001 and 2007, model testing provided quite interesting results. Two economic variables – resource (RESO) and unit labour cost (ULC) – and one control variable were significant. The variable RESO was marginally significant (10 per cent level) but the impacting direction changed from positive in the developing economy group to negative for the second time period. This result reflects the fact that the Asian economies under study as a whole were not resource rich and Chinese firms were not motivated to seek resources through FDI in these economies for the second time period. As with the result from the full sample testing, the variable ULC had a significant and negative influence for the second period, suggesting that it is in this period that Chinese firms became more profit-driven and mindful of cost reduction when involved in FDI activity. As was the case for the industrialized economy group, the control variable OPEN was significant and carried a positive sign, indicating that FDI outflows from China preferred economies with strong export orientation. This result demonstrates that Chinese FDI stock was used to serve other neighbouring markets and it may explain the non-significance of the market variables for the host economy (GDP growth and GDP per capita). Regarding results for institutional variables, a surprising finding is that the variable economic freedom (ECFREE) is significant, but its impact changed from positive for the full sample and industrialized economies to negative for this time period, suggesting that Chinese firms tended to locate their overseas operations in economies with which China had a smaller difference in economic regulative institutions. This result may be taken as a reflection of a positive change in China's economic regulative regime towards market-oriented economic freedom after China gained its full membership to the WTO in 2001.

Conclusions

This study investigates the impacts of traditional economic and institutional factors on the FDI location choice of Chinese firms. A conceptual framework is proposed by incorporating the two constructs of the eclectic paradigm and institutional approach and by including all three institutional pillars in a single model. Based on Chinese FDI outflows to eight Asian economies during the period 1995–2007, statistical testing of the conceptual framework was conducted. Empirical results demonstrated the importance of factors from both the eclectic paradigm and institutional approach in explaining location choice by Chinese firms in the Asian region, as eight of the nine main variables tested in the study, except GDP growth, have been found significant to some extent in affecting the location choice of Chinese FDI.

Two implications can be drawn from the empirical findings regarding FDI location choice. First, empirical evidence from this study suggests that while traditional economic factors have a major role to play in affecting MNEs' decisions on FDI location, institutional factors may matter more and demonstrate a higher level of complexity and diversity in determining FDI location choice. A comparison of findings from the modelling analysis on the full sample and four subsamples reveals that generally speaking, the influence of traditional economic factors is more stable and seems to have a more fixed pattern, and that the impacts of institutional variables are more diversified and dynamic, demonstrating more complex relationships between institutional factors and FDI location choice. The impacting directions of traditional economic variables are generally consistent across the full sample and subsample sections except for the variable resource (RESO) which is directly related to the endowment of natural resources in a host economy. On the other hand, impacts of institutional variables in model testing are less consistent and more complex across different sample sets. While all five institutional variables gained statistical significance, although to different extents, only the variable export (CEXPO) is highly significant across all sample sections. For the remaining four variables, the impacts are diverse and complex. The same institutional variables influence the location choice of Chinese firms towards different directions while crossing different sample sections. The location choices of Chinese firms result from different combinations of institutional variables and different impacting directions of these variables. As impacts of traditional economic variables are relatively more consistent and fixed, it can be inferred that institutional variables play a more dynamic and also more significant role in the FDI location choices of Chinese firms.

Second, based on the findings from this study, it can be suggested that while the mainstream FDI theories and frameworks regarding FDI location choice, which were generated mainly from studies on developed economies, are still applicable in the case for FDI outflows from China, some important theoretical modifications and extensions are needed in explaining FDI location choice by Chinese firms. Among the traditional variables, market size and potential have long been considered as the most important determinants for market-seeking FDI. Contrary to this, findings from this study reveal that absolute market size and market growth of the host economies did not affect or even negatively affected FDI location choices by Chinese MNEs. This finding raises a question of whether the motivation of market-seeking is valid for Chinese FDI in Asia. The question can be answered by the significant results of the two variables – Chinese exports to the host economy (CEXPO) and the openness of the host economy (OPEN). The variable CEXPO captures the economic ties between host and home economies and also reflects the intensity of business transactions between firms of the two economies. Highly significant and positive impacts of CEXPO demonstrate that market demand for Chinese exports, rather than absolute market size, plays a strong role in facilitating market-seeking Chinese FDI. The positive effect of the variable openness indicates that the market-seeking motivation of Chinese FDI was also actualized through serving new neighbour markets from the host economy and thus the host economy served as a bridge between Chinese-made products and the final markets. For variables representing three institutional pillars, the opposite directions of impacts from two regulative institutional variables (economic freedom and political influence) is quite unconventional and clearly demonstrates the impact of institutional forces in the home country on location choice. For economic regulative institutions, Chinese investors sought FDI involvements in economies with a higher level of market-oriented economic freedom. Chinese firms preferred locations where political and legal institutions resembled their home environment. Furthermore, the change of impacting direction from the variable economic freedom indicates the dynamic evolution of institutional forces at home. These empirical findings provide strong support for the notion that distinctive and highly dynamic institutional forces at home contribute to the uniqueness of FDI location choices by Chinese firms.

Several limitations need to be noted for this study, suggesting avenues for further investigation. First, variables used in this study may not accurately measure the institutional forces in play. A major issue here is the measurement of the cognitive pillar. The variable of exports to the host country was used as the variable of cognitive institutions, capturing the institutionalized behaviour pattern of managers in the home country. However, the variable of exports is more commonly used as an economic variable, measuring economic relations between the host and home countries, while social networks could be used as a variable of normative institutions, measuring normative institutional forces in a host country. There is the possibility that this study suffers from measurement errors. It is difficult to measure the behavioural pattern of investing firms using aggregate archival data. Thus, research at firm level may be more helpful to solve this problem. Second, the empirical testing of the conceptual framework was done in the context of Chinese FDI in the Asian region and this is a relatively narrow research setting. Future research could be done to examine if similar outcomes can be generated from a larger sample size of locations for FDI outflows from China and from a broad context of emerging economies, such as India, Brazil or Mexico.

6 The rising world status of China within the global economy in the 21st century

A cultural knowledge-based strategy for conducting successful businesses in China

John Saee

> He who knows his enemy and himself well will not be defeated easily.
>
> (Sun Tzu, *Art of War*)

Introduction

China is the fourth largest country in terms of size after Russia, Canada and the USA. It is now the world's second largest economy after the USA, if adjusted for differences in cost of living (purchasing power parity differences) (Economy Watch, 2010). China also represents the world's biggest emerging economy, and has already become the number one world champion with respect to international trade (UNCTAD, 2010). It is similarly the most important manufacturing location for firms with both local and foreign investment (Murray *et al.*, 2007).

Study shows that China's foreign exchange currency reserves have increased to about US$2.4 trillion in 2009, up by US$453 billion for the year. These stupendous figures – and the likelihood that the country's reserves will rise by a comparable amount this year – render China a superpower in terms of a financial, economic and geopolitical reality globally (Samuelson, 2010).

China's spectacular economic growth in recent decades has meant that it has been able to attract numerous entrepreneurs and multinational corporations to China and they have been keen on capitalizing on unprecedented businesses opportunities emerging from the Chinese market. However, cultural differences coupled with a lack of intercultural competence on their part have been the main reasons why many entrepreneurs and enterprises have been slow, and in some cases have failed, to achieve significant inroads into the Chinese market.

Broadly speaking, in an intercultural communication context, there are many barriers, which may emerge mainly due to the existence of stereotypes and ethnocentrism, leading to prejudice resulting in mistrust and hostility. Other impediments to effective intercultural communication include fear of change, fear of the unknown, fear of threatened identity, fear of rejection, and/or fear of contradictions to a belief system. Because many of these fears are deeply rooted in people's value systems, an important step in improving intercultural communication is for participants to admit these fears when they exist. It is natural for us to fear something that threatens our values. Moreover, in explaining incompetent intercultural communication situations, Tubbs and Moss (1987: 406) argued: 'Misunder-standings arise when people are unaware of cultural differences or even the pos-sibility of such differences.' This situation reflects a mono-cultural perspective. A mono-cultural perspective denies cultural differences, views cultural interactions as filled with errors not diversity, and forms cultural boundaries in which people remain their entire lives, unable to wander out (Pearce and Kang, 1987: 22).

Apparently, there are many outcomes of poor or ineffective intercultural com-munication and the most notable one is the culture shock:

> The mere shock of entering a different culture influences our abilities to communicate competently in those situations. For the participants, the results of poor intercultural communication are obvious. These include incorrect assumptions, lack of understanding, prejudices, anger, and disre-spect. One area of concern in intercultural communication is culture shock. Culture shock is a powerful result of poor intercultural communication skills. Culture shock is the emotional result of not being able to fulfil the basic need of understanding, controlling, and predicting others' behaviors.
>
> (Furnham, 1987; Saee, 2005, 2006)

Major obstacles to intercultural communication

The main source of misunderstanding among cultures is the differences in values and priorities. Challenges of cross-cultural difference have long been a focus of study by anthropologists, sociologist and psychologists. As a consequence, they separated a number of barriers that affect cross-cultural interactions, namely:

- communication barriers such as language (Guirdham, 1999; Hofstede, 1991) and cultural differences in communication, including non-verbal communication (Guirdham, 1999; Hall, 1976; Hodgetts and Luthans, 2000; Saee, 2005; 2006);
- behavioural barriers (Hofstede, 1991; Hodgetts and Luthans, 2000);
- psychological barriers such as stereotyping and ethnocentrism (Guirdham, 1999; Hewstone and Giles, 1986; Saee, 2006; Triandis, 1994); experiencing anxiety and uncertainty (Berger and Calabrese, 1975; Gudykunst, 1993; Stephan and Stephan, 1996) and culture shock (Harris and Moran, 1995; Lysgaard, 1955; Oberg, 1960);
- occupation-specific issues (Hughes-Wiener, 1986);
- organization-specific issues such as organizational culture (Adler, 1997; Saee, 2005).

Psychological barriers are the main impediments to effective cross-cultural com-munication. These include stereotyping and ethnocentrism, and a brief explana-tion of them here is warranted.

Stereotyping The tendency to create stereotypes – stable sets of preconceptions which members of one group hold about other groups – is considered to be a universal feature of any inter-group communication (Guirdham, 1999). Therefore, communication across cultures is often distorted by false assumptions grounded in rigid stereotypes (Hewstone and Giles, 1986; Muzychenko and Saee, 2004).

Ethnocentrism   The perception of one's own culture as superior is almost inescapable and subconscious, being bound by parochial or ethnocentric mentality instilled in the mind early in life, as 'schools in all cultures, whether they intend to or not, teach ethnocentrism' (Samovar and Porter, 1994: 245). Knowledge, just like any other element of culture (language, beliefs, value systems, rituals, etc.), is generated in a particular social context. Therefore, worthwhile knowledge is seen to be originating from within one's own cultural space, while the knowledge originating elsewhere is denigrated (Benn, 1996; Muzychenko and Saee, 2004).

To succeed in the burgeoning Chinese market, it is imperative to develop insight into the Chinese culture and Chinese business practices while developing intercultural communication competence.

Chinese socio-cultural system

The cultural and social roots of Chinese society can be traced as far back as 2,500 years and they are fundamentally predicated on the teachings and philosophical thoughts of Confucius.

Confucian philosophy has different perspectives on time management and power distance relationships, as compared with the Western world. This can engender differences in personal and organizational goals, organizational structures and management styles. With these differences in approach it would be very easy for misunderstandings to occur and it would take a great deal of cultural awareness and sensitivity on the part of Western business partners/entrepreneurs to avoid disagreements with Chinese business partners.

The most significant aspects of the Chinese cultural dimension which originate from Confucianism are preserving 'face' in public; cultivation and maintenance of Guanxi (relationship, network); experience of time as synchronous and subordinate to relationships; and limited legitimacy accorded to the rule of law in contrast to demonstrations of power.

According to Wilhelm (1994) social standing, called *lian* or 'face' in Chinese society, is pivotal for achieving wealth and power:

> Face involves both prestige and public standing. Failure to follow Confucius' moral code in business will lead to public disapproval, a powerful force that can negatively affect both aspects of face, jeopardizing prestige and, by impugning character, capability, and personal integrity, which is to say, reputation, jeopardizing as well the comfort and convenience that attends respectability.
>
> (Wilhelm, 1994: 32)

Confucianism societies like China are characterized by tight, close-knit networks among people and businesses, known in China as 'Guanxi'. In these groups, connections with the right people, not the price or quality of the product or service, are usually the main determinant of business decision-making (Yeung and Tung, 1996). Chen (1995) described Guanxi as relationships that imply a continual exchange of favours that need not be founded on friendship. When applied to organizations, Guanxi obligation tends to run counter to universalistic, performance-based values and systems, found in many Western organizations. Chinese nationals tend to rely heavily on personal relationships in business dealings (Chen, 1994). Sales force marketing, an activity heavily dependent on Guanxi, has become an increasingly popular and effective marketing means. Guanxi binds literally millions of Chinese firms into a social and business web that can be particularly useful for enterprises built on foreign investment in China (Jiang, 2006; Luo, 1995).

Consequently, Chinese business operates through a web of personal relationships and access to these networks requires connections with Guanxi that is based around trust, family relationships and friendship. A complete understanding of this aspect is absolutely essential to building business relationships; however, Guanxi like respect cannot be bought, and it must be earned. Without these relationships, it becomes virtually impossible for outsiders to conduct business successfully.

With the assistance of Guanxi, business relationships are built slowly and founded on trust rather than legally enforceable contracts. Without this trust there are no relationships and business ventures will flounder. This Chinese way of doing business is deeply affected by Confucian philosophy and knowledge of that philosophy will assist in understanding the Chinese psyche and in building the relationships required to conduct businesses successfully in China.

The Confucian values are distinctive, as their emphasis has always been on society and public administration and therefore the primary concern has been with public order.

Confucius (K'ung Fu-tzu), a teacher and bureaucrat, and his successor Mencius (Mang-tzeK'o) waged a philosophical war for the heart and soul of China's spiritual development. Their victory created a humanistic society and an outlook on life that believed in hard work; conservative adherence to traditional values; the dominance of society over individual and family over society; and a society in which there is a place for everyone, and everyone has his or her place and role to play in society (Haley *et al.*, 1998). It was Mencius who insisted that Confucian philosophy should be espoused from the inherent goodness of man, rather than the darker side.

Main features of Confucian doctrine

Confucianism is primarily concerned with the relationship between individuals in a given society, which is defined in terms of five virtues; they represent humanity/benevolence (*ren*) righteousness (*yi*), propriety (*li*) wisdom (*zhi*) and trustworthiness (*xin*) (Fan, 2002).

Developing an understanding of Confucian philosophy, one is able to understand how Confucianism traditionally manifests itself in modern Chinese business practices.

Confucian values divide society into a ruling class (thinkers) and a class who are ruled (workers), and provide an inherent respect for and acceptance of authority and maintaining the leaders in power. Further, Sebenius and Qian (2008) maintain that hierarchy, interdependence, and reciprocity represent the essential elements underlying Confucianism's five interpersonal relationship (relationships between: ruler and people being ruled, father and son, husband and wife, elder and younger siblings, and seniors and juniors). Failure to honour these characteristics can jeopardize interpersonal relationships as well as mutual trust among parties involved in business negotiations.

The role of family within Chinese society

At the very heart of traditional Chinese life lies the notion of the strong family, which emanates from Confucianism. *Harmony* in the family and within the wider society based on Confucianism is an integral feature of the Chinese culture. Harmony is the maintenance of one's *face*, that is, one's dignity, self-respect, and prestige. Treating others as one would like to be treated oneself is virtuous behaviour. *Virtue* with respect to one's tasks consists of attempting to obtain skills and education, working hard, not spending more than necessary, being patient, and persevering. It should be noted that individuals may have inner thoughts that differ from the group's norms and values; however, individuals may not act on those thoughts, because group harmony and not shaming the group is of paramount importance (Saee, 2005).

Chinese group orientation is another feature of Confucian doctrine that emphasizes ties of kinship and close personal relationships. Individuals exist for the benefits of the group and group pressure is applied to ensure conformity through eliciting shame (losing face) and conflict is handled through intra-group mediation (Fan, 2002).

Chinese business practices

The business practices of the Chinese arising from Confucian doctrine vary considerably from the way business is conducted in the West. If a person is interested in forming a business relationship with someone, where no previous relationship existed, connections are necessary. That person needs the assistance of an intermediary with whom he has Guanxi, and who in turn has Guanxi with the person with whom it is desired to discuss business. The function of the intermediary is not only to arrange the introduction but also to some degree vouch for the integrity of the person being introduced. Without such connections in business or society, a newcomer will find it very difficult if not impossible to enter the network and do business successfully.

A research study conducted by Braendle *et al.* (2005) confirms that in China a strong emphasis is put on social networks and a long-term horizon by pointing out that 'the Chinese view each event and transaction in the light of its possible effects on the social network because the maintaining of relations is almost always more important than the details of a single agreement' (Braendle *et al.*, 2005: 393).

The study investigated what role 'Guanxi' networks play in terms of corporate governance and whether they may hinder economic growth potential. 'Guanxi' is a central concept in China, which constitutes a social and cultural practice that is highly regarded and is based on complex social systems that facilitate mutually beneficial and reciprocal arrangements. It is ascribed to Confucianism, and is deeply rooted in the mindset of the Chinese people.

Understanding Chinese business practice requires some explanation and understanding of Guanxi and Chinese business networks; the two are intertwined and inextricably linked, and it is difficult to try and explain one without the other.

Networks

Networks as a mechanism are used by the Chinese to build trust, and speed decision-making, provide customer satisfaction and provide competitive advantage. Thus, networks have a number of traditional foundations. For example, network type(s) such as locality grouping embodies locality of origin in China, whereas clan grouping has as its foundation, the respective family surname.

Richter (1999) describes Chinese business networks in the following manner:

> Network members are connected to, trusting of, obligated to, and dependent on certain others. In networks, exchanges occur through neither contractual agreements nor hierarchical dictates, but through webs of individuals engaged in reciprocal actions. There are overlapping contacts, maintained through both reputation and friendship. Networks have overlapping relational characteristics, and a relative absence of quid pro quo behavior. This greatly enhances the acquisition and transmission of new knowledge.
>
> (Richter, 1999: 176)

The powerful economic nature of Chinese networks should not be underestimated, together with the overseas Chinese they form the biggest single FDI block in the world, and are at the heart of Asian economic development (Richter 1999).

Network is Guanxi in Chinese, a Mandarin word for which there is no precise English translation. Guanxi is essential to business relationships. It has similarities to goodwill, and arises from trust, family relationships and friendship, philanthropy, status, doing favours, receiving favours and reciprocating; it can be earned but like respect it cannot be bought.

There are several dimensions to the meanings of Guanxi. For example, there is an element of transferability in a business relationship based on Guanxi, i.e. if A has Guanxi and knows B, who knows C, then B can introduce A to C. Without such an introduction, A cannot deal with C.

Another feature of Guanxi is that it is fundamentally a reciprocal process of favours between persons having Guanxi so that each individual in a business relationship can only then maintain their social face/standing strategically. In addition, there is a personal and emotional element binding individuals through Guanxi (Richter, 1999).

The Chinese with their Confucian values tend to have different perspectives to those of the West. A summary of these values for China, based on the work of Hofstede (1991) on cross-cultural dimensions, is now described.

Geert Hofstede's analysis (1991) of China in terms of long-term orientation (LTO) shows that it has the highest-ranking factor (118). This dimension indicates Chinese society's long-term perspective on time and an attitude of persevering; i.e. overcoming obstacles with time, if not with will and strength. In contrast, most Western cultures scored in the 20s. Thus, occidental short-term perspective on time can often be a stumbling block for Western entrepreneurs and organizations doing business with their Chinese counterparts.

Similarly, using Hofstede's cultural dimension, the Chinese rank lower than any other Asian country in the individualism (IDV) ranking; at 20 compared to an average of 24. This reflects a traditional view of Confucianism prevalent in China, which is further reinforced by a high level of emphasis on a collectivist society by the Communist rule, as compared to one of individualism prevailing in the Western world.

The low individualism ranking is manifest in a close and committed member 'group', be that a family, extended family, or extended relationships. Loyalty in a collectivist culture is of utmost importance. The society fosters strong relationships where everyone takes responsibility for fellow members of their group.

On power distance, China ranks significantly higher with a power distance ranking of 80 compared to the other Far East Asian countries' average of 60, and the world average of 55. This is indicative of a high level of inequality of power and wealth within the society. This is an accepted traditional Chinese view of social hierarchy based on Confucianism representing the Chinese cultural heritage.

The masculinity (MAS) dimension focuses on the degree to which the society reinforces, or does not reinforce, the traditional masculine work role model of male achievement, control and power. A high masculinity ranking indicates that the country experiences a high degree of gender differentiation. This is the one dimension in which China most aligns itself to the rest of the world, and yet, it is often totally missed by Western businessmen, who think that the women in China are, for the most part, ignored.

Conversely, with respect to the uncertainty avoidance index, China scored at just 32. Confucianism places an emphasis on control behaviour via face saving, in contrast to elaborate Western laws relating to social behaviour (Hofstede, 2001; 2001).

Organization structure and management

In major contrast to Western organizations, Chinese organizations traditionally represent hierarchical and yet inflexible structures with the following characteristics:

- authoritarian but paternal management, where super-ordinates are expected to look after the interests of their loyal and respectful subordinates;
- autocratic leadership;
- communication top down, a long chain, with no bottom-up influence, although there maybe some horizontal and/or external communication via networks;
- conflict or dissent is unlikely to be displayed, due to respect for authority, seniority and loyalty;
- an inherent inflexibility, slowness to respond to changes in the external environment, with these factors offset to varying degrees by the information communicated via, and the flexibility provided by, the networks.

(Bolman and Deal, 1997).

It is imperative for the entrepreneurs to gain insight into Chinese culture in order to be able to understand the Chinese mindset. However, for the entrepreneurs to become fully competent in all intercultural encounters, it is necessary for them to master the multidimensional nature of intercultural competence, an explanation of which, based on sociological, anthropological and social psychological theories, is presented below.

The dimensions of intercultural competence

Competence is a multifaceted phenomenon. Being or becoming competent will depend on who we are, what we know, and how well we apply our knowledge. Bartlett and Ghoshal (1997) and Parry (1998) distinguish between internalized and externalized elements of competence. Internalized elements are 'deeply embedded personal characteristics, intrinsic parts of the individuals' character and personality' (Bartlett and Ghoshal, 1997) and are very unlikely to be affected in any way by training. Externalized elements can be acquired through training and include knowledge, experience and understanding, plus skills and abilities. The process of competence development through alteration of externalized elements will depend on a person's internalized characteristics; for example some individual qualities may have a direct effect on learning particular skills (Parry, 1998). Further, there will be interrelations between skills and abilities and knowledge components of competence. This is because knowledge facilitates the acquisition of skills and enhances abilities, and in turn, certain skills and abilities enhance the learning process that helps to constantly update the existing knowledge base. This thus prevents the individual from adhering to a set body of knowledge (Hughes-Wiener, 1986). This can be illustrated as in Figure 6.1.

Being competent means achieving the intended outcome. Cross-cultural competence theorists look at the outcomes across three dimensions, namely communication as a foundation of relationship-building with foreign individuals, psychological adjustment to the new culture, and doing well in one's job (Walter *et al.*, 1995, cited in Dodd, 1998; Saee, 2006). Walter *et al.* (1995, cited in Dodd, 1998) propose an E-Model of cross-cultural professional effectives that consists

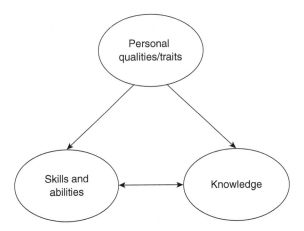

Figure 6.1 Generic competence dimensions.
Source: adapted from Muzychenko and Saee (2004).

of the three building blocks. These blocks are 'interpersonal relationships', 'adaptability' and 'task performance'.

Indeed, everything that people do involves interacting with others, and this interaction occurs through communication and building interpersonal relationships. Gudykunst (1991) and Spitzberg and Cupach (1984) argued that cross-cultural communication competence is about minimizing misunderstanding. Achieving that requires:

- culture general knowledge, or what is culture and what are its components (Lustig and Koester, 1993);
- culture-specific knowledge, or one's own and others' cultural attributes (in this case, the Chinese culture), including similarities and differences between the cultural groups (Lustig and Koester, 1993);
- knowledge of what is appropriate to do to have an effective communication outcome (Lustig and Koester, 1993; Ruben and Kealey, 1979);
- understanding of the dialectical perspective on multiple variables in cross-cultural communication (Martin and Nakayma, 1999), such as power, personality, social class, etc.;
- personal qualities such as empathy, respect, non-judgementalness, openness;
- ability to perform role behaviours;
- interaction management;
- ability to establish meaningful interpersonal relationships through understanding the feelings of others;
- ability to work effectively with others (Walter *et al.*, 1995, cited in Dodd, 1998);
- ability to deal with different social customs (Gudykunst *et al.*, 1977; Harris and Moran, 1995; Ruben and Kealey, 1979).

Meanwhile, psychological theories of intercultural communication look at intercultural communication in terms of individual behavioural adaptation. They focus on personal traits and attributes that help to generate internal psychological responses in the alien environment (Gudykunst and Hammer, 1983; Kealey and Ruben, 1983; Saee, 2006). The following abilities are associated with successful psychological adaptation in the new cultural environment through managing stress and reducing anxiety and uncertainty:

- being able to be mindful, to tolerate ambiguity and to calm ourselves (Berger, 1979; Gudykunst and Kim, 1997);
- being able to explain and make accurate predictions of strangers' behaviour (Gudykunst, 1991);
- being aware that stress, anxiety and uncertainty affect both sides of the intercultural encounter – the stranger and the host (Saee, 2006).

According to Walter *et al.* (1995, cited in Dodd, 1998) adaptability to foreign cultural environment depends on flexibility, maturity, knowledge of host culture, language skills, a non-judgmental attitude, patience, respect for culture, and appropriate social behaviour.

At the same time, according to Hughes-Wiener (1986) intercultural effectiveness of accomplishing a task depends on knowledge of the following:

- roles and role relationships of the task culture;
- intercultural interpersonal problems that might arise;
- situation variables that may affect job performance and satisfaction;
- occupation-specific issues, depending on the nature of the task involved.

However, Walter *et al.* (1995, cited in Dodd, 1998) claim that effective task outcomes are directly linked to:

- technical/professional performance;
- resourcefulness;
- imagination and creativity;
- ability to innovate
- performance evaluation;
- management of the task.

Thus, this study advances a proposition which argues that intercultural competence is a dynamic phenomenon and its dimensions (psychological adaptation, interpersonal communication, and task performance) are directly interrelated. This can be illustrated in Figure 6.2.

Further, interpersonal communication, psychological adaptation and task performance dimensions uncover the nature of intercultural competence from different perspectives. However, what they have in common is the reference to personal traits/ qualities, knowledge and skills/abilities that constitute the core of competence.

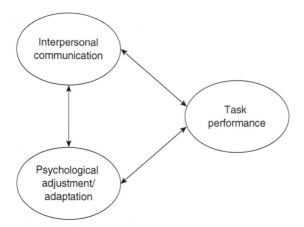

Figure 6.2 Intercultural competence.
Source: adapted from Muzychenko and Saee (2004).

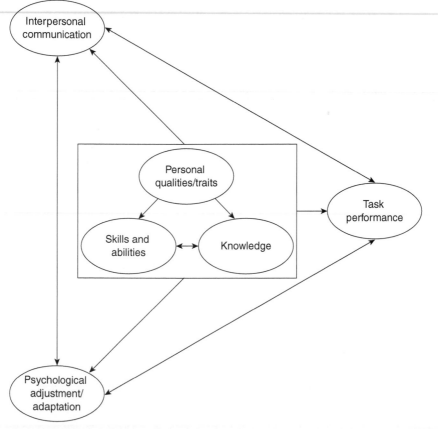

Figure 6.3 Modality of intercultural competence.
Source: adapted from Muzychenko and Saee (2004).

Therefore, we can derive particular personal traits/qualities, knowledge and skills/abilities that will correspond to each dimension of cross-cultural competence.

In view of the foregoing, the modality of intercultural competence as shown in Figure 6.3 is proposed.

In conclusion

Entrepreneurs globally wishing to establish business relationships in China have to deal with a couple of issues. First, they are outsiders (lacking Guanxi) and thus they need to establish connections. Second, there are, particularly for Westerners, huge challenges arising from cultural differences. Those cultural differences can cause difficulty in aligning corporate and personal goals, which may lead to differences in management style, and can lead to misunderstandings and mistrust. Consequently, it would take a great deal of developing cultural awareness and sensitivity on the part of the Western entrepreneurs so as to avoid such problems with Chinese business partners. Cultural adaptation to the Chinese cultural milieu on the part of the entrepreneurs and Western enterprises is recommended in terms of their corporate strategy and modus operandi.

Finally, developing globally intercultural competence can be of immense benefit to Western executives/firms in terms of promoting effectively international trade with China, one that is rapidly becoming a globally gigantic economic powerhouse in the twenty-first century.

7 The effects of a free trade agreement between Australia and China with special reference to the Australian textiles and service industries

John Saee and Ramiro Mora

Introduction

This chapter examines the effects of a proposed free trade agreement (FTA) between Australia and China. Reference will be made to the Australian textiles and services industries. An FTA is an agreement between two or more countries which give each other preferential market access (DFAT, 2006a). The term 'textiles' includes fibres, yarns, cotton, vegetable matter, wool and other material, which can be woven into fabrics (Pestana, 1996: 1). For the purposes of this research study, the textiles industry will also be classified, as the Textiles, Clothing and Footwear (TCF) industry and the terms will be used interchangeably.

An FTA with China is a contentious issue and as a result, both sides of the debate (i.e. pros and cons), will be examined throughout this chapter. Various issues including free trade negotiations, will also be considered, namely: the growing economic partnership between the countries; China's rapid economic growth; and the history and current state of the Australian textiles industry.

Theories, which justify free trade, will also be analysed with reference to an establishment of FTAs between China and Australia in the context of globalization – which is defined as the merging of national economies into an interdependent global economic system. Australia is a knowledge-based economy and would benefit from an FTA with China, which is a labour-intensive economy. This is because both countries would be focusing on their comparative advantages.

The negative consequences, which arise from FTAs, will also be discussed. It is argued that the theories that justify free trade are based on assumptions which do not reflect economic realities. This includes the assumption that jobs lost as a result of the liberalization of trade, through the lowering of protectionist policies, will be absorbed by other sectors in the economy. Textile industry employment in Australia has gradually decreased in the last 20 years as a result of China's grow-ing dominance in that sector. It is claimed that this phenomenon will be acceler-ated as a result of an FTA. China's labour force, labour polices and textile companies will also be examined.

Another contentious issue which will be addressed is that of granting China market economy status. As part of the FTA negotiations, Australia has agreed to grant China market economy status, whereas the European Union and the United

States have refused. Bilateral trades between China and the USA, as well as China and the EU with reference to the textile and clothing industries will also be explored respectively. The issue of market economy status will be examined in regards to dumping. It is suggested that granting China market economy status will make it easier for them to dump their goods into Australia at below market cost. The new protectionist policies introduced by the EU and the USA will also be examined in an attempt to answer why these regions have chosen to take a protectionist stance towards China while Australia is attempting to further open their markets to China.

The rate of assistance by the federal government is also addressed. The government has provided a number of assistance packages to help textile firms adapt and compete internationally. Programs provided in the 1990s to the present will be briefly examined. These programs have provided assistance to the offshoring processing of textiles as well as research and development (R&D).

Finally, this chapter considers innovations which have been adopted by the Australian textile industry. The investment into new technologies, the use of out-workers, and programs such as quick response have allowed the textiles industry to remain competitive against global competition in the face of gradual decreases in protectionist policies.

A conclusion summarizes the above arguments that have public policy implications.

A brief contextual background

China and Australia have been in free trade negotiations since the successful completion of their joint feasibility study in March 2005. The study concluded that there would be numerous benefits for both potential partners as a result of an FTA. To date, fifteen rounds of negotiations have been successfully completed and various issues have been addressed. Although China and Australia's political and economic systems are vastly different, both sides are keen on establishing an FTA. China has begun to assert itself on the world stage. It has been accepted into the World Trade Organization (WTO) and has completed a number of FTAs with other countries. It is in the process of completing other free trade deals as well. It has been argued that if Australia is to remain competitive, it must establish closer links with China, one of the fastest growing economies in the world.

It is further contended that globalization and the levels of trade and investment will continue to evolve regardless of whether or not an FTA with China is signed. As the economies of countries also evolve, they focus less on labour-intensive sectors and more on knowledge-based industries. Australia is a knowledge-based economy and it is therefore argued that they must take advantage of their strengths in knowledge-based industries, such as services, and focus less on labour-intensive industries. This is Australia's comparative advantage *vis-à-vis* other nations. It is further argued that labour-intensive sectors, such as textiles, will be forced to compete globally and as a consequence of which they will ultimately become more efficient.

There are numerous benefits in establishing FTAs. They are quicker to negotiate and concessions are easier to obtain, as there are fewer parties involved in the negotiation process. Competition and economic growth will also increase. Australia, in particular, has a lot to gain from an FTA with China, including lower prices and a greater variety of choice for consumers, as well as increased business opportunities for exporters. Although employment losses in the labour-intensive TCF sector will inevitably occur, there is a case to be made that the Australian Government should pursue policies which assist those industries that have been adversely affected. If the government pursues trade policies while supporting industries adversely affected by free trade, the benefits will offset the negative aspects of trade.

It is further argued that tariffs and quotas will inevitably be phased out, regardless of whether or not an FTA with China is signed. Tariffs are customs duties on imported merchandise and give a price advantage to locally produced goods over similar imported goods (WTO, 2010a). Quotas are a target number that cannot be breached. Australia has successfully established four FTAs which have reduced tariffs and quotas on numerous good and services – including textiles. Australia is also currently negotiating FTAs with Malaysia and the Association of Southeast Asian Nations (ASEAN) and a FTA feasibility study with Japan. Australia is further committed to the Asia-Pacific Economic Cooperation (APEC), which is based on free and open trade and investment in the Asia-Pacific region. APEC's current goal is to be achieved through the elimination of tariffs.

Opponents of an FTA with China acknowledge that tariffs and quotas will likely continue to be reduced; however, they believe that an FTA will cause irreversible damage from which the Australian TCF industry will be unable to recover. It is claimed that Australia can neither compete with the Chinese labour force, the largest in the world, nor with their questionable labour practices which results in extremely low wages. China has not ratified any international conventions regarding compulsory or unfair labour practices and has no obligation to address these practices. It is further argued that the theory of free trade is flawed. It is based on numerous assumptions that ignore economic realities such as unemployment and unequal production, including labour-cost between the two countries.

A substantial amount of job losses will also occur in the TCF industry, as a result of the FTA with China. Although economic modelling suggests that the market will absorb retrenched workers, mobility figures of TCF workers demonstrate otherwise. In order to protect domestic workers, the EU and the USA have established protectionist policies, in the form of increased tariffs and quotas, against China. They have also refused to acknowledge China as a market economy. As part of free trade negotiations with China, Australia is required to recognize China as a market economy, for anti-dumping purposes. It is believed that being recognized as a market economy will make it easier for China to dump its goods, textiles in particular, into Australia at below market value.

The Australian TCF industry experienced a substantial amount of change throughout the twentieth century. The industry has managed to stay internationally competitive and generate a substantial amount of revenue and employment. Government assistance packages have helped TCF firms adapt to the realities of global competition. There has been a great amount of money and effort placed in technological advancements. The industry has also begun innovative practices, such as 'quick response', which focus on consumer responsiveness. Offshoring and outworkers have also been used by the industry. Problems that the industry faces, including firm size and lack of coordination coupled with a lack of investment into new technologies, can, however, be overcome with the assistance of the government. Whether or not the Australian TCF industry can cope with the changes resulting from a FTA will ultimately depend on its flexibility.

Free trade negotiations with China – planting the seed

This section will summarize the historical negotiation processes between China and Australia, which has led to a proposed FTA between them. Both countries undertook a feasibility study in October 2003 that concluded that a FTA would result in numerous economic benefits. The first round of negotiations began in May 2005. Fifteen successful rounds have been completed (DFAT, 2010a).

The joint feasibility study in perspective

Australia is arguably an experienced trade negotiating country, as it has successfully negotiated six FTAs with New Zealand, Singapore, Thailand, the USA, ASEAN and Chile. However, Australian negotiators have a difficult road ahead of them, as there are major differences between Australian and Chinese administrative and political regimes. In the recent Global Competitiveness Report 2010–2011, Australia was ranked 13 in *legal framework efficiency* whereas China was ranked 51 due to its inefficient and cumbersome legal framework (World Economic Forum, 2010).

Whilst Australia is a liberal, free market democratic country, China, often accused of serious human rights violations, is arguably still controlled by the Chinese Communist Party with no apparent democratic principles.

Despite these differences, on 24 October 2003, Australian Prime Minister John Howard and Chinese President Hu Jintao signed the Australia–China Trade and Economic Framework. Part of the framework was committed to a feasibility study as to the possibility of an FTA between Australia and China. The feasibility study was completed in March 2005 and concluded that there would be numerous benefits for both potential partners as a result of an FTA (DFAT, 2010a).

The free trade negotiations in historical perspective

The first round of negotiations for the FTA began on 23 May 2005, in Sydney. Trade Minister Mark Vaile represented Australia, while Wei Jianguo, Vice Minister of the Chinese Ministry of Commerce, headed the Chinese delegation. The immediate issues of concern included negotiation procedures that would facilitate future negotiations. The successful completion of the first round of negotiations resulted in a second round of negotiations, in Beijing, which commenced on 22 August 2005. The meeting was centred around four working groups which represented the service sector, investment interests, agriculture and trade in goods. This meeting focused on an open discussion of each country's expectations with respect to the proposed FTA. Australian representatives emphasized the importance of including all major sectors previously agreed to in the negotiations. The Chinese, for their part, have accepted this.

Australian and Chinese negotiators met again in August 2005, in Beijing. A wide range of information exchange regarding each country's trade and investment regimes occurred during this meeting (TFIA, 2005b: 1). China's primary focus included foreign direct investment and anti-dumping issues (TFIA, 2005b: 1). There is no set deadline for the negotiations. In regards to the free trade negotiations, Peter Hendy, Chief Executive of the Australian Chamber of Commerce and Industry stated that:

> [a] successful outcome would place us in a unique position and one in which we would be the envy of our trading competitors – as the only country in the world with comprehensive free trade agreements with both China and the United States.
>
> (cited in DFAT, 2010b)

The successful completion of the third round of negotiations in Beijing from 2 to 4 November 2005 resulted in the launch of a fourth round of negotiations, which focused on market access for each country. The results of this round formed the centrepiece for market access in trade in goods for the proposed FTA. A fifth round of negotiations took place in Beijing from 22 to 24 May 2006. This meeting was centred on the shape and content of the proposed FTA (DFAT, 2006b). Numerous proposals were tabled including intellectual property rights and rules of origin. China agreed that provisions on investment and government procurement should be included in the FTA and that negotiations on these topics should be negotiated in the sixth round of talks (DFAT, 2006b). The sixth round of negotiations took place in Beijing on 31 August to 6 September 2006 and it dealt with the provisions on access to their respective markets. The seventh round of the Australia–China FTA negotiations was held in Canberra, from 11 to 15 December 2006. This also centred around access for goods (including agriculture).

The eighth round of the Australia–China FTA negotiations was convened from 26 to 30 March 2007 in Beijing, with continued dialogue and negotiation on market access. This was followed by a ninth round, which was held from 18 to 22 June 2007 in Beijing, with no conclusive movement on market access. Later in the same year, the tenth round of the negotiations was held and this resulted in narrowing the respective differences on some issues. The eleventh round of negotiations was held in Beijing from 16 to 20 June 2008. This was the first round since the Australian Prime Minister had agreed with his Chinese counterpart in April 2008 on the 'unfreezing' of the negotiations,.

The twelfth round of negotiations was held in Canberra from 22 to 26 September 2008. As foreshadowed at the eleventh negotiating round, the two sides began more intensive discussions on their respective sensitivities to tariff liberalization. Australia pressed China to explain why it was characterizing a range of agricultural products of interest to Australia as sensitive. The thirteenth round was held in Beijing from 1 to 5 December 2008. With respect to market access for goods, the two sides continued the discussion on their respective sensitivities to tariff liberalization.

The fourteenth round of negotiations was held in Canberra from 24 to 26 February 2010. Further progress was made in relation to the trade in goods, rules of origin, sanitary and phytosanitary (SPS) issues, technical barriers to trade (TBT) and customs procedures. This was followed by the fifteenth round, convened in Beijing from 28 to 30 June 2010. The main topics for discussion included an institutional framework relating to intellectual property and electronic commerce related issues (DFAT, 2010a).

Throughout the FTA negotiation processes, the Australian Federal Government has been in consultation with the interested parties, receiving their inputs regarding the proposed agreement. The list of parties includes Australian industry associations, business groups, state and territory governments, trade unions, community groups and members of the general public (DFAT, 2010b). As such information will influence how negotiations with China are undertaken, this consultation process will continue throughout the negotiation process.

The Victorian Government's position

The Victorian Government also undertook a study on the impact of a proposed FTA with China. This study examined the effects of tariff and non-tariff barrier removal (TFIA, 2005a: 3). The Victorian Government has emphasized minimum conditions that must be addressed before the completion of an FTA. Some of these conditions include effective measures against the dumping of goods into Australia, a free moving exchange rate in China and free association of labour, also in China (TFIA, 2005b: 2). The Victorian Government also recommends support packages, safeguards and phase-in periods to assist the manufacturing sectors in adjusting to the impacts of an FTA.

In summary

In brief, although Australia and China have vastly different political and administrative systems, fifteen successful rounds of negotiations have been completed, reflecting the likelihood of the establishment of an FTA between the two nations in the near future. Various critical issues, including intellectual property rights and rules of origin, have been addressed throughout the course of the negotiations. A mutual understanding between the parties has clearly been established, as various issues have and continue to be addressed as talks intensify. However, in order to fully understand how the parties reached this stage, a brief history of China's economic rise in the twentieth century is provided in the next section.

China – the rising star

The fact that Australia, a highly-developed country, and China, still a developing country, are negotiating an FTA demonstrates the enormous changes that have occurred within China. Despite experiencing historically a tremendous upheaval, in the form of the Great Leap Forward and the Cultural Revolution, China has gradually changed its economic policies. It has established FTAs with other countries and joined international bodies, such as the WTO. China has become one of the fastest growing economies in the world and is the world's second largest recipient of FDI after the USA. China appears to have unlimited immediate growth potential. As a result, it is argued that Australia would benefit from an FTA with China as it would have greater access to China's markets. This section will summarize China's history throughout the twentieth century, its economic rise and the agreements it has established with current and future trading partners.

China's history in the 20th century

China has experienced enormous domestic upheavals in the twentieth century. The two largest political campaigns were the Great Leap Forward (1958–1960) and the Cultural Revolution (1966–1976). The disastrous Great Leap Forward was an attempt to modernize economically, as quickly as possible. The subsequent Cultural Revolution was a social experiment, which led to political chaos, educational and economic disasters. This turbulent era came to an end when Chairman Mao died in 1976.

The post-Mao period began when Deng Xiaoping was given power by the Communist Party Central Committee in 1977. This handover of power officially ended the Cultural Revolution. The post-Mao political order was given its first vote of confidence at the Eleventh National Party Congress in 1977 (Poon, n.d.).

By 1978, reformers restored individuals to power who had fallen out of favour because of the turmoil of the Cultural Revolution. By 1979, the Eleventh National Party Congress Central Committee retracted the party theory, which was based on class struggle, and promoted the four modernizations. The four modernizations consisted of industry, agriculture, science and technology, with the objective of advancing China to industrial nation status (Poon, n.d.). In the same year formal diplomatic recognition was established between China and the United States.

The objectives of China's national goals were now economic and not political. Farmers and peasants were given more power in relation to production and distribution, thus marking the end of collectivized agriculture. China's second revolution, in the 1980s, was dubbed 'reform'. This was a gradual approach to economic reforms, which continues to this day. It was based on economic reform, governmental reform and cultural reform and led to profit incentives and bonuses for individuals (Poon, n.d.). By the early 1980s, foreign interests began to invest heavily in China. Joint ventures with foreign conglomerates were also being established. The government gradually introduced capitalist economic practices including international bank loans. Self-autonomy was also increased for state enterprises. Financial systems were reformed, including wages and taxes. For the first time in its history, a rational body of law was codified in China. This has lead to a stable domestic economic environment. Special economic zones were also designated and developed during this time.

Although China was an original signatory of the General Agreement on Tariffs and Trade (GATT), it was not until 1986 that it resumed its status as a member.

China joined the Multi-Fibre Arrangement (MFA) in 1983 and was formally accepted into the WTO in 2001, after years of negotiations. As part of the agreement, China has sought to liberalize its regime in order to integrate itself into the world economic community. It has attempted to do so by offering a stable trade and investment domestic environment. China provided non-discriminatory treatment to all WTO members and eliminated the dual pricing practices and treatment between goods produced in China and goods produced for export (WTO, 2001).

A special Transitional Safeguard Mechanism was put in place for a 12-year period, commencing from the date of China's ascension into the WTO. This safety mechanism is to be used against goods of Chinese origin, which could cause market disruption to other WTO members. Conversely, import restrictions against China, which were inconsistent with the WTO, were phased out or were to be dealt with by mutually agreed terms (WTO, 2001).

With regards to textiles, China automatically became a party to the Agreement on Textiles and Clothing (ATC). Although quotas on textiles came to an end in 2005, a safeguard mechanism was put in place until 2008. This was established to assist countries in regards to any possible disruptions which might occur as a result of Chinese exports.

China's other trade partners

Free trade agreements have recently grown in importance the world over. As of September 2005, 334 regional trade agreements have been notified to the WTO, with the core of these agreements dealing with the removal of tariffs (bilaterals. org, 2006a). China has also made FTAs its priority. From the period 2001 to 2005, China has been in negotiations with 27 countries and regions in an effort to establish free trade (bilaterals.org, 2006a). China has established a Closer Economic Partnership Arrangement (CEPA) with Hong Kong and Macau and has established an 'early harvest' program with Pakistan. China has also been seeking FTAs with ASEAN, the Gulf Cooperation Council, the South African Customs Union and New Zealand (bilaterals.org, 2005).

Free trade talks with New Zealand began in December 2004. The FTA between New Zealand and China (NZ–China FTA) entered into force on 1 October 2008. The NZ–China FTA was signed on 7 April 2008 in Beijing, bringing to the end a negotiation process that spanned fifteen rounds over three years. The NZ–China FTA is a treaty between New Zealand and China that liberalizes and facilitates trade in goods and services, improves the business environment and promotes cooperation between the two countries in a broad range of economic areas. Hence, New Zealand is the first OECD country to sign a comprehensive FTA with China (NZMFAT, 2010).

China is New Zealand's fourth largest trading partner accounting for NZ$1.6 billion of New Zealand's merchandise exports and over NZ$1 billion in services.

An FTA is expected to add between NZ$240 million and NZ$280 million to the economy of New Zealand over the next 20 years while increasing exports by 40 per cent (Allen and NZPA, 2006).

China has also completed an FTA with Chile, which was signed in November 2005. It was the first FTA between a Latin American country and China. The essence of the FTA with Chile was greater access to Chilean copper production, as China is the world's largest copper importer and accounts for 22 per cent of the world's consumption (Hua, 2005). Access was granted through joint ventures between Chilean and Chinese companies.

In summary

China experienced tremendous growth in the latter part of the twentieth century. It has overcome political turmoil and is becoming economically focused. It has been accepted into the WTO and is in the process of completing numerous free trade deals with various regions across the world. China is beginning to assert itself on the world stage and it has been argued that in order for Australia to remain competitive and have greater access to China's market, an FTA is necessary. In order to fully comprehend FTAs, a short history of globalization and theories supporting it are discussed in the next section.

The march of globalization

This section will provide a brief history of globalization with reference to foreign direct investment (FDI) and FTAs as indicators of the rate and pace of globalization. Trade is a fundamental feature of globalization and has numerous economic benefits. The evolution of economies will also be discussed. As economies evolve they tend to focus less on labour-intensive industries and more on knowledge-based industries. As a result of its high labour costs, it has been concluded that Australia must focus less on labour-intensive industries, such as textiles, and focus more on services. As globalization continues to intensify, it can be argued that Australia needs to embrace this process by endorsing policies that facilitate trade, including the establishment of FTAs.

A brief glimpse into the history of globalization

The world is moving towards an economic system where national economies are merging to become interdependent global economic systems. This phenomenon is referred to as globalization. Globalization is the integration of economies across the world and includes features such as trade, capital movements, including the movement of private capital, the movement of people from one country to another and technology through FDI and technical innovation. Advances of telecommunication technologies have accelerated the process and have had a profound effect on national borders (Saee, 2005, 2007). It is also claimed that global markets allow people access to larger markets which would otherwise be unattainable. Globalization brings capital flows, technological innovation and lower prices on imports (IMF, 2000).

Globalization began to take shape in the nineteenth century. From the period 1880 to 1913, world trade grew eleven times faster than world output and embraced 155 trading areas from all continents (Hoogvelt, 2001). Immediately before the commencement of the Second World War, in 1938, world exports totalled US$22.6 billion (Hoogvelt, 2001: 77). However, it was not until the end of the Second World War that a general consensus to reduce protectionism and move towards freer trade was established. As a result, FDI and international trade increased rapidly. This also led to the creation of GATT (1948), the European Economic Community (Common Market, 1957) and the North American Free Trade Agreement (NAFTA) in 1993, between Canada, Mexico and the USA (Answers.com, 2010).

The WTO, which superseded GATT, was also created during the Uruguay Round in 1995. The WTO has become an internationally recognized governing institution entrenched in law. It brings together treaties, codes and clauses and binds them into a single package (Hirst and Thompson 1996: 137). All members of the WTO have legal obligations, which bind them, and decisions are based on majority voting. Under the WTO, multilateral trade liberalization took four directions:

1   ongoing work by all WTO members to commit to the Uruguay Round;
2   negotiate to bring more countries into the WTO;
3   efforts to further liberalize trade through sectoral initiatives;
4   preparations for a new round of multilateral negotiations.

(DFAT, 2001a: 106)

Foreign direct investment

The rate of FDI is a significant indicator of the rate of globalization. It is claimed that FDI, which began in latter part of the 1960s, can generate employment, raise productivity and enhance exports (UNCTAD, 2006).

The rate of FDI substantially increased in the early 1980s. Between 1983 and 1990, FDI grew an average of 34 per cent compared with an average annual rate of 9 per cent for global merchandise (Hirst and Thompson 1996: 55). Currently, foreign affiliates of an estimated 77,000 transnational corporations generate 62 million jobs (UNCTAD, 2006).

As a result, governments throughout the world recognize the benefits of FDI and compete to attract investors by improving their investment climates through the reduction of trade restrictions (UNCTAD, 2004).

Free trade agreements

As globalization has become increasingly pervasive throughout the world, the number of FTAs has increased. FTAs increasingly gained prominence in the 1990s and by 2001 there were 239 regional trade agreements (Urata, 2002; 21).

Free trade agreements are entered into between countries in order to remove tariffs and import quotas. They can secure markets, which will provide export opportunities. They also liberalize markets, which leads to increased competition that then eliminates weak domestic competition. FTAs are also popular because they require less time to implement trade liberalization than through the WTO. They are justified and entrenched in Article 24 of GATT.

Although FTAs discriminate against non-members by nature, they are allowed to exist under the WTO as an exception to most favoured nation (MFN) treatment prescribed in GATT Article 1 if they meet the following criteria:

1   trade barriers are not higher than they were before the FTA was entered into;
2   trade barriers are to be abolished for substantially all trade; and
3   the FTA must be completed within a reasonable time.

(Urata, 2002)

As a result of an established international organization that monitors trade and trade laws, the number of international agreements has increased. Bilateral treaties, for example, increased to 1,856 in 1999 (Saee, 2005, p. 11). Global trade has grown from US$250 billion, in 1965, to over US$7.4 trillion in 2005 (Saee, 2005, p. 13). In 1960, the total ratio of foreign trade to gross domestic product (GDP) was 25 per cent. By 1999, this number had soared to 52 per cent (Urata, 2002). In 2009, total world trade in goods accounted for US$12.15 trillion while world trade in services represented US$3.31 trillion (WTO 2010b).

Evolving economies

Economies are constantly evolving. It is asserted that adjustments to the TCF industry will occur, as a result of global pressure, regardless of any assistance that may be rendered by the government. In a Market Access Study, it was stated:

> It is clear that no developed economy, even countries that have been consolidating their position in the international market ... can escape the contraction in local textile and garment production. Further trade liberalization will only accelerate the decline of local apparel production. Australia is no exception to this.
>
> (Commonwealth of Australia, 2003: 19)

The growth in services

The global economy is also experiencing dramatic changes, as a result of knowledge-based industries and technological advancements. Industrial economies are becoming more service-oriented and highly skilled in order to meet the demands of their populations (IMF, 2000).

There has also been a global movement towards services at the expense of agriculture and manufacturing. In the 1970s, services accounted for a quarter of world FDI stock, by 2002, services rose to 60 per cent (UNCTAD, 2004: 98). This was due in large part to the expansion of public utilities and the expansion of educational services. The Australian service sector increased from 55 per cent in 1980 to 61 per cent in 2000. For the then G7 nations, services grew from 45 per cent of employment in 1960 to 70 per cent of employment in 2000 (DFAT, 2001a: 26–27).

Knowledge-based economies

Labour-intensive industries have been replaced by skill-intensive industries in the major OECD countries. This has resulted in these countries becoming knowledge-based economies. Knowledge-based industries are those which have intensive input in human capital and technology. Taiwan is a recent example of how a country can transform itself from a labour-intensive economy into a knowledge-based economy. Taiwan was made famous for its cheap manufacturing from the 1960s to the 1980s. Since 1990, the majority of Taiwan's labour-intensive industries have relocated to China, resulting in the manufacturing sector's share of GDP falling from one-half to one-third (DFAT, 2001a: 30). At the same time Taiwan began to focus on knowledge-based industries such as information technology and is now a world leader in that field. Australia is also becoming a knowledge-based economy. Such industries comprised 48 per cent of Australia's GDP in 2000. Australia was also the third fastest growing advanced economy between 1996 and 1999 (DFAT, 2001a: 33).

In summary

Generally speaking, the process of globalization will continue. The levels of FDI and the number of FTAs and trade agreements will also continue to increase. Australia, as a developed country, has already embraced this by focusing on less labour-intensive industries such as the TCF industry and moving towards knowledge-based industries. In order for Australia to benefit from globalization, it must facilitate trade and capital movements. This includes establishing FTAs with countries, such as China, in order to capitalize from its competitive advantage. The next section will discuss theories which explain, endorse and justify free trade amongst nations.

International trade theories

The free trade theories justifying globalization of national economies are briefly examined here and include mercantilism, Adam Smith's absolute advantage, David Ricardo's comparative advantage and modern theories based on economic efficiency. In a modern context it can be argued that Australia, as a developed country, would benefit from an FTA, with China, if it focused on its strengths in knowledge-based industries, such as services. While China, as a result of its abundant cheap labour force, would benefit if it focused on labour-intensive sectors, such as the TCF industry. As a result, both countries would be benefiting from their respective comparative advantages. By reducing protectionist policies, such as tariffs and quotas through an FTA, the governments of each country would facilitate this process.

Mercantilism

Mercantilist theory of international trade was prevalent from the mid-1500s to 1800. It was based on the notion of encouraging exports and discouraging imports. Wealth was measured by gold reserves, which were acquired by exporting more than importing. Government control over imports was deemed to be necessary in order to accumulate gold. Trade was a zero-sum game where gains by one nation were at the expense of another (Saee, 2005).

Adam Smith and the 'absolute advantage'

Adam Smith's work entitled *Wealth of Nations*, published in 1776, has formed the basis of modern economic theory. Smith believed that the sovereign government should provide a legal framework based on justice and property rights. The sovereign government was not to interfere with an individual's pursuit of self-interest, which he believed took precedent over everything else. Smith believed that a nation could become wealthy through economic liberty, which included the removal of artificial barriers to trade, both internal and external (Backhouse, 1985). These ideas were first espoused in the seventeenth century by John Locke who held that an individual had a right to use property freely, subject to well-defined laws (Wolf, 2004).

Smith adopted the 'absolute advantage' theory, which occurs as a result of commodities being produced wherever they can be produced more cheaply. This theory is based on the assumption that capital and labour are mobile among and within countries. Differences in production costs are based on the premise that different countries have different advantages in land and natural resources. A nation, ideally, should specialize and trade only in those goods and commodities in which it was seen to have the absolute advantage – that is, for being the most efficient (Saee, 2005). Smith believed that international trade served as a way to dispose of surplus products (Backhouse, 1985).

David Ricardo's 'comparative advantage'

David Ricardo's theory of comparative advantage arose in 1819, some time after Smith's work, but was equally as influential. This theory formed the basis for the justification of international trade. The theory is based on the principle that if a home country can produce a good at a lower cost than a foreign country, and that foreign country can produce a good at a lower cost than the home country, then the cheaper goods should be traded as it would benefit both parties involved in free trade with each other (Suranovic, 2004).

Ricardo used England and Portugal as an example. He claimed that if England specialized in producing one good (cloth), and Portugal another (wine), the result would be a total world increase in the output of these goods. The specialization for a good should be only for a good for which that country has a comparative advantage in production. To ascertain the comparative advantage, opportunity costs of producing goods across countries must be considered (Suranovic, 2004). This occurs where a good can be produced at a lower opportunity cost than another country.

To illustrate this further, if Portugal is three times more productive than England in producing wine and four times more productive in producing cloth, it has a comparative advantage in producing cloth. England on the other hand, would have a comparative advantage in wine as it is disadvantaged least in regards to that product.

Modern economic perspectives on free trade

There have been numerous modern theorists who support free trade. Former director-general of the WTO, Mike Moore, for example believed that the growth of villages was a direct result of specialization and that this specialization led to civil organization. The surpluses of time, crops and animals led to the flourishing of riches, ideas and technologies. Moore states that protectionist policies exist because those who grant them are rewarded by the few who benefit from them. He asserts that competition is essential for society and that monopolies are exploitive and less innovative. He further stated that lack of competition can lead to price-fixing and cartel behaviour (Moore, 2003).

Perhaps the most revered modern proponent of international trade is Milton Friedman. In his article entitled *The Case for Free Trade*, Friedman stated that since Adam Smith, there has been unanimity among economists that free trade is the best option for countries and that, despite this, tariffs still exist. Protectionist measures have been implemented throughout the world on numerous products. The justification for these measures is that they are a reaction to unfair international competition. But Friedman asserted that it was the consumer who ultimately suffered. He stated that 'protection' really meant exploiting the consumer (*FreeRepublic*, 1997). Cheaper and a greater abundance of goods would be the result of a reduction in protectionist policies.

Friedman further believed that few arguments have been advanced in favour of tariffs. The national security argument, where certain industries are protected, such as the domestic steel industry, is often a rationalization for certain tariffs rather than a reason for them (*FreeRepublic*, 1997).

The 'infant industry' argument holds that newly established industries must be protected while they mature. However, Friedman argues that most firms experience losses in their early years but will recuperate them in later years. If the original entrant cannot recuperate their losses, then, Friedman believes, it is probably not worthwhile for the community to make such an investment.

Another argument, in favour of tariffs, occurs when a country is a major producer of a product and seeks to control production of that product through tariffs or by joining a number of other producers thus creating a monopoly, such as the

Organization of Petroleum Exporting Countries (OPEC). This can be viewed positively by the OPEC countries, as it creates export taxes on the product(s) but this also leads to cartel behaviour and eliminates benefits to consumers. The final argument against reducing protectionism is that not all countries practice it equally; thus it is not in the best interest of a country to completely do so. However, Friedman believed that by imposing tariffs, a country is harming itself. He believed in the freedom of international trade and that when there is economic freedom and countries intend to cooperate, international trade will work effectively.

In summary

Smith's absolute advantage theory is based on economic efficiency. Commodities are to be produced wherever they can be produced more cheaply. Ricardo's comparative theory is also based on economic efficiency as goods are to be produced and traded wherever they can be more cheaply, relative to another country. Modern theorists state that protectionist policies, such as tariffs and quotas, lead to economic stagnation, reduce competition and make economies less innovative. All theories have a common thread in terms of advocating minimal government intervention, while governments around the world are pursuing favourable government policies that promote free trade.

Policies that endorse free trade will directly benefit consumers, as they have a greater variety of goods to choose from at competitive prices. Competition leads to innovation, thus it can be deduced that reducing protectionist policies will make an economy more efficient. Australia will benefit through greater trade, free trade in particular, as its firms will have to compete internationally and only the efficient ones will thrive. In order to fully understand the benefits of a proposed FTA with China, a closer examination of Australia's economic relationship with an emphasis on textiles, is provided in the following section.

A close economic relationship between Australia and China

Australia and China have a well-established economic relationship, which has led to negotiations on a proposed FTA. There has been a great deal of economic integration in the form of trade and investment between the countries. It can be argued that the relationship has reached a point where an FTA between the countries is the next logical step. This section will summarize the relationship with a focus on the textile industry.

Establishing the relationship

As a result of geographic proximity, Asian countries have been of particular importance to Australia. Having a good relationship with this region is beneficial to the Australian economy. This is particularly true of China, which is quickly becoming a global economic giant. China's growing power will undoubtedly influence the region for years to come. Although Australia only established diplomatic relations with the People's Republic of China in 1972, the partnership has strengthened in a relatively short time. In regards to investment, as of August, 2003, China approved 6,703 direct investment projects by Australian companies, which accounted for US$3.421 billion (CEDA, 2005). At a media conference in Beijing, in 2004 Australian Foreign Minister Alexander Downer stated: 'We agree that Australia and China would build up a bilateral strategic relationship, that we would strengthen our economic relationship and we would work together closely on Asia-Pacific issues, be they economic or security issues' (CEDA, 2005).

Economic integration

It is propounded in certain circles that Australian industries will be challenged by their Chinese counterparts whether an FTA is signed or not. In 2004, China was Australia's third largest trading partner and accounted for 8 per cent of Australian exports and 11 per cent of imports (DFAT, 2010b). Australia accounted for 2 per cent of China's exports (TFIA, 2005b). This was due to China's increased share of world merchandise exports that jumped from less than 1 per cent in 1980, to 6 per cent in 2003 (CEDA, 2005). Australia's merchandise exports to China in 1979–1980 were an estimated A$845 million or 4.5 per cent; by 2003–2004, Australian exports to China had arisen to A$9.9 billion, accounting for 9.1 per cent of total exports (CEDA, 2005). And in the period 2009–2010, Australian merchandise exports to China amounted to the astonishing amount of A$46.5 billion (DFAT, 2010c). In 2004, trade in manufactures between the two countries totalled US$13.79 billion and comprised 30 per cent and 86 per cent of total merchandise exports from China and Australia, respectively (DFAT, 2005a: 9). As illustrated in Table 7.1, Australia has become one of China's most important trading partners. In 2009, Australia ranked 11 among China's merchandise export destination countries, and 7 in regard to China's sources of merchandise imports (DFAT, 2010c). And it is expected that in the following decades the development of an increasingly strong economic relation between China and Australia will continue, and China will play the most dominant role in terms of Australia's economic partnerships (CEDA, 2010). Table 7.1 illustrates China's merchandise trade relationships on a global scale.

Textiles integration

Australia currently imports 50 per cent of its wool from China, while China imports up to 75 per cent of its wool from Australia. This number is expected to increase as Chinese demand for wool is expected to equal 62 per cent of the world's total demand (AWI, 2006). It is estimated that full liberalization of trade will lead to an increase in the volume of greasy wool exports by 20 per cent, which would increase Australian exports, by US$600 million.

In regards to cotton, China is the world's fourth largest producer of cotton in the world, accounting for an estimated 25 per cent of the world's production (DFAT, 2005a). Australia is China's fourth largest supplier of cotton and provided

Table 7.1 China's merchandise trade relationships on a global scale

China's key export destination countries			China's key import sources		
Rank	Country	%	Rank	Country	%
1	USA	18.4	1	Japan	13.0
2	Hong Kong	13.8	2	Republic of Korea	10.2
3	Japan	8.1	3	Taiwan	8.5
11	*Australia*	*1.7*	7	*Australia*	*3.9*

Source: adapted from DFAT, 2010c.

6.3 per cent of China's total cotton imports between 2001 and 2003 (DFAT, 2005a). Australia currently applies zero tariffs on wool and cotton. China has a tariff on wool and wool tops as well as cotton imports. In 2004, China had a tariff quota volume of 287,000 tonnes and 894,000 tonnes on wool and cotton, respectively (DFAT, 2005a: 34).

In regards to clothing, China is a dominant world player. China accounted for US$61.6 billion total exports in 2004 compared with Australia's clothing exports amounting to US$0.2 billion in 2003 (DFAT, 2005a: 36).

China's export of clothing and textiles to Australia, in 2004, were US$1.4 billion and US$0.4 billion, respectively, while clothing and textile imports from Australia amounted to US$17.1 million and US$28.2 million (DFAT, 2005a: 36).

Through an FTA, Australia would have even greater access to cheap Chinese textiles, while being provided greater access to China's domestic market.

In summary

Consequently, Australia and China are gradually becoming more economically integrated. An FTA, which appears to be the next logical step, will undoubtedly increase the already close economic ties between the countries. Some immediate advantages to Australia, as a result of an FTA, would be China's increasing demand for Australian cotton and wool as their economy continues to increase. Australia would also gain greater market access to China's domestic market and Australian consumers would have a greater variety of goods to choose from. However, to fully understand the numerous advantages of an FTA with China, a more comprehensive look at FTAs is provided in the next section.

The advantages of FTAs

This section will address the numerous advantages that can result from FTAs. FTAs are quicker to negotiate and concessions are easier to obtain, as there are fewer parties involved in negotiations. An FTA also provides access to the markets of other members. This, however, depends on the terms of the agreement; having the right framework is critical. FTAs also eliminate protectionist policies such as tariffs and quotas, which will benefit the community as a whole. Competition and economic growth will also increase. Employment losses in labour-intensive industries of developed countries, e.g. Australia, will inevitably occur, but governments should pursue policies which assist those industries that have been adversely affected. If governments pursue free trade policies while supporting industries adversely affected by free trade, the benefits will generally offset the negative aspects of free trade amongst the countries involved.

Benefits of FTAs

Parties to FTAs are able to secure advantages that may be more difficult to obtain in bigger forums, such as through the WTO. They are also quicker to negotiate, as there are fewer parties involved (DFAT, 2001b: 19). For example, the main outcome of the Uruguay Round of negotiations, in 1995, was to reduce tariffs in developing economies with an emphasis on textiles and agricultural goods. There were many key issues that were still not addressed, including labour standards and human rights and by the late 1990s, world trade was still plagued by protectionism (Meredith and Dyster, 1999). It was clear that international agreements had to be reviewed, as the most powerful countries had not changed their policies in regards to protectionism.

FTAs have been most effective when parties have had different economic structures that give them comparative advantages against each other (DFAT, 2001b).

It has been claimed that Australia would benefit if China exported its textiles into Australia. Australia would then be able to focus on less labour-intensive industries, such as services, to export into China. Economic trade modelling by the Department of Foreign Affairs and Trade (DFAT) further demonstrates that more trade would benefit the world community. Global welfare gains from further multilateral trade were estimated at about US$400 billion (DFAT, 2001a).

Supporting displaced workers

Globalization has resulted in severe job losses with reference to the labour-intensive sectors of developed countries, but has provided more jobs for workers in less developed countries who work at a fraction of the standard Western salary. However, it is argued that rather than slow the process of globalization, governments should pursue policies which facilitate it while at the same time assisting those industries which have been adversely affected by it. This should be done through education and vocational training that will ensure that workers have the opportunity to acquire the skills needed for changing economies (IMF, 2000).

The Federal Government of Australia provides assistance for displaced workers through the *New Start Allowance Program* which provides income support to job seekers (Commonwealth of Australia, 2003: 146). The level of payment depends on the income of both partners as well as their assets. *The Job Network,* another service provided by the federal government, helps displaced workers find employment. Initiated in 1998, *The Job Network* now encompasses over 100 public and private organizations that are awarded business through tenders (Commonwealth of Australia, 2003).

The price of protection

In 1993, it was estimated by the US International Trade Commission (USITC) that liberalization of all US quotas on textiles and apparels would have resulted in a gain of up to US$10 billion to the US economy, with job losses of 57 000, mainly in the apparel sector (Industry Commission, 1997). Lowering assistance, it is suggested, will benefit the community as a whole. Assistance to selective industries is at the expense of other sectors. Greater competition also leads to improved productivity. It has been stated that:

> Data on world trade] show a definite statistical link between freer trade and economic growth. All countries, including the poorest, have assets – human, industrial, natural, financial – which they can employ to produce goods and services for their domestic markets or to compete overseas. ... Simply put, the principle of 'comparative advantage' says that countries prosper first by taking advantage of their assets in order to concentrate on what they can produce best, and then by trading these products for products that other countries produce best.
>
> (Industry Commission, 1997: 332)

Although tariff revenue raised from the Australian TCF industry was an estimated A$950 million, in 2001–2002, it is believed that the increase in imports, as a result of freer trade, will offset the loss of revenue (Commonwealth of Australia, 2003). Tariffs and federal government assistance provided protection worth an estimated A$13,000 a year, per each TCF worker in 2003 (Commonwealth of Australia, 2003: 23). Members of the TCF industry are aware of the cost of protection.

In regards to the federal tariff cuts, Gloweave's David Same stated that:

> Interestingly enough, because of the Government's action in the quota dropping and the tariffs, the industry that has survived is probably a better industry, a more capable industry than anywhere else in the world. We're flexible. We can import from anywhere because there's no quota.
>
> (cited in Ashton and Ryan, 2000)

In summary

There are numerous advantages in establishing FTAs that far outweigh protectionist policies. FTAs are quicker to negotiate and can lead to more concessions among members as there are fewer parties than in larger forums such as the WTO. The price of protection in numbers is substantial. Protectionist policies are created at the cost of other industries, which receive no protection. As a result, governments should pursue policies that reduce protectionism and assist those workers who become displaced by them. The next section will outline what Australia specifically stands to gain from an FTA with China.

The advantages of an FTA with China

China's growth rate over the last 20 years has been remarkable and has touched all sectors of their economy. This has been a result of the growth of non-state enterprises, which have been fuelled by substantial amounts of FDI. Non-state enterprises have become an integral part of China's economy. Australia can obtain numerous benefits in forming an FTA with China. This section will examine those benefits, including lower prices, greater investment and increased business opportunities.

China's economy – unlimited potential

Although China's economic reform has been gradual, its economic growth has been enormous. Measured on a purchasing power parity (PPP) basis, China stood as the second-largest economy in the world after the USA at US$8.182 trillion, in 2005 (2005 est.) (CIA, 2006).

China's real growth rate was 9.3 per cent in 2005 and its labour force of 791.4 million in 2005 was the largest of any country in the world (CIA, 2006). Its real GDP has increased by over 9 per cent per annum over the last 20 years (CEDA, 2005). In regards to China's growth, Trade Minister Mark Vaile stated that:

> China's economic growth forecasts over the next decade are phenomenal so it is imperative that Australia positions itself to take advantage of this major export market opportunity. We also want to ensure we maintain our competitive edge as China's trade with the world expands.
>
> (DFAT, 2010b)

Non-state enterprises have now become an increasingly important contributor to the Chinese economy. The contribution to GDP by non-state enterprises rose to 63.37 per cent in 2001 from 53.57 per cent in 1992 (China Internet Information Center, 2006a).

China's recent economic surge has also attracted substantial FDI. The Chinese Government has encouraged investment by foreign businesses. Foreign firms are taxed substantially less than domestic firms and in 2001, 63 per cent of the total volume of imports and exports were by foreign invested enterprises (China Internet Information Center, 2006a). In the first two months of 2006, FDI grew nearly 8 per cent from the previous year and totalled US$8.6 billion (*People's Daily Online*, 2006). China attracted US$60.3 billion in FDI in 2005 and US$60.6 billion in 2004 (*People's Daily Online*, 2006).

China's outward investment has also increased. In 2005 China's foreign investment was an estimated US$6 billion, up from US$620 million in 2000 (*People's Daily Online*, 2006).

Table 7.2 shows China's FDI flows within the period 1985–2004 in comparison to the FDI activities of the United States, developing economies and the whole world. It clearly illustrates that in the past decades China has steadily gained

Table 7.2 FDI flows for the period 1985–2004, selected countries

FDI flows	FDI overview, selected years (millions of dollars)				
	1985–1995 (Annual average)	2001	2002	2003	2004
China					
Inward	11 715	46 878	52 743	53 505	60 630
Outward	1 687	6 885	2 518	−152	1 805
United States					
Inward	44 109	159 461	71 331	56 834	95 859
Outward	43 102	124 873	134 946	119 406	229 294
Developing economies					
Inward	49 868	217 845	155 528	166 337	233 227
Outward	21 580	78 571	47 775	29 016	83 190
World					
Inward	182 438	825 925	716 128	632 599	648 146
Outward	203 256	743 465	652 181	616 923	730 257

Source: adapted from UNCTAD, 2005.

relevance as an FDI host country. According to the *World Investment Report 2010*, in 2009, China's inward FDI stock increased to an amount of US$95 billion, and its FDI outflows accounted for US$ 48 billion (UNCTAD, 2010).

The growth of China's TCF industry

China's TCF industry is growing at 30 per cent per annum and this trend is expected to continue into the near future (TFIA, 2005b).

China is also the world's largest producer of sheep and accounted for 15 per cent of the world's total sheep production in 2004 (DFAT, 2005a: 29). Private Chinese companies accounted for 58 per cent of capital investment in the TCF industry, followed by 34 per cent by foreign direct investment (TFIA, 2005b).

China's primary export markets include: Japan and Hong Kong, which comprise 32 per cent of total exports; the USA, which accounts for the 22 per cent of exports; and the EU which accounts for 18 per cent of exports (TFIA, 2005b).

How Australia stands to gain?

The economic modelling in the Joint Feasibility Study, by the Australian DFAT and the Chinese Ministry of Commerce, endorses the proposed free trade agreement by claiming that numerous economic advantages will result from it. These benefits include lower prices, a greater variety of choice for consumers and increased business opportunities for exporters (DFAT, 2005a: 28). The removal of tariffs will also add 0.012 and 0.006 percentage points or A$1.3 billion and RMB13.3 billion to Australia's and China's average annual real GDP growth rates, respectively (DFAT, 2005a: 28). It is further claimed that net employment will grow as a result of an FTA. In regards to services, Australian service exports reached A$1.3 billion in 2004, largely driven by education, tourism and transport services (DFAT, 2010b).

Further, adjustment costs to sensitive sectors, such as clothing and textiles will be offset by either domestic reform or globalization. The cotton, wool and textiles and clothing sectors are used as economic modelling examples.

Australia is China's fourth largest supplier of cotton, representing 6.3 per cent of China's total cotton imports (DFAT, 2005a: 29). Although there are no tariffs for cotton into Australia, China's cotton imports are subject to tariffs. A possible FTA will further liberalize China's cotton industry as well as increase Australia's production and supply capability (DFAT, 2005a: 29). China is currently the world's largest importer of wool, with Australia as its major provider. From 2001 to 2003, Australia exported 0.15 million tonnes of wool to China, which represented 62.9 per cent of China's average annual wool imports. These imports are subject to tariffs (DFAT, 2005a). Australia does not apply tariffs to wool imports. Independent economic modelling confirms that liberalization will further increase exports from Australia into China. The differences in wool production between Australia and China will also lead to the further development of China's wool production, as well as an increase in Australia's production and supply capabilities (DFAT, 2005a).

Currently, both Australia and China apply tariffs on textile and clothing products ranging from 5 to 17.5 per cent for Australia and 5 to 25 per cent for China (DFAT, 2005a). Economic modelling suggests that the Australian textiles industry will experience an increase in production as well as employment, due to greater market access by 2015 (DFAT, 2005a). Imports from China are also projected to increase. The proposed FTA could also lead to an increase of Australian manufacturers investing in China, as well as new opportunities in supplying specialized textiles.

In summary

China has become one of the fastest growing economies in the world. It has low-value-added industries, which require little capital or barriers to entry. It also has an enormous labour force and low labour costs as well as favourable policies, which endorse foreign investment. Australia has a lot to gain through an FTA with China, particularly in the TCF industry, where it is one of China's most important trading partners. Reduced tariffs will provide excellent opportunities for Australian companies supplying specialized textiles, as well as for domestic consumers who will have more goods to choose from. Although it is recognized that an FTA would reduce employment, this would be offset by the adjustments made as a result of domestic reforms – in the form of governmental assistance. Australia has successfully completed six FTAs and has major regional commitments. It will be contended in the next section that protectionist policies on tariffs have already been eroded through such FTAs. Further, Australia would have to reduce their protectionist measures in order to comply with their regional agreements, irrespective of signing an FTA with China.

Australia's other commitments

Overall, Australia has successfully established six FTAs that have reduced tariffs on numerous good and services – including textiles. For example, the Thailand–Australia Free Trade Agreement (TAFTA) and the Australian–United States Free Trade Agreement (AUSFTA), touched upon the reduction of tariffs on the textiles industry. On the topic of FTAs, Mark Vaile, Minister for Trade stated:

> The Government's FTA agenda is one of the most exciting and dynamic developments in Australia's trade policy history. Our pursuit of high quality and comprehensive FTAs reflects an integrated strategy for promoting global free trade that, in the long-term, benefits all Australians.
>
> (DFAT, 2006a)

This section will examine those agreements, as well as Australia's commitment to APEC, which is based on a free and open trade and investment regime in the Asia-Pacific region.

A closer economic relations (CER) agreement

The closer economic relations (CER) agreement, between Australia and New Zealand came into force in 1983. It was established in order to progressively eliminate barriers to trade. This agreement was a culmination of a series of agreements between the two countries. Since its inception, the CER agreement has undergone three reviews, which resulted in all tariffs and restrictions being eliminated, the inclusion of services into the treaty and the harmonization of non-tariff measures, including quarantine and customs (DFAT, 1997).

This has resulted in the CER agreement becoming one of the most comprehensive FTAs in the world.

The Singapore–Australia Free Trade Agreement (SAFTA)

The Singapore–Australia Free Trade Agreement (SAFTA) commenced in July 2003 after ten rounds of negotiations. The agreement eliminated tariffs and increased market access for the Australian service sector (DFAT, 2006c).

Areas such as competition policy and intellectual property have as a result become more open and predictable.

The Thailand–Australia Free Trade Agreement (TAFTA)

The TAFTA commenced in January 2005 and will result in Thai tariffs, on Australian goods, being eliminated by 2010. Thailand has already eliminated tariffs on 2,934 items which accounted for 78 per cent of all imports from Australia (DFAT, 2006d). The treaty provides a framework for numerous bilateral activities including law enforcement, tourism and natural resource management in agriculture. Australia has eliminated tariffs on 2,003 items that accounted for 47 per cent of imports from Thailand (DFAT, 2006d).

In regards to textiles, Australia has reduced tariffs, on 239 items, previously at 25 per cent, to 12.5 per cent which will hold until 2010. These items will then be reduced to 5 per cent until 2015, when they will be eliminated (DFAT, 2006d). Textiles, clothing and leather items with tariffs of 10 or 15 per cent were reduced to 5 per cent at the commencement of the FTA and will hold until 2010 (DFAT, 2006d). Textiles with 5 per cent tariffs have been reduced to 3 per cent as a result of the FTA and will be eliminated in 2008 (DFAT, 2006d).

The Australian–United States Free Trade Agreement (AUSFTA)

The Australian–United States Free Trade Agreement came into force on 1 January 2005. The treaty has increased trade and investment with the USA, which is one of Australia's most important two-way trading partners. In 2003, the two-way trade relationship was worth A$40.9 billion, with A$14.2 billion worth of goods and services exported to the USA, and A$26.7 billion imported to Australia (DFAT, 2005b). The potential benefits for Australian industries are substantial, as the USA is the world's largest market with a GDP of almost US$14 trillion (DFAT, 2010d).

Despite the significant increase in trade and the reduction of barriers, there were exemptions on both sides. The main exemptions of the agreement for Australia were in defence strategic purchasing, which dwarfs all other Australian Government procurement, government advertising, and motor vehicles (Burgess, 2004). American exemptions included defence, air travel and oil for the US strategic petroleum reserve. Both countries have also exempted foreign aid and research and development in services (Burgess, 2004).

Major advantages of AUSFTA

The potential economic advantages to Australian industries are substantial. Independent analysis suggests that AUSFTA will generate around A$6 billion in economic benefit to Australia and see the creation of over 30,000 jobs for Australian workers (Switzer, 2004).

Since the agreement took effect, more than 97 per cent of US tariffs applying to Australia's non-agricultural exports have been eliminated (DFAT, 2005b). The FTA also gives Australian industry access to the US$200 billion US Federal Government procurement (DFAT, 2005c).

The FTA has resulted in bids from Australian companies for contracts with the US Government to be considered in the same way as those from American businesses. US businesses will also retain the right to bid for Australian Government contracts (DFAT, 2005b).

In regards to textiles and clothing, the agreement automatically eliminated 30 per cent of US tariffs on textiles with remaining duties being eliminated by 2015 (DFAT, 2006e). The rate of tariff reduction depends on the category under which certain textiles have been placed. Under the agreement only textiles made from materials originating from Australia or the USA will be eligible for tariff reductions. Textiles exported to Australia will receive a two-percentage point reduction until the end of 2009 (DFAT, 2006e).

There are remedies for importing parties who have been adversely affected as a result of the elimination of customs duties under the agreement. The damaged party may apply for an increased rate of custom duty on the goods which equals the MFN applied rate at the time the action is taken (DFAT, 2010d). The level of damage is to be measured by considering factors such as output, utilization of capacity, exports and wages. An importing party may take emergency action if imports are causing or threaten to cause substantial damage. This measure is not to exceed 200 days under which time the claim is to be investigated. Each party retains their rights under Article XIX of GATT 1994 and the Safeguards Agreement and the Agreement on Textiles and Clothing (DFAT, 2010d). Both parties are also required to cooperate in enforcing laws related to the origin of goods, under the agreement.

ASEAN–Australia–New Zealand Free Trade Agreement (AANZFTA)

The agreement establishing the Association of Southeast Asian Nations (ASEAN)–Australia–New Zealand Free Trade Area (AANZFTA) was signed by the Minister for Trade, Simon Crean, and his ASEAN and New Zealand counterparts, on 27 February 2009 in Hua Hin, Thailand. AANZFTA is the largest FTA Australia has concluded. ASEAN and New Zealand together account for 20 per cent of Australia's total trade in goods and services, which were worth A$112 billion in 2008. This is by far the largest FTA than Australia's trade with any single country (DFAT, 2010e).

AANZFTA contains regional rules of origin and substantial tariff reduction and elimination commitments, as well as WTO-plus commitments in other areas such as services, which will provide commercially meaningful benefits to Australian business and further strengthen Australia's commercial ties with ASEAN.

AANZFTA came into effect on 1 January 2010 for eight of the twelve countries that signed the agreement: Australia, New Zealand, Brunei, Burma, Malaysia, the Philippines, Singapore and Vietnam (DFAT, 2010e).

The agreement is designed to reduce progressively and/or eliminate at least some products tariffs facing Australian goods exported to ASEAN countries and vice versa (DFAT, 2010f).

Australia–Chile Free Trade Agreement (ACI-FTA)

The Australia–Chile Free Trade Agreement (ACI-FTA) is a significant market opening agreement which will result in the immediate reduction of tariffs on 97 per cent of goods currently traded. It is anticipated that tariffs on all existing merchandise trade between Australia and Chile will be eliminated by 2015 (DFAT, 2010g).

The agreement will foster new trade and investment opportunities to Australia. The FTA covers trade in goods, services and investment and is truly liberalizing with commitments that go beyond both countries' WTO commitments.

The FTA is designed to deliver the most comprehensive outcome on goods in any such agreement negotiated with another agricultural producing country since the CER agreement with New Zealand. Tariffs on all existing merchandise trade – in both directions – will be eliminated by 2015. The vast majority of Australian goods exported into Chile – and Chilean goods exported to Australia – will enter duty free from entry into force of the FTA on 6 March 2009. Chile is currently Australia's third-largest trading partner in Latin America. Two-way trade between Australia and Chile is growing rapidly – up from A$857 million in 2007 to A$1.4 billion in 2008. Australia is the fourth-largest foreign investor in Chile, with around US$3 billion of direct investment. The FTA will offer Australian exporters opportunities across the board (DFAT, 2010h).

Australia's Commitment to APEC

It is also contended that protection in the form of tariffs and quotas will have to continue to decrease as a result of Australia's commitment to APEC. APEC was formed in 1989. It aims to strengthen regional links by promoting trade and economic goals. The twenty-one Asian Pacific members meet annually to discuss ways in which to strengthen regional development. The *Bogar Declaration*, in 1994, provided an outline for trade liberalization regarding APEC members. Article 24 stated APEC's goals, which include:

a)   a commitment to liberalization towards free and open trade in the region;
b)   a target date for achieving free and open trade in the region;
c)   a requirement of consistency with GTT/WTO rules and principles;
d)   details to be worked out by APEC Ministers.

(Garnaut, 1996: 82)

To justify discrimination in favour of APEC members, a free trade agreement on virtually all products would need to be established between the members (Garnaut, 1996). APEC also has three pillars that form the basis of its work; they consist of trade and investment liberalization, business facilitation, and economic and technical cooperation (DFAT, 2010i). APEC's current goal is of a free and open trade and investment regime in the Asia-Pacific region, by 2010 for industrialized countries and 2020 for developing countries (DFAT, 2006f).

In order for this to be achieved, tariff and non-tariff barriers must be removed. The average tariff rates were reduced from 12 per cent in 1995 to 8 per cent in 2000 and will continue to decrease (DFAT, 2006f).

APEC members are important to Australia as these economies purchase three-quarters of Australia's merchandise exports and provide access to over 2.5 billion customers (DFAT, 2006f).

In summary

Protectionist policies, such as tariffs and quotas, have already been substantially reduced as a result of FTAs with other countries. Both TAFTA and AUSFTA reduced Australian tariffs on textiles and will ultimately eliminate them. Further, Australia is committed to APEC, which seeks to establish a free and open trade and investment regime in the Asia-Pacific region through the reduction of tariffs. To date, on top of free trade negotiations with China, Australia is negotiating FTAs with Malaysia, Japan, Korea, Indonesia and the Gulf Cooperation Council, which comprises six member states, namely, Bahrain, Kuwait, Oman, Qatar, Saudi Arabia, and the United Arab Emirates. In addition, Australia has undertaken a feasibility study with India (DFAT, 2010j).

An FTA with China will not stop the reduction of tariffs. However, it can be argued that further opening up of Australia's market to China will cause irreversible damage to Australia's TCF industry. Australia simply cannot compete with China's enormous labour force and questionable labour policies, and this will ultimately result in substantial job losses in the TCF industry. These issues will be discussed in the following section.

China's questionable labour practices

Although tariffs and quotas will inevitably be phased out, regardless of whether an FTA is signed with China or not, it has been claimed that an FTA with China will cause irreversible damage from which the Australian TCF industry will be unable to recover. International competition is an expected result of free trade; however, it is argued that Australia simply cannot compete with the Chinese labour force, the largest in the world, or with their questionable labour practices which results in extremely low wages. This section will examine China's textile industry, including its companies, its labour force and labour practices.

Unions take a stand

At a recent International Confederation of Free Trade Unions (ICFTU) congress, the European Division advocated that China has made repression of workers' rights a systematic part of state policy. Independent trade unions are outlawed in China where only one state-controlled trade union centre is allowed to operate. Any strikes are rapidly repressed. Factory workers, who are mostly rural immigrants, who show any interest in trade unions face losing their permit to stay as well as the deposits they are (illegally, but very frequently) required to pay their employer. Workers' protections exist on paper but are rarely enforced by local officials and judges.

As a result working conditions in Chinese special economic zones have already reached the bottom and millions of jobs are moving from other developing countries to China. Worse, this threatens to unleash a 'race to the bottom' in other countries (TCFUA, 2005).

Asia's influence within the global textile and clothing sector

Asian developing countries have gradually taken over global textiles and clothing production. From 1980 to 1995, the value of textile exports from Asia increased by 298 per cent compared with 177 per cent for the world average (Industry Commission, 1997). This increase was due to China, which has expanded its textiles industry tremendously. China's growth was initiated by the movement of the Hong Kong clothing market to the mainland to take advantage of its cheap and abundant labour force.

China's textile industry

The Chinese Government has established free trade zones in the southern part of the country and these host 19 million workers whose wages range from A$96 to A$112 per month (TCFUA, 2005: 6). These policies have had a substantial effect on the provinces of Guangdong, Zhejiang and Jiangsu, in particular. Guangdong has a population of 110 million people with migrants accounting for 31 million and women accounting for the majority of the labour force (IAMAW, 2005). Guangdong's township – Xiqiao – has a giant commune of 2,000 textile workers. It is now a powerhouse of textile manufacturing in China.

A quarter of Zhejiang's population come from other parts of China. Pockets of textile producing communities have sprung up throughout China. Yangzhou City, in Jiangsu, had 296 textile and clothing companies with an output value of 12.6 billion Yuan, in 2003 (N.N., 2010). This textile cluster produced 205 million metres of cloth, 2.85 million metres of woollen cloth and 63.67 million clothing articles, in 2003 (N.N., 2010).

The basic formula is that one group will take the initiative, which will then result in hundreds and sometimes thousands of copycat manufacturers. As a result, Chinese textiles account for 6 per cent of the world's total exports, worth more than US$340 billion (Fishman, 2005).

China's leather factories are the world's largest providers of shoes and clothing. There are six thousand companies which specialize in leather and produce a total of 460 million tanned hides, 5 billion pairs of shoes and 70 million clothing articles a year (Fishman, 2005: 69). Guangdong and Wenzhou are the first and second largest footwear producing regions in China. Zhejiang province's 8,000 companies make 8 billion pairs of socks a year which equates to one-third of the world's total (Fishman, 2005: 70). Yue Yuen, just north of Hong Kong, is home to the world's largest shoe factories. Yue Yuen factories accounted for 18.7 million pairs of athletic shoes and 11.1 million shoes in 2003 (IAMAW, 2005).

Chinese textile companies

For the purposes of illustration, *The Youngor Group Co., Ltd*, a garment company that was incorporated in China in 1979, is briefly mentioned here,. Across China, the Youngor Group's network encompasses over 100 branch offices as well as over 400 company-owned stores operating a total of more than 2,000 outlets. Its product line, including shirts, trousers, suits, ties, casual jackets, as well as T-shirts, officially ranks among China's leading and most popular national brands. The Group's annual capacity has achieved the biggest market penetrations in relation to shirts and suits for fourteen and nine consecutive years, respectively.

The company has grown to a workforce of over 50,000 employees and has generated RMB21.4 billion sales revenues. Within the Chinese garment industry, the company has generated the highest revenue and profit for eight years in a row, which also made it more competitive on the international market. Due to its extraordinary performance the Youngor Group was listed among the 'Top 100 Chinese Companies 2008' (Youngor Group Co., Ltd, 2008).

The *Wuhan Yudhua Group Co., Ltd* is another well-established Chinese company with 3,692 employees and an annual production of 15,000 tons of cotton yarn, 40 million metres of cotton fabrics and 900,000 sets of knitted dresses. The company is involved in spinning, weaving, knitting, printing and dyeing and garment manufacturing (Department of Commerce Hubei Province, 2006). Perhaps its greatest asset is the fact that it has been authorized as a textile and garment export production base by the state, which facilitates the export process.

Chinese textile companies have also established themselves through alliances with international partners. *Nantong YINGLAN Fashion Co. Ltd,* in Jiangsu Province, is a joint venture with Japanese company MEIFU Co. Ltd Established in 2000, the company boasts modern computerized embroidery and sewing machines from Japan. The company had a turnover in 2005 of US$5,000,000 (Alibaba.com Corporation, 2006).

The Chinese textile sector has also established itself into successful clusters. Numerous textiles companies have been successfully established in the province of Jiangsu, such as, the *Jiangsu Textile Industry (Group) Import and Export Co., Ltd (Sutex)* which was founded in 1985. The company's product line of nearly a thousand products comprises ten categories such as fabrics, garments, and textile raw materials. In consecutive years, the Bank of China, Jiangsu Branch has rated Sutex as a 'Class AAA Credit Enterprise' (Sutex Co., Ltd, 2010).

The *Jiangsu YuLun Textile Group Co., Ltd* produces cotton carded and bleached yarn and consists of five spinning factories, four trading companies, two cotton purchasing and processing subsidiaries, as well as one weaving factory (YuLun Group Co., Ltd, 2010).

The *Jiangsu Lianfa Textile Co., Ltd* is a large-scaled textile group, which manufactures yarn, yarn-dyed fabrics and shirts. The company employs more than 5,000 people and its total assets amount to RMB1.107 billion. The Lianfa Group is the largest and best-performing company among the yarn-dyed companies within Jiangsu Province (Lianfa Textile Co., Ltd, 2010).

Ignoring international conventions

The International Labour Organization (ILO) defines minimal standards regarding labour practices and human rights. Australia, like most developed countries, is a signatory to the ILO and is therefore obliged to follow the ILO statute. Some of the rights stated in the statute include the elimination of forced or compulsory labour and the effective abolition of child labour (Hamilton, 2001).

It is argued that trade can only be deemed fair when these rights are adhered to by the signatories. China has never ratified conventions 87 and 98 of the ILO, which grant the right to organize and the right to collective bargaining, respectively. Article 2 of convention 87 states:

> Workers and employers, without distinction whatsoever, shall have the right to establish and, subject only to the rules of the organization concerned, to join organizations of their own choosing without previous authorization.
>
> (IFBWW, 2001)

Article 1 of convention 98 states:

1 Workers shall enjoy adequate protection against acts of anti-union discrimination in respect of their employment.
2 Such protection shall apply more particularly in respect of acts calculated to:

>   (a) make the employment of a worker subject to the condition that he shall not join a union or shall relinquish trade union membership;
>   (b) cause the dismissal of or otherwise prejudice a worker by reason of union membership or because of participation in union activities outside working hours or, with the consent of the employer, within working hours.
>
> (IFBWW, 2001)

As a result of China not being a signatory to the ILO, numerous worker manifestations have been brutally suppressed in China. At the Guangyuan Textile Factory in Sichuan, for example, 1,000 workers went on strike, resulting in the arrest of more than a dozen of its leaders (TCFUA, 2005: 6). There is no recourse for employees who are fired, let alone arrested. It is claimed that this situation will continue as long as the massive workforce remains disorganized. Labour, in China, is simply a commodity. When one worker leaves, there are numerous others who will fill the void.

China's labour force

China's estimated population is around 1.3 billion people, though the exact figure is impossible to calculate, as there are numerous people who are unaccounted for, including children and ethnic minorities as well as wondering workers with no fixed address. It is further estimated that 90 to 300 million Chinese are migrating from the countryside to the cities, and more importantly, to the factories (Fishman, 2005). This steady stream of cheap labour has had an enormous impact on China, especially in the free trade zones in the south.

Women labourers

Young women are preferred to their male counterparts in factory jobs, as they are considered to be more docile and are thus willing to work for lower wages. Shenzhen, China's fourth largest city, with a population of 7 million, had 4.75 million factory jobs in 2002, of which 3.5 million were filled by women (Fishman, 2005). Young female rural workers typically have to pay a bond to obtain employment, which results in a debt that they are unable to pay. Once they receive employment, they do not have a say as to their working conditions or their pay. Living conditions for female employees in Shenzhen are minimal. These women live in cramped dormitories and work 7 days a week for 70 hours and earn 72 dollars per month (Fishman, 2005). It is argued that these millions of women are undermining the TCF industries of developed and developing countries the world over.

The Laogai

China also uses prison labour as a way to produce cheap goods. The reform through labour system, known as the Laogai, boasts 1,000 to 6,000 prison camps and 10–20 million inmates (TCFUA, 2005: 7). These prisons force inmates to work up to 15 hours per day for the duration of their incarceration. The goods produced are then exported to international markets. As a result of China's labour practices, there are huge discrepancies between labour costs in Australia and labour costs in China. The comparative labour costs of the TCF industries of Australia and China, in 2005, are shown in Table 7.3.

In summary

China has the world's largest labour force and provides extremely low wages that Australia cannot compete with. China has not ratified the ILO and has no obligation to address the forced, compulsory or unfair labour practices which it practices. China's TCF industry is growing along with their private enterprises. However, it is not only China's labour force and policies that have a negative impact on the Australian TCF industry; the underlying theory of free trade itself has been criticized. The next section will address this issue.

Flaws inherent in free trade theory

In order for Ricardo's theory of comparative advantage to work, there are numerous assumptions which must be considered. First, there must be perfect competition in regards to a large number of buyers and sellers. Second, there must be zero unemployment. Third, the production of goods will not involve pollution or other costs (Hamilton, 2001).

Ricardo's model, for example, is based on the assumption that labour is the only factor of production and that goods are homogeneous across countries. It

Table 7.3 Comparative labour costs of the Textiles, Clothing and Footwear (TCF) industries in China and Australia, 2005

	Labour costs (in US$)	
	China, hourly wage	Australia, hourly wage
Weaving		
Skilled personnel	1.45	14.98
Unskilled personnel	0.66	11.51
Knitting		
Skilled personnel	1.64	14.98
Unskilled personnel	0.93	11.51

Source: adapted from TCFUA, 2005.

also assumes that goods can be transported freely and labour can be reallocated freely, as well as there being full employment (Suranovic, 2004). In reality, there is never full employment and there are differences in production technology across borders which results in different prices.

Free trade is never 'free'

Free trade is not literally free, as tariffs and quotas remain sensitive issues. Governments are able to choose which sectors will be exposed to free trade. For example, the most glaring omission of AUSFTA has been that towards the Australian sugar growers. Australia's sugar access to the USA remained unchanged at 87,402 tonnes (DFAT, 2005b). Australia's world-class fast ferries have also been left untouched by the FTA (*The Canberra Times*, 2004).

Although the FTA has allowed access to Australia's A$45 billion government procurement market, open competition for procurement contracts will be distorted when huge US corporations compete with small Australian bidders (*The Canberra Times*, 2004).

The same argument can be used with regard to the proposed FTA with China. As Australia is the smaller partner, it is much more likely to make concessions than China. China has already stated that agriculture is a sensitive area and it is unlikely that there will be many concessions made regarding this sector. China may also demand greater concessions from Australia. This may include greater access to Australia's domestic markets. China has already demanded that Australia recognizes it as a market economy and Australia has obliged.

Other negatives aspects of FTAs

FTAs can also increase the transaction costs for businesses through complicated rules of origin (DFAT, 2001b). Different rules can be negotiated under different regimes, which must be adhered to by businesses. Free trade may also be deemed unfair if one of the parties does not adhere to the labour standards to which the other party does. As China is not a signatory to the ILO convention, it does not have to meet any basic labour requirements and Australia, for its part, does not intend to question China's alleged human rights abuses.

In summary

The theories in favour of free trade make assumptions that are not representative of reality. Competition is never perfect, employment is never absolute and there are differences in production methods. China's labour-intensive industries constantly undercut those of Australia's. Free trade is never free, as the stronger partner usually dictates the terms, as was done in AUSFTA.

Regardless of the benefits of an FTA with China, the negative effects on employment for the Australian TCF must also not be ignored. This issue will be addressed in the next section.

The impact on employment in Australia's TCF industry

Regardless of the perceived benefits of an FTA with China, it has been argued that the negative effects on employment in the Australian TCF will be irreversible. This section will examine the inevitable job loss that results from FTAs, as a result of the reductions in tariffs and quotas. The problem of worker mobility in the TCF industry is a particular problem and needs to be addressed before an FTA with China can be ratified.

Job losses and the results

In 1985, there were 67,000 full-time female jobs. This had been reduced to 30,000 in 2002. Male full-time jobs over the same period fell from 37,000 to 31,000 (TCFUA, 2005). Economic predictions for employment in the clothing industry suggest that an FTA would result in an 11.9 per cent reduction in jobs by 2015 (TCFUA, 2005). In a recent survey taken of those who were retrenched it was discovered that only 54 per cent had found work and only one in five found work comparable with their former textile, clothing and footwear jobs in terms of hours, pay and conditions (TCFUA, 2005: 14). The weekly earnings of respondents were A$409.44 as compared to A$360.24 during post-retrenchment (TCFUA, 2005).

Worker mobility

Australia has a mobile workforce, as people can change employers relatively easily. In 1991, Australia had the shortest tenure of employment, three and a half years, among OECD nations (Industry Commission, 1997: 134). Most job changing that occurred in Australia in 1994, occurred within the same industry. However, TCF employees have been generally less mobile than other workers. Between 1988 and 1996, 10 to 14 per cent of people employed in the TCF industry had changed their employment within the previous 12 months, whereas 14 to

19 per cent of workers for all manufacturing and 18 to 25 per cent for all industries had done so within the previous 12 months (Industry Commission, 1997: 135). In 2002, 11 per cent of TCF workers changed jobs compared to 15 per cent of workers in all industries (Commonwealth of Australia, 2003).

The adjustments by displaced workers may be more difficult as their skills are usually sector-specific and educational levels low (Commonwealth of Australia, 2003: 43). In 2001, two-thirds of TCF workers lacked tertiary qualifications. Over 40 per cent had not completed the highest level of secondary schooling (Commonwealth of Australia, 2003: 46). On the topic of labour mobility, economist David Bassanese stated:

> Economic models generally assume a fully employed economy in which labour can move almost effortlessly from one sector to another. Almost by definition, these models would show gains from an FTA – even if we get squat from the other side. It's virtually impossible for them to show a country losing from an FTA. But the real world is more complicated. We can't teach car makers, for example, to become computer programmers overnight. In reality, such sectoral change is often generational and comes at the cost of leaving a rump of newly redundant workers on welfare for the rest of their working lives.
>
> (TCFUA, 2005: 14)

In summary

The Australian government's economic modelling fails to take into account the cost of job loss to the TCF industry as a result of the reduction of tariffs and quotas that is necessary in establishing FTAs. Unemployment in the TCF industry is further compounded by the low mobility of retrenched TCF employees, which is attributed to their low levels of education and specialized labour. Australia is not alone in having to face mass unemployment as a result of the surge of Chinese textile exports – regardless of whether an FTA is signed or not. This is a problem that affects a significant number of countries throughout the world. The following sections will deal with world reaction to China's growing textile market. The policies of the EU and the USA specifically will be examined.

International reaction to China's textile threat

As China's economy continues its unprecedented rate of growth, numerous textile industries throughout the world are becoming, or will soon become, unable to compete. This section will provide an example of a coordinated global reaction, in the form of the Istanbul Declaration, which sought to prevent China from becoming a monopoly in the TCF industry. It will also focus on the EU's protectionist policies towards China since global quotas on textiles came to an end in 2005. The negative effects on Italy's textile market will also be examined.

China versus the world

China's enormous growth and potential in the textile and clothing industries have posed a threat to the world. For example, the termination of the Multifibre Agreement (MFA) was expected to result in China's share of world textiles to increase from 17 per cent, in 2003, to over 50 per cent by 2007 (*The Economist*, 2004). As a result, trade associations from more than 50 countries have ratified the 'Istanbul Declaration'. Co-founded by the USA and Turkey, the Istanbul Declaration is aimed at preventing the market monopoly of the textiles industry by China. Members include countries from Europe, Africa, South America, North America and Asia. The group has sought to extend the phasing out of global tariffs in textiles. The declaration states that:

> China's massive growth has come at the expense of virtually all other participants in the market, especially the least developed and the developing countries which are poised to lose as many as 30 million jobs due to the quota phase-out.
>
> (GAFTT, 2006)

Chinese textiles in the EU

China's share of the EU's market in textiles has gradually increased from 43 per cent in 2002, to 55 per cent in 2003, to 60 per cent in 2004 and 74 per cent in 2005 (Kan-Softek Solutions Pvt. Ltd, 2005). Quotas on apparels were removed by the EU, which resulted in China's market share into the EU increasing from 27.1 per cent to 48.4 per cent. It was predicted that if these rates were to continue, China would have 70 per cent of the EU's market share by 2006 (Kan-Softek Solutions Pvt. Ltd, 2005).

The Agreement on Textiles and Clothing (ATC), which was established in 1995 to eliminate textile quotas, came to an end in January 2005. As a result of the dissolution of the quota regime, Chinese exports to the EU have soared. The number of imported cotton trousers, cotton T-shirts and blouses, and cotton underwear, in the first quarter of 2005, rose by 1,573 per cent, 1,277 per cent and 318 per cent, respectively (*The Economist*, 2005a). In anticipation of the expiration of the quota system, the EU signed an agreement with China for new quotas on ten types of textiles. This was implemented despite the fact that on 7 April 1998, the EU deleted China from a list of 'non-market-economy countries', granting China the status of 'special market economy country' (China Internet Information Center, 2006a).

The agreement did not however rule out the possibility of dumping claims (China Internet Information Center, 2006a). It is regarded as merely giving European manufacturers time to adjust to the increase of Chinese imports. Shortly after the agreement was signed, China exceeded its quotas, which resulted in millions of garments piling up at customs checkpoints and warehouses. As a result, quotas on Chinese apparels were reintroduced in 2005 and capped at 25.4 per cent (Kan-Softek Solutions Pvt. Ltd, 2005).

Although this figure appears substantial, it barely covers one-fifth of China's apparel exports and will ultimately not halt China's exports into the EU (*The Economist*, 2005a). The EU trade commissioner at the time, Peter Mandelson, also contemplated imposing limits on imports of yarn and T-shirts, which had soared since the end of the quota regime. A 4.8 per cent provisional tariff was also imposed by the EU, on Chinese leather shoes in 2006 (China Daily Information Company, 2006). These tariffs were justified by the European Commission that stated that it had clear evidence that there was unfair state intervention in China regarding the leather footwear industry, which included cheap state loans and tax breaks.

Italy: A case study in point

Italy, Europe's leading market for clothing and footwear, is a prime example as to how China has altered the textile industry in Europe. Italy has almost 600,000 jobs in the textiles industry, resulting in a significant financial contribution to the Italian economy (*The Economist*, 2006). However, this number has gradually decreased as Chinese imports have increased. In the province of Varese, which hosts an enormous industrial cluster, the number of workers in textiles and clothing has almost halved between 1981 and 2001 to 27,300 (*The Economist*, 2006). These job losses can be attributed to the increase of cheap goods imported from China. Italy has adapted to low-cost competition from China, by moving production to China. Clothing maker Benetton, for example, once produced almost 90 per cent of its clothes in Italy. That number is currently down to 30 per cent and is expected to decrease to 10 per cent over the next few years (*The Economist*, 2006).

In summary

China's massive growth has come at the expense of both developed and developing countries, as stated in the Istanbul Declaration. The EU, for its part, has taken a protectionist stance towards China and its growing economic presence in the textile industry. The termination of the quota system and the exceeding of export quota limits into the EU by China resulted in a reintroduction of quotas in 2005. The EU seeks to protect its remaining textile industries, which have been severely affected by Chinese imports, as demonstrated by the Italian textiles industry. The USA has also adopted protectionist measures against China. America's shift towards free trade and their policies against China will be examined in the next section.

US policy towards free trade and China

The USA has actively sought FTAs with numerous countries. However, there has been a gradual shift towards more protectionist policies. This has been especially pronounced in its relationship with China. The USA has imposed safeguards on Chinese textiles and limited imports of Chinese textiles through an agreement with China. Despite having substantial trade with China, the USA recently introduced a bill to impose stiff tariff rates on Chinese goods to counter China's currency manipulation. This section will address all of these issues.

A shift towards free trade

The USA has been a strong proponent of FTAs. Before the year 2000, it had three FTAs with Canada and Mexico, as part of NAFTA, and Israel. Since 2000, it has established FTAs with Australia, Bahrain, Chile, Jordan, Oman, Morocco, Singapore, Peru and the six Central American members of CAFTA (Costa Rica, Dominican Republic, El Salvador, Guatemala, Honduras and Nicaragua) (bilaterals.org, 2006b). The USA is currently in free trade negotiations with a dozen other countries from Asia, Africa, the Middle East and South America.

However, at the same time there has been a gradual shift towards a more protectionist stance. The fears of many Americans came to fruition after the implementation of NAFTA, as numerous manufacturing plants relocated to Mexico. Free trade was also blamed for the outsourcing of jobs and the growing trade deficit (Answers.com, 2010). This has resulted in former free trade advocates, such as the Democratic Party, to seek tougher measures in order to ensure compliance with other trading partners. CAFTA, the FTA between the USA and Central America was almost defeated in the US congress, as the labour and environmental standards set were deemed to be too low.

A stance against china

The USA has also taken a more protectionist stance towards China. In 1999, America signed an agreement with China, regarding safeguards, before China's acceptance into the WTO. By demonstrating that Chinese imports caused material injury, a member state could impose safeguards, which, under the terms of China's accession into the WTO, were justifiable. These safeguards included shirts, sheets, underwear and pants and were set to expire at the end of 2004.

The USA is also a party to the ATC, which was established in 1995. Its main purpose was to eliminate quotas in North America and Europe by 2005. However, the textile industry lobbied the government on the eve of the 2004 US presidential election and was ultimately successful in maintaining the safeguards. The USA imposed safeguard quotas that have limited the rise of seven categories of Chinese textiles and also limited the rise in imports to 7.5 per cent (*The Economist*, 2005b). As a result of the new restrictions imposed, Chinese textile exports to the USA shrank substantially in the beginning of 2005. The safeguards also restricted the annual growth of imports for certain Chinese textile products.

The USA also signed a comprehensive agreement with China in 2005 which limited US imports on 34 categories of Chinese textiles (The Istanbul Declaration Coalition, 2005). Although safeguards can be renewed on a yearly basis, in regards to the agreement, the Executive Director of the American Manufacturing Trade Action Coalition (AMTAC) stated that:

this deal is a significant improvement over the deal signed by the European Union and China earlier this year. The U.S. agreement will prevent market disruption through the end of 2008 while the EU deal only does this through the end of 2007, and it is far more flexible towards China.

(The Istanbul Declaration Coalition, 2005)

This agreement was signed despite the robust trade relationship in textiles between the two countries. In 2005, the USA imported US$88.2 billion in textiles throughout the globe, US$20.6 billion of which was imported from China (The Istanbul Declaration Coalition, 2005).

No more currency manipulation please

China is also accused by America of keeping their currency artificially low. The US Treasury Department has made the currency issue a central part of its engagement with the Chinese Government. In particular it seeks to open the Chinese financial sector to more private companies. It also seeks to introduce currency futures and allow greater foreign participation in China's credit and capital markets (Frisbie, 2006). It is often claimed in the USA that China keeps its currency artificially low in order to boost exports and keep the trade balance with the USA in their favour (Frisbie, 2006). As a result of these allegations, China has failed to meet the requirements of a market economy under US law, which states that a country's currency must be convertible into other currencies (Frisbie, 2006).

The 'Schumer Bill' was also recently introduced into the US congress as a way to counter China's currency manipulation which has resulted in an American trade deficit of more than US$200 billion in 2005 (Stewart, 2006). The bill intended to impose a 27.5 per cent tariff rate on Chinese goods unless the Chinese Government allowed its currency to float (Bown, 2009). China responded by revaluing its currency in July 2005, thus making the bill obsolete.

In summary

The USA has taken a more protectionist stance towards China by establishing safeguard quotas on numerous categories of Chinese textiles. The 'Schumer Bill' was also introduced to increase the tariff rates on Chinese goods. The US Government and the EU are becoming more protectionist towards China, since the end of global tariffs on textiles. This is occurring while Australia is intending on further opening its markets to China. The USA and the EU have also refused to grant China market economy status, which Australia has agreed to do as part of the negotiations leading to an FTA. This contentious issue will be addressed in the next section.

Granting market economy status

As part of negotiations for an FTA with China, Australia is required to recognize China as a market economy. This is mainly for anti-dumping purposes. It is believed that being recognized as a market economy will make it easier for China to dump its goods, textiles in particular, into Australia at below market value. This section will outline China and Australia's current position on dumping, as well as international legislation. The issue of whether China is a market economy will also be addressed.

Market economy status – requirements

Recognizing China as a market economy would mean that China would no longer be treated as an 'economy in transition' (EIT), in regards to Australia's anti-dumping legislation (DFAT, 2005d). EIT provisions were introduced to address the economies of China and countries of the former Soviet Union who were moving away from non-market economies. EIT status allows Australian authorities to assess the normal price of goods by comparing the prices of a third country.

Changes were made regarding EIT provisions in 2003. It was argued that it was harder for the TCF sectors to assess anti-dumping actions as there are more one-off shipments along with a greater diversity in products than in other sectors (Industry Commission, 1997). As a result, the price control test was replaced with a price influence test, where several tests can be applied to establish price influence. The burden of proof was also placed on the exporter, who now has to demonstrate that domestic prices are not influenced by the government (PACIA, 2004).

Australia's current position

Australia currently has domestic laws at its disposal to counter an anti-dumping threat by China. Under subsection 269TAC (5D) of the Australian Customs Act, the Minister of Trade can determine the normal value if he/she is satisfied that the country of export is an EIT and market conditions do not prevail in the exporting country (PACIA, 2004). Subsection 269TAC (5F) states that the minister may determine the normal value by examining:

1   the price of domestic sales of like goods in the third country;
2   the price of export sales of like goods in the third country;
3   the cost of production, plus administrative, selling and general costs, of like goods in the third country;
4   the price of like goods produced in Australia.

(PACIA, 2004)

The Australian Federal Government has also stated that it would clarify and tighten anti-dumping regulations. This resulted in the 'clarification of anti-dumping administration' document, which was produced on 4 March 2005 (Callick, 2005). The document stated that Chinese governmental influence on costs and prices would be considered. In particular, it stated that 'when issues of government-owned enterprises are raised by applicants, Customs will have clear operational guidance that these issues must be considered' (Callick, 2005).

Rights under the WTO

The Australian Government can also currently protect its industries under WTO agreements against anti-dumping, to which it is a signatory. As part of its entry into the WTO, China agreed that other WTO members could treat it as a non-market economy until 2015 (Green, 2004).

China was also granted a 12-year Transitional Safeguard Mechanism that omit-ted it from meeting certain WTO membership obligations. Section 15 of the Chinese Protocol of Accession states that an importing WTO member may use a method which is not based on the domestic prices in China, if the producer is unable to demonstrate that market economy conditions prevail (PACIA, 2004).

The WTO also provides members with a framework to impose anti-dumping measures on other members. Article 2 of the Anti-Dumping Agreement provides the following criteria to establish nominal value:

1   the price at which the goods are sold, in the ordinary course of trade, in the domestic market of the exporting country;
2   the price at which the like goods are sold to a third country;
3   the cost of production in the country of origin (including reasonable amounts for administrative selling and general costs and for profits);
4   a constructed cost based on an export price where the goods are subsequently sold to an independent buyer; or
5   such reasonable basis as the authorities may determine.

(PACIA, 2004)

Is China a market economy?

The question of whether China is a market economy is debatable. Chinese authorities believe that China is a market economy because a large number of Chinese firms operate within market environments. Furthermore, they believe that using surrogate third-party countries is deemed unfair, as no other country possesses as large a labour pool as China. China's competitiveness, it is claimed, is based on its low cost labour force and not on government subsidies.

Nonetheless, there are numerous instances that demonstrate that China is not a market economy. The Chinese Government frequently intervenes in the market; it provides hidden assistance to companies and artificially values its currency (TCFUA, 2005: 2). It is also claimed that banks provide soft loans to state-owned companies. China was subject to 232 separate anti-dumping measures in 2003, the most of any country (Green, 2004). Determining the true market price in China may prove a difficult task for Australian authorities. Commodities and interest rates are still controlled despite price liberalization in most sectors (Green, 2004).

China is the world's largest iron ore consumer and involves itself in yearly iron ore price negotiations with BHP Billiton, CVRD and Rio Tinto. The 2006 negotiations were prolonged due to the Chinese Government's lack of position during these talks. China has threatened to manipulate iron ore imports if the current price negotiations come to an 'unreasonable' conclusion (Interfax Information Service, 2005).

The *Index of Economic Freedom*, which is published annually by the Heritage Foundation and *The Wall Street Journal*, measures the economic freedoms of all sovereign nations. Societies are considered to be economically free when their 'governments allow labor, capital and goods to move freely, and refrain from coercion or constraint of liberty beyond the extent necessary to protect and maintain liberty itself' (The Heritage Foundation, 2010a).

The index measures countries based on ten specifications of economic freedom which range from corruption to non-tariff barriers to trade to labour market regulations, and they are as follows:

- freedom from corruption;
- business freedom;
- trade freedom;
- investment freedom;
- financial freedom;
- fiscal freedom;
- property rights;
- government spending;
- monetary freedom;
- labor freedom.

(The Heritage Foundation, 2010a)

Each of these components of economic freedom is rated on a scale ranging from 0 to 100, with a higher score indicating more economic freedom.

In 2010, Australia ranked three with a score of 82.5 while China ranked 135 with a score of 52.0 (The Heritage Foundation, 2010b). This figure suggests that China represents to a much a lesser degree being a free market economy.

Seeking international recognition

Despite China's best efforts, only a total of seven countries (New Zealand, Singapore, Malaysia, Thailand, Benin, Togo, Kyrgyzstan) have recognized China as a market economy (China Daily Information Company, 2004).

The EU rejected market economy status for China in 2004. China failed to satisfy the EU's criteria for market economy status, which includes certain levels of state intervention, bankruptcy legislation and accountancy law (China Internet Information Center, 2006b). This was despite the fact that the EU and China have a strong trading relationship, which was worth €210 billion in 2005 (China Internet Information Center, 2006b).

China has been pressing the EU for market economy status recognition ever since its initial rejection. Chinese Foreign Ministry spokeswoman Zhang Qiyue recently stated that the EU should grant China market economy status as it would further boost expansion in Sino-EU cooperation (China Internet Information Center, 2006b). She further added that because China opened up to reform over 25 years ago and is a member of the WTO, it has become a market economy. The non-public sector of China, she stated, has also grown rapidly. More than 90 per cent of goods are produced by this sector. The Chinese Government has also amended almost 3,000 laws, policies and recommendations which transformed government functions to private enterprises (China Internet Information Center, 2006b).

European Union Trade Commissioner Peter Mandelson recently stated that China has made progress towards EU recognition as a market economy; however, he emphasized that the EU would first demand greater access to the Chinese market before such status would be granted (EUbusiness Ltd, 2006).

Does market economy status for China really matter?

The question is ultimately whether shifting China's status from an EIT to a market economy will have any impact on anti-dumping issues. Shifting China to market economy status would result in China being added to Schedule 1B of the Australian Customs Regulations. This is a list of countries for which EIT provisions for the purposes of anti-dumping would not apply (DFAT, 2005d). This would result in China being treated as any other country for anti-dumping purposes.

The Australian Government takes numerous factors into account when determining whether market conditions prevail in the country in question. The exporter is required to cooperate fully with the Australian investigation process. If market conditions do not prevail, Australian Customs can calculate the value of goods being exported by comparing another exporter's domestic price, sales to a third country, or by a constructed nominal value (DFAT, 2005d). Regardless of whether the exporters under investigation are from an EIT or a market economy, Australian Customs must be sure that the information being provided is accurate. When this is not the case, Customs can fall back on a surrogate third country (Stoler, 2004). The same steps are involved in gathering information regarding surrogate third country information regardless of whether the country in question is an EIT or not (Stoler, 2004). Thus removing China from its current EIT status should not have any negative effects on Australia's ability to protect its industries from dumping.

As part of joining the WTO, China has allowed itself to be treated as a non-market economy. However, China has not accepted that inaccurate or indefensible dumping margins may be used against them. China possesses the right to challenge any dumping margin it chooses through WTO processes (Stoler, 2004).

Customs must justify its calculations, in spite of whether a country is an EIT or not. Customs can fall back on a surrogate third country with both 'normal' and EIT countries. It has thus been argued that granting China market economy status will have little impact on dumping issues.

In summary

Although the Chinese Government has demanded that Australia recognizes it as a market economy as part of the FTA negotiations, China is not a market economy. The Chinese Government frequently intervenes in the market and figures suggest that there is little economic freedom in China. Furthermore, only a handful of countries recognize China as a market economy. Granting market economy status has been interpreted as granting China the freedom to dump its goods into the country granting them that status. Thus, it serves as a powerful tool for those who are opposed to an FTA with China. However, this may be of little consequence, as removing China from its current EIT status should not have any negative effects on Australia's ability to protect its industries from dumping.

The Chinese Government's goal may be not to achieve a fully open domestic market but rather a 'socialist market economy with Chinese characteristics' (Brown, 2005). The constitution, which has undergone three amendments since China has begun to reform explicitly, states that 'China practices a socialist market economy' (China Internet Information Center, 2006b). Perhaps the key issue is not whether granting China market economy status will have a negative effect on the Australian TCF industry, but rather can the Australian TCF industry cope with an FTA with China. With this in perspective, a brief history of the Australian TCF industry is given in the next section.

A history of Australian textiles

The TCF industry has had a long history in Australia. Wool, cotton and flax played an important role from settlement to federation. However, it was not until the First and Second World Wars that the TCF industry began to play an important international role. This section will examine those events, as well as the policies of federal governments in the latter half of the twentieth century, with an emphasis on the withdrawal of protectionist policies. By examining a brief history of the Australian textiles industry, it is hoped that a better understanding will be gained as to how the TCF industry has coped with global change and also whether it is capable of surviving further reductions of protectionism through an FTA with China.

History – before federation in Australia

In the late 1830s, Australia's footwear and clothing were mainly produced in convict establishments, while fashionable products, such as silks and satins, were imported from Britain. Female convicts also played a significant role in the production of wool. Looms were established in Parramatta, New South Wales, in the early 1800s to accommodate female prisoners. This was a result of numerous agreements with government-selected weavers. One of the earliest private mills to spring up was at Blackwattle Bay, Sydney, in 1832 (Australian Science and Technology Heritage Centre, 2000). By 1838 there were seven woollen mills in New South Wales (Australian Science and Technology Heritage Centre, 2000).

By the mid-1800s the textiles industry began to expand. By 1852, New South Wales had four woollen mills, and this doubled in 1880. Woollen and cloth manufacturing began in Geelong, Victoria, in 1868, and was followed by South Australia, Queensland and Tasmania in 1870 and Western Australia shortly thereafter. Cloth also began to be produced in the Waverley Woollen Mill at Distillery Creek, near Launceston, Tasmania in 1873. At the same time, government-sponsored protectionism resulted in the flourishing of clothing workshops in Victoria, South Australia, Tasmania, New South Wales and Queensland.

History of wool in Australia

From the initial 26 merino sheep brought from South Africa in 1797, the Australian sheep flock grew to over 140 million in 1985/86 and Australia entered the twenty-first century as the world's largest wool producer, accounting for an estimated 25 per cent of the world's production (Australian Science and Technology Heritage Centre, 2000).

History of cotton in Australia

The cotton industry was not as successful as the wool industry. Growing cotton was unsuccessful due to climatic factors. Labour was too expensive and there were no convenient markets at the time. Cotton only became a viable agricultural business in the early twentieth century and it was only during times of war and world shortage that the Australian cotton industry flourished. The first cottonseed was brought to Australia in 1788, although it was not until the American Civil War (1861–1865), that Australia gained some prominence on the world market, as they attempted to fill the void left by US growers (Cotton Australia, 2010a).

By the mid-1950s, the cotton industry in Australia was still almost non-existent. However, it gradually began to gain prominence. Limited cotton production commenced in southwest Queensland in 1960 (Cotton Australia, 2010a). In 1966, in New South Wales, a cotton mill was established in the Macquarie Valley and cotton production began at Bourke. By 1975, Australian cotton production reached 110,000 bales. This number reached 435,000 bales in 1980, 2.2 million bales in 1992 and 2.9 million in 2005 (compared to China's 28 million in the same year) (Cotton Australia, 2010a).

Federation and beyond

The period of federation was marked by government protection. This policy was introduced in order to create self-sufficiency in textiles for Australia. Federation also resulted in uniform customs tariffs throughout Australia, which stimulated the wool-manufacturing industry (Australian Science and Technology Heritage Centre, 2000). This was further endorsed during the First World War which was a period marked by tariffs. Cotton textiles were also developed prior and during the First World War.

Clothing manufacturing also experienced growth after federation. Factory employment doubled to 60,000 by 1923. Clothing manufacturers were able to meet 84 per cent of Australia's clothing needs (Pestana, 1996: 4). At the end of the First World War, the federal government took active steps to protecting the textile industry. This resulted in a total of 4,575 textile and garment manufacturers in Australia, with Victoria representing the largest share at 2,087 (Australian Science and Technology Heritage Centre, 2000).

In the 1920s, 25 per cent of the factory workforce of Australia worked in the textiles industry. This declined to 18 per cent in the mid-1950s and 14 per cent by 1969 (Pestana, 1996: 5). During this period, cotton tweed manufacturers were established, first in Sydney and then in Melbourne. By 1939 there were 333,000 spindles and 4,384 looms, which turned out 3 million pounds of yarns and 32 million yards of cloth (Pestana, 1996). At the same time the production of rayon, a synthetic fibre, was produced for the first time. This was followed by the production of nylon a few years later.

The Second World War, much like the First World War, stimulated the textile industry. At the onset of the war, there were 90 woollen and tweed mills staffed by an estimated 20,000 employees (Australian Science and Technology Heritage Centre, 2000: 299). By the end of the Second World War there was over-capacity and demand for woollens stabilized to around 30 million square yards over the next 20 years (Pestana, 1996). Many textile products, which were introduced as a result of the war, continued to be manufactured after its end. Australian domestic products also displaced foreign products; for example, Australian wool barathea replaced silk from Europe (Australian Science and Technology Heritage Centre, 2000).

Government policy after the Second World War was geared towards import substitution. Import licences were a common feature during this time but were eventually replaced by tariff protection in the 1960s (Australian Science and Technology Heritage Centre, 2000). However, by 1966 the Tariff Board and the Industries Assistance Commission (IAC) began to openly question the tariff regime (Webber and Waller, 2001: 16). Within the protected environment, the textile industry relied on a steady flow of low cost migrant workers. In 1971, 36 per cent of women employed in textiles and 45 per cent employed in clothing and footwear were from non-English speaking backgrounds (Webber and Waller, 2001: 49).

A new policy initiated by the USA in the 1950s, to restrict cotton textile exports from Japan, the MFA provided a framework for restricting clothing exports into developing countries. Restrictions to the MFA have gradually been added as the agreement had been regularly updated. During the Uruguay Round of negotiations, an agreement was established to gradually phase out the quantitative restrictions by 2005. Australia, for its part, stopped being a signatory to the MFA in the 1970s.

Whitlam's policies

In the 1960s, rates of assistance ranged up to 45 per cent. This was reduced to 35 per cent by the Whitlam government. In the early 1970s, the Whitlam government introduced a 25 per cent tariff reduction; this was coupled with an increase of wages for female workers and a revaluation of the Australian dollar. This resulted in Australia losing some of its market share to Southeast Asian nations. Employment in textiles and clothing fell more than 20 per cent (Pestana, 1996: 5) This also resulted in the imports of textiles and clothing increasing by 43 per cent and 63 per cent in 1973 and 1974, respectively (Australian Science and Technology Heritage Centre, 2000).

The textiles industry in the 1970s

The cotton industry experienced considerable growth in the 1970s and this led it to becoming an export commodity. During this time, millions of dollars were also being spent on plant modernization. This included upgrades on weaving equipment and spinning and dyeing equipment. Global tariffs were also introduced, in 1976, to assist the apparel industry. The Australian Federal Government imposed global tariff quotas, which were within GATT rules, in 1976. These tariffs were in place for four years. However there were still significant job losses. Between 1971 and 1981, 55,000 jobs were lost (Pestana, 1996: 6). This was due in large part to low wages for female workers in Asia. Between 1974 and 1977, 38,400 Australian textile jobs were lost (Australian Science and Technology Heritage Centre, 2000).

At the same time the IAC published a draft report, in 1977, calling for an end to protectionism.

Assistance withdrawn

By 1982, the federal government created a seven-year plan, which called for a substantial reduction in TCF industry protection. Although some quotas were removed, a bounty on yarn production was implemented to compensate the industry as well as to keep prices down. Synthetic fibres, bed-linen, clothing and footwear remained subject to tariff quotas (Pestana, 1996: 5). There was also a consolidation of five large textile and footwear companies in the mid-1980s. This merger resulted in a concentration of 8 per cent of textiles companies employing 70 per cent of the sectors workforce (Pestana, 1996: 6).

In 1986, the federal government made the decision to reduce quotas to 40 per cent consumption tax, based on textile, clothing and footwear products, as well reducing tariffs to 60 per cent for clothing and 50 per cent for footwear (Pestana, 1996). However, the federal government also provided a A$200 million compensation package, which was to be used to develop manufacturing plants. The IAC's 1986 report further recommended that beginning in 1988, the rate of protection should fall by 12 per cent per year to reach 50 per cent by 1996 (Webber and Waller, 2001: 59). The effective rate of assistance during the mid-1980s was 75 per cent, which fell to 28 per cent by the 1990s, and will fall to an estimated 15 per cent by 2008/09 (Webber and Waller, 2001).

The Button Plan, initiated by then Industry Minister, John Button, was implemented in 1989 and ended in 1996. It sought to gradually remove quotas and lower tariffs and make the textiles industry more competitive. This included a gradual phasing of the highest tariffs, which were to fall to 60 per cent, while quotas were to be eliminated altogether (Industry Commission, 1997). The plan also emphasized the investment in labour-saving technology which had been initiated by the Capitalization Grants Programme, introduced by the federal government in 1990. In justification of the Button Plan, it was stated:

> Many companies are undercapitalized as a result of many decades of non investment because high tariffs made this unnecessary. ... The tariffs have in the past sheltered and protected and have been a disincentive to modernize an unbelievably old fashioned and inefficient industry.
>
> (Industry Commission, 1997: 21)

As a result of the implementation of the Button Plan, exports in clothing and footwear quadrupled, reaching A$250 million in 1993 (Pestana, 1996).

In 1997, the IAC was asked to review the TCF industries. It recommended that tariffs should continue to be cut to bring them level with other manufacturing sectors (5 per cent) by 2008/2009 (Webber and Waller, 2001: 61). Despite this recommendation, the government froze tariffs at their 2000/2001 level until 1 January 2005 when textiles will be reduced to 17.5 per cent and textile products will be reduced to 7.5–10 per cent (Webber and Waller, 2001).

In summary

The Australian TCF industry has experienced a substantial amount of change throughout the twentieth century. Protectionist policies, during and after the First and Second World Wars, quickly gave way to a reduction of tariffs and quotas, which began in the 1970s. The TCF industry has had to cope with the reduction of protectionist policies and job loss, which appear likely to continue regardless of whether an FTA is signed with China. In order to assess how well the TCF has adapted to the gradual reduction of protectionist policies, a closer examination of the current state of the industry will be provided in the following section.

The TCF industry and current problems

Australia's TCF industry is internationally competitive and generates a substantial amount of revenue and employment. However, the industry is besieged with a number of problems. First, there is a lack of coordination between producers and processors. This leads to the second problem; that is the majority of firms represent small-sized producers. Finally, the lack of investment in new technologies has posed a problem for the industry. This section will address these issues in order to assess if the TCF industry can cope with an FTA with China.

The Australian TCF sector in the global context

Australia's TCF industry is competitive as compared to other OECD countries. In 1990, Australia was ranked third lowest for prices of clothing, fourth lowest for household textiles and sixth lowest for footwear, compared to other OECD countries (Pestana, 1996: 25). The average tariff rates for the TCF sector was 68 per cent in 1987 and 17.5 per cent since January 2005. They will further reduce to 5 per cent in 2010 (TCFUA, 2005: 9).

Industry snapshot

Australia's TCF industry generates a great deal of revenue and employment. In 2000–2001, the TCF sector accounted for more than A\$9 billion in generated revenue (Commonwealth of Australia, 2003: 7). Informal employment estimates suggested a figure of 70,000 formal factory employed positions and 25,000 outworkers (Commonwealth of Australia, 2003). Australia's yearly cotton production averaged 0.5 million tonnes from 2001 to 2003 and accounted for 2.3 per cent of total world production (Commonwealth of Australia, 2003: 29). Australia is the world's largest wool producer and exports over 90 per cent of its wool. The average annual production of wool from 2001 to 2003 was 0.6 million tonnes which equalled 27 per cent of the world total (Commonwealth of Australia, 2003: 29). The majority of Australia's flock, which was 100 million head in 2003, was from the merino breed.

Current problems confronting the industry

It is claimed that Australia does not take full advantage of its productive base because of the lack of coordination between producers and processors. For example, the government has encouraged the processing of wool, as Australia mainly exports 'greasy' wool, which is in an unprocessed state. In 1996, 37 per cent of Australian wool clip was processed at an early stage, but only 13 per cent was processed at the top stage (Industry Commission, 1997).

The same problem is prevalent in the cotton industry where only less than 10 per cent of Australia's cotton was further processed in Australia, before it was exported (Industry Commission, 1997).

Greater interaction between procurement officers and industry representatives is required. International examples demonstrate that this can be achieved with positive results. For example, the Canadian Defense Force shares out work among TCF manufacturers that results in cost efficiencies as well as maintaining a domestic industry presence (TCFUA, 2005).

Firm size in the TCF industry has also been a problem. More than 80 per cent of Australia's TCF firms have less than 20 employees (Industry Commission, 1997). The wool sector, for example, has suffered due to the large number of small growers in the industry. In 1991 there were more than 60,000 producers above the value production of A\$20,000 and an average of 60 bales of wool produced (Industry Commission, 1997).

Small business owners may also be unwilling to change their operations and in the process become less likely to gain access to capital markets. However, their size may also be an advantage as small businesses can adapt quicker and establish niche markets. By developing alliance clusters, similar to those in the USA and Italy, the TFC industries can overcome their coordination problems. This does not mean firms must form alliances. They can simply share information through computers and the internet.

Another problem facing TCF firms is the lack of technological investment. Although the federal government provides R&D and grants for new technologies, the number of firms investing in technology is relatively small. Fewer than one in three TCF manufacturers undertook technological innovation between 1991 and 1994 (Industry Commission, 1997).

The Cooperative Research Centre for Advanced Composite Structures stated that:

> ... insufficient attention is given by the Industry to education and research and development in the use of these materials [advanced textiles], which have excellent potential for developing viable, high-technology industries in Australia. Most of these advanced textiles are imported from Europe, USA and Japan. They are excellent examples of high-technology, high-value-added, industrial textiles.
>
> (Industry Commission, 1997: 32)

In summary

The Australian TCF industry is competitive internationally and provides a substantial amount of raw material, such as cotton and wool, into the international markets. Although the industry must address certain problems, such as coordination in the supply chain, firm size and investment in technology, these issues can be overcome with the assistance of the government. Government assistance programs will now be examined.

Australian government assistance

The Australian Federal Government has gradually implemented tariff and quota reduction policies, which have lead to retrenchments and the closure of firms in the TCF industry. However, it has also provided a number of assistance packages to help TCF firms adapt and compete internationally. This section will summarize the assistance, which the federal government has provided from the 1990s to the present. The government has also introduced a TCF Post-2005 Assistance Package, comprising numerous programs running to 2010 and 2015. This assistance package will also be examined.

A history of industry assistance

Although there have been significant cuts in tariffs and quotas, the federal government has provided assistance to the TCF industry in the form of the TCF 2000 package. This was a A$45 million package to assist in providing quality management, quick response manufacturing, information programs for potential investors, training centres and the establishment of international intelligence networks (Webber and Waller, 2001: 65). The Overseas Assembly Provisions (OAP) was established in 1992 to assist in the offshore processing of textiles. As a result of this program, Australian textile producers can now produce Australian-made cloth in neighbouring countries at a fraction of Australian labour costs. Another significant program, which was created by the government, was the Export Market Development Grant (EMDG) Scheme. This scheme encouraged Australian companies to establish overseas markets. In 1993–1994, EMDGs totalling A$205 million were paid to 3,250 claimants with the majority of recipients being small to medium enterprises.

The Federal Government has also provided assistance packages through Austrade and the Australian Wool Research and Promotion Organization (AWRAP). In the late 1990s, Austrade provided A$54.4 million to more than 200 projects (Pestana, 1996: 40). AWRAP funds research and development through a 0.5 per cent tax on the gross value of sales by growers, which is matched by the Commonwealth Government (Industry Commission, 1997).

Government assistance up to 2005

Perhaps the most significant assistance package provided by the government was the Strategic Investment Program (SIP) that was implemented in 2000 and ran until 2005. The program, which was capped at A$678 million, was available to all TCF manufacturing entities with a minimum spending threshold of A$200,000 over more than one year (Commonwealth of Australia, 2003: 67). The types of grants that were available included grants for new equipment and grants for research and development.

Post-2005 assistance

The TCF Post-2005 Assistance Package, announced in 2003, is a A$747 million package of assistance provided by the Australian Government to the TCF industry (DIISR, 2010). This package consists of numerous programs including the TCF Post-2005 Strategic Investment Program Scheme, the TCF Product Diversification Scheme, the TCF Structural Adjustment Program, the TCF Small Business Program Determination 2005 and the Expanded Overseas Assembly Provisions Scheme (DIISR, 2010).

Each assistance program focuses on a particular aspect of the TCF industry. For example, the TCF Post-2005 Strategic Investment Program Scheme, which came into effect in July 2005 and runs until 2015, is a A$575 million program established to assist the TCF industry in investment projects (Treadstone, 2010).

The TCF Product Diversification Scheme, a 10-year A$50-million program, is provided for the period, namely, from 2006/2007 to 2015/2016 and assists local textile manufacturers in internationalizing their sourcing arrangements (Productivity Commission, 2008).

The TCF Structural Adjustment Program is another 10-year A$50-million project and the Small Business Program is a 10-year A$25-million program which is provided from 2006/2007 to 2015/2016 (Productivity Commission, 2008).

The Expanded Overseas Assembly Provisions Scheme, administered by Australian Customs and which ended in 2010, enabled participants to assemble goods overseas. Once these goods had been assembled, they could be imported back into Australia with duty payable only on the overseas processing and content costs (AusIndustry, 2003). This scheme ended in 2010. There were also limitations to participation. The participant had to both export the fabric or leather and import the assembled goods and the value of non-Australian fabric or leather could not be greater than 20 per cent (AusIndustry, 2003).

In summary

The assistance programs introduced by the Federal Government have allowed TCF firms to adjust to the realities of global competition. These programs have provided assistance to the offshoring processing of textiles as well as R&D and will run into the future. These programs have been essential for the survival of the TCF industry as they negate the negative aspects of lowered protection for the industry. Though governmental assistance is fundamental in assisting TCF firms, there are also other possible solutions in ensuring the survival of TCF firms. These are discussed next.

Other forms of assistance

As stated previously, governmental assistance is necessary in order to help TCF firms adjust to global competition. However, there are other forms of assistance, such as investment in new technologies and programs such as quick response, which will give domestic firms an advantage over international competitors. The government can assist in funding and promoting such programs. This section will discuss the current global trend of the TCF industry and outline ways in which the government can assist TCF firms in adjusting to these changes.

Technological advancements – a history

The processing of wool has undergone enormous changes in Australia. At one time, wool was sorted by hand and separated by length and quality of the fibres, which depended on which part of the body the wool was taken from. Impurities were removed by scouring and were then placed in the sun to dry. When dry, the wool was beaten by rods, this process was known as willeying (Australian Science and Technology Heritage Centre, 2000). It was then picked at, by hand, to ensure all contaminants were removed. Short fibres were then carded (the separation of fibres) to produce woollen yarns, while long fibres were combed to produce worsted yarns (Australian Science and Technology Heritage Centre, 2000).

As combining machines gained widespread use in the early nineteenth century, this led to a more efficient way of processing the wool. What used to take 110 hours by hand, to manufacture one kilogram of yarn on a spinning wheel, was reduced to 60 hours by the manually operated spinning jenny and 9 hours by the mechanized jenny. It currently takes 36 minutes by a modern spinning machine (Australian Science and Technology Heritage Centre, 2000).

The uniformity and quality of fabric has substantially improved due to the preparation of fibres as well as more control in spinning. After the introduction of synthetic fibres in the 1930s, textile manufacturing became an industry dominated by cotton and synthetics. Synthetic dyes are of excellent quality and more resistant to fading. Australian textiles have also been at the forefront of technological advancement. Zipper fastening machinery was developed in the early 1980s and this produces 10 feet of zipper a minute. This technology has been exported to the USA and Mexico (Australian Science and Technology Heritage Centre, 2000).

Current new technological emphasis

The Federal Government has also recognized the importance of promoting the investment in new technologies. From the early 1990s to 1996/1997 TCF investment in technology has increased by 23 per cent. The majority was aimed at labour-saving equipment, including programmable sewing machines, computer-aided design (CAD) and computer numerically controlled (CNC) cutting systems, and modern warehousing and distribution systems (Industry Commission, 1997).

The Council of Textile and Fashion Industries of Australia (TFIA), in conjunction with the Victorian Government, have established the VicStart Program. This program was established to develop the collaboration between TCF firms and various research organizations to uptake new technologies, products and innovative ideas (TFIA, 2005b: 9). Under the program, new technologies are assessed and then matched to companies that can develop them. Networking opportunities are also provided, both nationally and internationally. Sportsknit, a division of the Australian Fashion Group, for example, was able to reduce its average pre-production time for garment design from 21 to 15 days as a result of new software that allows clothing sketches to be scanned, production costs to be compared and projects to be overviewed at any time (Industry Commission, 1997: 61).

The Australian cotton industry has had a long-standing tradition of investing in research for new technologies. Australian cotton growers pay a compulsory research levy of A$2.25 per bale (Cotton Australia, 2010b). These funds are used to research new technologies such as water and pesticide use. The Cotton Research and Development Corporation (CRDC) invested A$20 million in research projects during the period 2005–2007. This has been used for crop protection research projects, farming systems and breeding and technology (Cotton Australia, 2010b).

The CRDC project has been coupled with the Commonwealth Scientific and Industrial Research Organization (CSIRO). This is a cotton breeding program which started in 2005 to increase cotton yields (Cotton Australia, 2010b).

The State Government of Victoria has also provided funds for technological advancements. It provides a service known as network facilitation. This is a database which consists of TCF and non-TCF companies, researchers and financers with similar R&D interests. Network staff facilitate correspondence between the parties to ensure the best possible outcomes. This is done through wide-scale matching and identification – nationally and internationally (DIIRD, 2006).

A quicker response time

Australian TCF businesses have an advantage over their international competitors in the form of quicker delivery times. This has been established through the 'quick response' system which consists of short supply runs, better quality control and life cycle costing for procurement (TFIA, 2005a: 5).

The adaptation of 'quick response' has allowed firms to move closer to their customers (Industry Commission, 1997: 59). This is done through Electronic Data Interchange (EDI) technology. Manufacturers have now become more flexible with quicker response times.

Retailers in Australia strive to reduce their inventory costs by modifying their purchasing strategies, which results in smaller, but more regular orders throughout the year (Industry Commission, 1997). This benefits small businesses, as they are able to adapt quicker to changes whereas overseas producers require longer cycles. Coles Myer, who works with suppliers to pursue quick response, has stated that:

> because of their proximity and flexibility, Australian suppliers are generally better at responding to Quick Response than overseas suppliers, that have long lead times, production runs have to be booked into often inflexible schedules and most are sea freighted to Australia.
>
> (Industry Commission, 1997: 60)

Quick response – an international example

Gildan Activewear Inc., a T-shirt manufacturer, based in Montreal, Canada, is in direct competition with Chinese textile manufacturers. Aware of China's increasing export power, Gildan began to research the future price of cotton shirts six years before the end of the quotas imposed by the WTO's Agreement on Textiles and Clothing. As part of their long-term strategy, Gildan began to gradually reduce the price of cotton T-shirts, in anticipation of the lowered future benchmark. Sewing facilities were moved to Honduras and Mexico in 1998. State of the art textile factories were also built in the Dominican Republic in 2001.

Although the average Honduran garment worker earns an estimated US$100 per week, quadruple the amount of their Chinese counterparts, their wages are substantially lower than those in developed countries (Sanford, 2005: 55). The low wage and high tech combination allows Gildan to undercut their Chinese counterparts on price. Their strategic location allows them to avoid duties to anywhere in North America, and to ensure a quick response, Gildan has established distribution centres in each of its major markets. This has resulted in an estimated 375 million garments being produced every year (Sanford, 2005: 55).

Outworkers

Outworkers are increasingly being used in the Australian TCF industry, as well as in other developed countries. Through outworkers, firms are able to respond quickly to consumer demands. Outworkers work from their homes, which allows them to combine income earnings with family responsibilities. In 1995 it was estimated that there were 300,000 outworkers in the Australian clothing industry, with more than half of them of Vietnamese descent (Gare, 1995). It has been estimated that they work for as little as A$2 an hour (Gare, 1995).

However, as a result of their circumstances, outworkers are often exploited. Outworkers often speak little English and are intimidated by contractors to whom they are tied. It is alleged that if they do not do what they are told they will be refused work. As a result, numerous contractors have established unregulated home-based factories where recently arrived immigrants work 14 hours a day, 7 days a week with no holiday pay, sick leave or superannuation (Gare, 1995). The Australian Tax Office estimated that the textile black market has resulted in a loss of more than A$100 million in revenue (Gare, 1995).

An Australian success story

Saul Same inherited the Comfort Shirt and Underclothing Manufacturing Company in 1950 as a result of the death of his father-in-law. This company was renamed Glo-Weave. Glo-Weave placed a great deal of time and effort on research and development to make its shirts different from the competition. Investment in R&D ultimately resulted in the *Glo-Stripe, Glo-Check* shirts, in 1953 and *Royal Suede* in the early 1960s (Ashton and Ryan, 2000: 14). Glo-Weave's production rose 390 per cent from its inception in 1954 to 1964 (Ashton and Ryan, 2000: 23). The Glo-Weave production plant was also moved during this time to accommodate the increased production.

By the end of the 1960s, Glo-Weave had a strong export market to numerous countries, including Singapore, Fiji and Hong Kong. They had also established a mill in Fitzroy, Victoria, in order to meet production demands. However, as a result of the Whitlam government's policies in the early 1970s, Glo-Weave's costs doubled within a 14-month period and it was forced to scale back its domestic market (Ashton and Ryan, 2000: 75).

Once again, Glo-Weave used its expertise as an innovator and created the *Ram* short sleeve shirt, which sold well for five years after its introduction. It also acquired the licence to produce French label Guy Laroche and later Pierre Cardin. In the late 1970s Glo-Weave also leased the Medding shirt-maker factory and numerous other operations which were owned by Paterson, Reid and Bruce, who were closing down their operations (Ashton and Ryan, 2000: 82). However, with the abolition of quotas, as a result of the Button Plan, cheap garments from Asia began to flood Australia. Glo-Weave was forced to sell its mill.

Glo-Weave also began to manufacture in Indonesia in conjunction with the company P T Great River International (Ashton and Ryan, 2000: 88). Shortly after, in 1982, Glo-Weave began to manufacture shirts offshore, for the first time. The number of staff was subsequently reduced by 380 employees (Ashton and Ryan, 2000: 91). By 1994 P T Great River was licenced to produce shirts for sale in Indonesia, Malaysia, Singapore and Brunei (Ashton and Ryan, 2000: 91). In 2000, Glo-Weave moved a division of their manufacturing offshore. This resulted in unbranded garments being supplied to Target and Yakka (Ashton and Ryan, 2000).

Although further tariff reductions by the newly elected Liberal Party were postponed until 2005, as a result of rigorous lobbying by the TCF industry, the Glo-Weave factory was unable to remain trading. Its factory was forced to close in 1997 which led to a further 80 staff redundancies. By the end of 2000, Glo-Weave staff numbered 50 (Ashton and Ryan, 2000).

However, Glo-Weave is still successfully trading. It has established quick stock delivery through a vendor refill program, which resulted in 90 per cent of Glo-Weave's business being 'in the same or next day' stock delivery all over Australia This is accomplished through a highly integrated warehousing system. Glo-Weave has found its niche, through the 'quick response' system and through offshoring and hence has been able to successfully compete with other international textile companies (Ashton and Ryan, 2000).

In summary

The clothing and footwear sectors are more labour-intensive and this has led to a shift, in the last 20 years, of production to low-labour-cost countries, such as China. The majority of imports are outsourced from China. This is usually achieved through joint ventures or direct investment. This is a dilemma that affects all developed countries. As world markets become further integrated, whether through FTAs, regional agreements or through global organizations, such as the WTO, this process will undoubtedly continue. However, the Australian TCF industry has demonstrated its resilience in regards to global competition. There has been a great amount of money and effort placed in technological advancements. There has also been a focus on consumer responsiveness through innovations such as 'quick response'.

Offshoring and outworkers have also been used to assist the industry. Glo-Weave is an excellent example as to how a textiles company has adapted to the increase of global competition. They have reduced their workforce and saved costs by establishing offshore manufacturing bases. They have also become a niche company by focusing on quick stock delivery. This section demonstrates that the Australian TCF has been able to adapt to the seemingly irreversible trend of globalization by establishing innovative concepts. An FTA with China will ultimately have little effect on the changes that have been made, and will be made in the future, by the industry in order to compete internationally.

Concluding remarks

There are numerous benefits that may arise from free trade agreements. They are quicker to negotiate and it is easier to obtain concessions, which would otherwise be unattainable in global forums such as the WTO. China is one of the world's fastest growing economies in the world and through an FTA, Australia will have increased access to China's markets. This is particularly beneficial for Australia's service sector. Australia can increase its FDI in China and domestic businesses will have greater export opportunities.

China has begun to assert itself as a leader in the global economy. It has joined the WTO and signed FTAs and is in various negotiations in order to establish more. Australia would be at a great advantage if it were one of the first developed countries to establish an FTA with China. There is already a vast amount of trade and investment between the countries, especially in regards to textiles. There is the fear that China, as a larger partner will impose itself on Australia and seek more concessions than it is willing to give. However, Australia has negotiated numerous FTAs, including an FTA with the USA, which resulted in safeguards and a gradual reduction in tariffs and quotas.

The reality is that the world has gradually become more economically integrated and it appears that this trend will continue. Australia has embraced this by opening up its markets to international trade and investment. Australia has successfully completed six FTAs and these have led to a reduction in tariffs and quotas. It is also in the process of establishing numerous other agreements. Australia is also a party to APEC, which is based on free and open trade and investment among its members. This is to be achieved through the reduction of tariffs by all members. Tariffs and quotas have been and will continue to be reduced regardless of whether an FTA is signed with China or not. However, Australia would benefit enormously from an FTA with China, as it can focus less on labour-intensive industries, such as textiles, and more on knowledge-based industries, such as services, where it has a comparative advantage over China.

Both the EU and the USA have taken a flawed position in regards to their protectionist stance towards China in recent years. They have both refused to grant China market economy status. Australia, on the other hand has agreed to grant China market economy status as part of the free trade negotiations. China is not a market economy, as stated in its constitution. The Government frequently intervenes in the market, as demonstrated by their currency manipulation. However, changing China's status from an EIT to a market economy will have little impact on dumping issues as the same steps must be followed when making an anti-dumping claim.

Certain assumptions must be made in order for the theories in support of free trade to work. For example, it is presumed that job losses, as the result of trade will be absorbed by other sectors. In reality, the TCF industry is not as mobile as other manufacturing sectors, as workers tend to be less educated and more specialized. However, this does not negate the positive aspects of an FTA with China, nor does it lessen the resilience of the industry. The TCF industry has faced reduced protection since the 1970s. It was recognized by the IAC and previous federal governments that Australia had to reduce its tariffs and quotas on textiles. International competition has resulted in a more efficient industry as firms that could not compete have been eliminated.

Tariffs and quotas, which maintain uncompetitive firms, do so at the expense of society as a whole. It is unfair to other manufacturing sectors for an uncompetitive firm to remain trading. If a firm is unable to recuperate their losses, then it is not worthwhile for the community to make such an investment. It is unfair to consumers as well. Friedman argued that protection really meant exploiting the consumer. Prices increase as a result of protectionism while product variety decreases. In Australia, the price for protecting one worker in the TCF industry was estimated to be in the thousands.

The longer an industry remains under protective policies, the more uncompetitive it becomes. It has been recognized by TCF firms that quota and tariff dropping has resulted in a better industry. Those firms which have survived have become more capable and flexible. Australian firms can import from anywhere because there are no quotas. The EU, by contrast, has provided too much protection to its textiles industry. When tariffs were abolished in 2005, the EU quickly established new ones as their industry was unable to cope with the increase of Chinese imports. The EU's TCF sector cannot compete internationally as a result of their protectionist policies. The US Government also protects its TCF industry through tariffs and quotas, which have also been reintroduced after global quotas came to an end in 2005. The fear in America is job loss in particular. This is an emotional argument with little economic basis.

It must be recognized that job losses will occur in labour-intensive industries. This will become more pronounced when tariffs and quotas are further decreased if and when an FTA with China is established. However, as noted, the reduction of protectionist policies has been occurring in Australia since the 1970s. In the last 20 years, there has been a shift to low-labour-cost countries and numerous employees have been laid off and numerous firms have ceased trading. The success of an FTA ultimately depends on what the macro-economic conditions are at the time of its implementation. International trade does not exist in isolation from economics and the chances of retrenched employees finding quality employment ultimately depends on macro-economic policies and circumstances at the time, both national and global.

Australia cannot compete with China in regards to labour costs; however, the Australian TCF industry has demonstrated its resilience. It is internationally competitive and generates a substantial amount of revenue and employment. There has been a great amount of money and effort placed in technological advancements. There has also been a focus on consumer responsiveness through innovations such as 'quick response'. Offshoring and outworkers have also been used to assist the industry. Glo-Weave is an excellent example as to how a textile company can adapt to the various aspects of global competition. They have reduced their workforce and saved costs by establishing offshore manufacturing bases. They have also become a niche company by focusing on quick stock delivery and on specialized textiles.

Globalization will neither end nor decrease. FTAs and FDI between countries will continue and a FTA between Australia and China is likely to occur. There will be numerous benefits for Australian businesses – services in particular, as outlined above. The proposed FTA will not be as beneficial to the TCF industry of Australia in regards to employment. However, the Australian TCF industry will be able to cope with these changes as it has in the past – with resilience and innovation.

8 Potential determinants of China's research and development

Li Ping, Gaston Fornes and Yu Guocai

Introduction

The potential determinants of China's increasing research and development (R&D) expenditure, which jumped from 0.62 per cent in 1987 to 1.42 per cent in 2006, are investigated. Most of the existing literature surrounding R&D addresses productivity and growth issues[1] but studies on R&D's determinants are scarce. This chapter attempts to address this gap by exploring the determinants of China's increasing R&D expenditure within a comprehensive framework.

A common idea is that R&D and innovation are the main engine of technological progress and productivity growth in the long run, which leads to one of the main questions in economic development: why is the R&D investment rate as a share of GDP, a proxy for innovative activity, relatively low in most developing countries? For example, Latin American countries post relatively low R&D investment rates with an average of roughly 0.4 per cent of GDP, whereas most OECD countries invest on average around 2 per cent of their GDP in R&D.[2] However, China's investment in R&D has been growing dramatically in recent years, and therefore the analysis of the potential determinants of this phenomenon is an area in need of further research.

The rest of the chapter is organized as follows. The next section reviews the literature on the determinants of R&D, followed by a methodology section. The chapter finishes by explaining the results and drawing some conclusions.

Review of the literature on the determinants of R&D and other contributing factors

The literature on the potential determinants of R&D is rather limited, though studies suggest various contributing factors: demand pull on innovation, technology transfer facilitated by trade and foreign direct investment (FDI) and patent protection. A review of these streams follows.

Potential determinants of R&D

Previous studies on the determinants of R&D worth mentioning are Lee (2003), focusing on the determinants of R&D intensity at industry level, Lederman and

Maloney (2003), tracing the evolution of R&D expenditure along the development process using a new global panel data set, Maloney and Rodriguez-Clare (2007), exploring the relationship between R&D investment rates and specialization patterns, and Alvi *et al.* (2007) examining whether patent protection and technology transfer facilitate R&D with a semi-parametric model.

Lee (2003) found that the intra-industry determinants of R&D intensity are mainly four categories of factors: consumer preference over quality and price; factors representing the cost of R&D, such as R&D production cost and industry-wide technological opportunity; the appropriability of R&D; and market competition represented by market structure or the degree of firm density in the market. The predicted positive relationship between firm density and industry R&D intensity was empirically tested.

Lederman and Maloney (2003) focused on developed countries with high R&D investment rates, like Finland, deviating from the predicted trajectory and displaying impressive R&D takeoffs, and concluded that the depth of domestic credit markets, educational variables, the extent of protection offered to intellectual property rights (IPRs), the ability to mobilize government resources, and the quality of complementary academic institutions tend to influence cross-country differences in R&D.

Maloney and Rodriguez-Clare (2007) suggested that R&D investment is, like other capital investments, determined by the economy's pattern of specialization, as well as by the overall economic incentives and distortions. They concluded that R&D investment rates vary across sectors and that the natural-resource-abundant economies of South America are not expected to invest as much in R&D as the manufacturing-oriented countries of East Asia, and that low R&D investment rates – at least for some countries, like Chile – could just be part of a more general capital accumulation problem.

The results of Alvi *et al.* (2007) showed thresholds in patent protection and technology transfer; patent protection has a positive effect which weakens as the protection level grows, and FDI has a positive effect only if the country is FDI-dependant.

The application of these frameworks/results to China presents two main challenges: first, whether a static analysis is suitable to explain China's low but increasing R&D investment rate; and second, how to consider the influence of technological transfers, since China, as a developing country, has benefited from developed countries' investments. For these reasons, a comprehensive analysis and a time-varying model will be attempted.

Other contributing factors

This section reviews three main streams of research on other contributing factors to determinants of R&D.

Demand pull on R&D

Theory of demand-induced innovation considers that innovation is pulled by external demand forces (Scherer, 1982; Schmookler, 1966), and that variations in sales and profits stimulate R&D investments (Judd, 1985). This influence has been described as the price advantage effect (Greenwood and Mukoyama, 2001) and market size effect (Zweimuller, 2000). Other studies have found that enterprises' R&D investment is correlated with per capita income (Reinthaler and Wolf, 2004), income distribution (Murphy *et al.*, 1989; Reto and Zweimuller, 2006), and exports (Bebczuk, 2002).

The micro-mechanism of demand influence on innovation can be a price advantage effect (Greenwood and Mukoyama, 2001) or a market size effect (Zweimuller, 2000). First, Greenwood and Mukoyama (2001) concluded that the division of income could simulate the motivation of innovation under a partial equilibrium frame. Then, Reto and Zweimuller (2006) suggested that income inequality could influence a country's independent innovation through both price and market size effects, i.e. the higher the degree of inequality, the more purchasing power the high-income groups will have for innovative products, which may in turn stimulate enterprises' R&D investment and innovation. In this context, Acemoglu and Newman (2002) and Jakob and Damania (2001) proposed the wage-induced effect where an increase in wages appears to give enterprises a stimulus to increase investments in equipment and R&D. Also, Jaff (1988) suggested that the enterprises' factor endowment seems to promote R&D investments, as the ability to get abnormal profits (part of endogenous demand) is an important determinant of R&D investment due to imperfections in capital markets.

Technology externality

A second stream asserted that enterprises' technological capacity drives innovation (Dosi, 1982), and that the determining factors include the discovery of basic science technological opportunities, the efficiency of research departments, and the cost of opportunity of investments (Dosi, 1988; Rosenberg, 1974); this is called 'supply push'.

More recent studies within this stream have concentrated on externality (Romer, 1990), namely technology transfer and spillovers, where the most commonly referred to channels are trade-based: trade in intermediate goods (Caselli and Wilson, 2004; Coe *et al.*, 1997; Keller, 2002), foreign R&D spillovers (Coe and Helpman, 1995; Keller, 2002; van Pottelsberghe de la Potterie and Lichtenberg, 2001; Zachariadis, 2004) and imitation (Mukoyama, 2003; Papageorgiou, 2003; Perez-Sebastian, 1999), all with empirical evidence illustrating the positive effect on domestic R&D investments.

Empirical findings for FDI as a potential R&D determinant are controversial (Li, 2006). Contrary to the commonly accepted positive influence, Nonaka and Takeuchi (1995) suggested that FDI could cause a serious reverse loss of talent, which hinders the improvement of the host country and its R&D capabilities. In this context, Aiken and Harrison (1999) found from panel data of Venezuelan enterprises that FDI would bring negative impact to domestic enterprises' R&D. Also, Jiang (2004) studied how the multinational companies' participation in domestic markets could influence Chinese enterprises' financing capacity, and concluded that competition brought by multinational companies would deteriorate the R&D motivation and capacity of domestic-funded enterprises.

Absorptive capacity is another area related to technology transfers and R&D investments. The adoption of existing technology is costly and firms and countries need to develop an 'absorptive' or 'national learning' capacity; these, in turn, are hypothesized to be functions of R&D investment. Cohen and Levinthal (1989), among others, added that knowing where the technology frontier is and figuring out what adaptations are necessary is the 'second face' of R&D. Investment in pure research is also important for developing countries (Pavitt, 2001). However, most empirical studies in this area have focused on how R&D affects the absorptive capacity (Griffith, *et al.*, 2004).

Patent protection

Economic theory suggests that advancing innovation through patents is not always straightforward. The costs of disclosure can more than offset the private gains from patenting (Horstmann *et al.*, 1985). For example, the effects of 'stronger' patent protection on incentives to innovate is not apparent, as a 'stronger' patent protection framework may mean that not only is the protection to a given firm's patent stronger, but also that of its rivals (Gallini, 2002; Jaffe, 2000). In this context, Heller and Eisenberg (1998) said that associating associating the patents and patent-holders with just one new product is so numerous that the necessary negotiations for subsequent development and commercialization may be excessively costly. Similarly, Shapiro (2000) suggested that for complex products (Cohen *et al.*, 2000) firms often possess numerous and overlapping patent rights, giving rise to 'clusters' where transactions costs can impede innovation. Building on these ideas, Hunt (2006) developed a model of overlapping patents showing that in R&D and patenting intensive industries where patents overlap (thus conferring rights to rivals' innovation rent streams) making patents less costly to obtain may reduce firms' incentives to invest in R&D.

Most previous studies using aggregate cross-national data have found a positive and significant effect (Chen and Puttitanum, 2005; Falk, 2006; Kanwar and Evenson, 2003; Lederman and Maloney, 2003; Park and Ginarte, 1997). To address the limitation of most of these studies that patent policy may be endogenous with respect to innovation, Lerner (2002) employed an instrumental variables approach and found that strengthening patent protection appears to have few positive effects on patent applications by domestic entities. In addition, Eaton and Kortum (1999), in a general equilibrium model of the impact of R&D, innovation, and diffusion, considered the impact of patents on R&D and growth and concluded that eliminating patent protection would reduce R&D and economic growth.

These empirical analyses of the relationship between either patenting activity or patent strength, and measures of innovation or innovative activity – usually R&D – have been conducted either at the firm level or at an aggregate level. The latter is also analysed in this chapter, aiming at reflecting aggregate impacts and potential offsetting effects (including negative effects on R&D incentives of diminished R&D spillovers to which patents may contribute).

All in all, most of the previous studies on contributing factors to R&D and innovation have a focus on demand pull, technology transfers, or patent protection; however, studies combining all three to systematically examine their effect on R&D investment are scarce. This is the main objective of this chapter, to consider the effects of demand pull, technology capacity and patent protection, ceteris paribus, on China's expenditure on R&D.

Methodology

The main R&D determinants were identified using an ordinary least square model (OLS) and the dynamics of the major contributing factors' influence were illustrated with a state space model using data from 1987 to 2006. In this context, the index of technology capacity calculated through data envelopment analysis (DEA) was used as a proxy for supply push, and the index of patent protection (IPP) was included, following Ginarte and Park (1997) but adapted to China's special situation. Finally, the dynamics of major contributing factors' influence was illustrated with a state space system model.

As the companies' R&D expenditure is a function of the expected profits from innovation profits (and following Jaffe's (1988) conclusions that the effects on R&D intensity of technological opportunity, market demand, and R&D spillovers at the firm level have significant effects on R&D demand), a patent protection variable was added due to its influence on a country's innovation and technology capacity in firms' R&D investment instead of on technology spillovers, even though the capacity may be partly affected by spillovers.

The demand for innovation is determined by domestic demand, including GDP, income distribution, exports, price, and other factors. Among them, innovation demand is positively related to GDP and exports negatively to price, but the effect of income distribution is complex to assess since the poor usually cannot afford the products of innovation which are more in demand, by contrast, by the richer part of the population. This idea can be expressed as:

$$Q^D = F\left(Gdp, Ex, Gini, P\right) \tag{1}$$

where Q^D and P denote the demand and price for innovation products; Gdp, the gross domestic product, Ex is the abbreviation for exports and $Gini$ is the Gini index, a proxy for income distribution.

The supply side of innovation products is based on the enterprises' R&D stock, technology capacity, and price, as well as on the human capital input. In this context, it is reasonable to assume a Leontief's relation between R&D personnel and expenditure due to the low degree of substitution between the two elements; therefore, human capital for R&D efforts is not considered here. Innovation supply as a function of R&D stock, technology capacity and price, can be expressed as:

$$Q^S = G\left(D, Tech, P\right) \tag{2}$$

where D denotes the R&D stock and *Tech* the technology capacity of enterprises for the whole economy.

The market equilibrium occurs when the demand is satisfied by the supply:

$$Q = Q^D = Q^S \tag{3}$$

Therefore,

$$Q = Q(Gdp, Ex, Gini, D, Tech, P) \tag{4}$$

On the other hand, the enterprises' multi-stage optimal programming can be expressed as:

$$\underset{R_t}{Max} \sum_{t=0}^{\infty} \frac{Q_t - P_t' R_t}{(1+r)^t} \tag{5}$$

$$s.t. \; D_{t+1} = R_t + (1-\delta)D_t$$

where R_t denotes the R&D investment, P_t' is the R&D capital's price and r is the interest rate.

Calculating the equation:

$$L = \sum_{t=0}^{\infty} \left\{ \frac{Q_t - P_t' R_t}{(1+r)^t} + \lambda_t [R_t - D_{t+1} + (1-\delta)D_t] \right\} \tag{6}$$

where λ_t is the multiplier, indicating R&D shadow price in period t. By differentiating R_t and D_t we have

$$P_t' = \mu_t \tag{7}$$

$$\frac{\partial Q_t}{\partial D_t} = r\mu_{t-1} + \delta\mu_t - \Delta\mu_t \tag{8}$$

where $\mu_t = \lambda_t (1+r)^t$ to represent the current price.

Transversality condition:

$$\lim_{t \to \infty} \mu_t D_{t+1} = 0 \tag{9}$$

which means that the current value of R&D stock in the infinite tends to zero.

From equations (7) and (8):

$$\frac{\partial Q_t}{\partial D_t} = rP_{t-1}' + \delta P_t' - \Delta P_t' \tag{10}$$

The left-hand side of equation (10) represents the expected profits of R&D, and the right-hand side is the cost for R&D efforts (rP'_{t-1} is the opportunity cost, $\delta P'_t$ is the discount part, and $\Delta P'_t$ is the change in R&D capital price).

The R&D price change is assumed to be constant, P'. The elasticity of R&D capital with respect to production, $Q_D D/Q$, is assumed to remain constant due to the constant return scale (CRS) of the production function, α. This results in the optimal R&D stock in period t:

$$D_t = \frac{\alpha}{(r+\delta)P'} Q_t \tag{11}$$

$$R_t = \theta\left(Q_{t+1} - (1-\delta)Q_t\right) \tag{12}$$

where $\theta = \dfrac{\alpha}{(r+\delta)P'}$.

From equations (4) and (12), the framework for the empirical analysis is obtained:

$$s_t = \theta * \phi_t(Q, Gdp) * \left(g_{t+1}(Gdp, Ex, Gini, D, Tech, P') + \delta\right) \tag{13}$$

where, $s_t = R_t/Gdp_t$, $\phi_t = Q_t/Gdp_t$ and $g_{t+1} = Q_{t+1}/Q_t - 1$.

Equation (13) shows that R&D investment as a share of GDP is a function of GDP, exports, income distribution, and technological capacity. Namely,

$$s_t = s_t(Gdp, Ex, Gini, Tech) \tag{14}$$

Logarithms of equation (14) are taken to identify the elasticity with respect to R&D investment (namely each factor's contribution):

$$\ln s = c + \beta_1 * \ln Gdp + \beta_2 * \ln Gini + \beta_3 * \ln Ex + \beta_4 * \ln Tech + \beta_5 * \ln IPP + u \tag{15}$$

where *IPP*, denotes patent protection and u the error term. Patent protection was added to analyse its influence as reported by previous studies, although it is not a market force and consequently was considered as an exogenous variable.

Data and method

The large and medium-sized industrial enterprises' expenditures on science and technology (S&T) activities as a share of GDP was the dependent variable, denoted by *Erd*[3] and China's expenditure on R&D as a share of GDP, denoted by *R*, was chosen as the independent variable to test variables' different reactions to market forces.

As the enterprises' investment decisions were not driven by market forces before the enlargement of the enterprises' independent authority in 1987, the data range covers only 1987–2006. All the data of large and medium-sized industrial enterprises' expenditures on S&T and China's expenditure on R&D were sourced from *China Statistical Yearbooks* and *China Science and Technology Statistical Yearbooks*.

The data for *Gdp* and *Ex* are from *China Statistical Yearbooks* and adjusted to 1985 prices. *Gini* data are from standard income distribution data (SIDD) (Babones and Alvarez-Rivadulla, 2007). Technology capacity *Tech* is measured by China's technology distance to the frontier represented by leading countries like the United States and Japan, and the method for measurement and result are described in the next subsection. *IPP*, the index of patent protection, is measured similarly to Ginarte and Park (1997) with some modifications addressing China's special situation.

Technology capacity

Technology capacity or state refers to the capacity of supplying the same amount of products with different inputs, or yielding a different number of products with the same inputs.[4] Different countries' technology states can be seen in the different product output with the same labour input, much like the total factor productivity in Solow's (1956) model. This chapter uses technology distance instead of total factors productivity (TFP) for technology state, as each country's capital stock is necessary to make estimations and non-comparable due to the heterogeneity of cross-country data. The DEA Malmquist index to measure technology state was calculated, in a similar way to how Fare *et al.* (1995) calculated the TFP. Data envelopment analysis (DEA) was proposed by Charnes *et al.* (1978). The purpose of DEA is to use linear programming methods to construct a non-parametric envelopment frontier over the data points such that all observed points lie on or below the production frontier to be able to calculate efficiencies relative to this surface.

The DEA was introduced by a ratio form. For each decision making unit (DMU) a measure of the ratio of all outputs over all inputs is obtained. To select optimal weights, such as the efficiency measure of the *i*-th DMU the output quantities are proportionally expanded without altering the input quantities used. Then, the model is specified with the multiplier form of the linear programming problem, or the equivalent envelopment form of this problem. The envelopment form involves fewer constraints than the original programming problem, and hence is generally the preferred form to solve.

$$Min_{\theta,\lambda}\,\theta,$$

$$s.t. - y_i + Y\lambda \geq 0,$$

$$\theta_{X_i} - X\lambda \geq 0,$$

$$\lambda \geq 0$$

Table 8.1 Technology state of the USA, Japan and China

Year	USA	Japan	China	Year	USA	Japan	China
1987	1	0.731	0.051	1997	1	0.752	0.086
1988	1	0.754	0.055	1998	1	0.722	0.089
1989	1	0.767	0.055	1999	1	0.707	0.092
1990	1	0.786	0.048	2000	1	0.721	0.098
1991	1	0.792	0.052	2001	1	0.721	0.104
1992	1	0.771	0.057	2002	1	0.718	0.11
1993	1	0.762	0.064	2003	1	0.718	0.118
1994	1	0.758	0.07	2004	1	0.719	0.125
1995	1	0.764	0.076	2005	1	0.72	0.136
1996	1	0.765	0.081	2006	1	0.726	0.148

The value of θ obtained will be the efficiency score for the i-th DMU. It should satisfy $\theta \leqq 1$, with a value of 1 indicating a point on the frontier and hence a technically efficient DMU.

All of the defined efficiency measures are measured along a ray from the origin to the observed production point. One advantage of these radial efficiency measures is that they are invariant units, i.e. changes in the units of measurement do not change the value of the efficiency measure. In this context, the DEA can independently form the productive function and avoid result bias due to wrong definitions of the model.

Each country's GDP is considered the output and the total labour force input; then, the distance to the technology frontier takes a value between zero and one, providing an indicator of the degree of technical efficiency of the economy. A value of one implies that the economy is fully technically efficient. A comparison between China, and, the USA and Japan was carried out, as these two countries are currently the world leaders in technology development. The results can be seen in Table 8.1.[5] In the table it is possible to see that compared with the USA and Japan, China has a lower technology state but with an upward trend. This could be due to international technology spillovers and domestic technology accumulation over the last 20 years. Also, through international trade, overseas patent application, and FDI, China may have absorbed technology spillovers from advanced economies. In addition, the accumulation of human capital through education may have impacted positively on the technology state with a better labour output performance; improvements in quality and updating of physical capital may have also indirectly enhanced the state.

Index of patent protection

The Ginarte and Park (1997) index (GPI) is widely accepted as a measure of a country's patent protection level. As it tends to be more suitable for countries with relatively more developed legal systems, it was adjusted to address China's

Table 8.2 Index of patent protection (IPP) in China

Year	1987	1988	1989	1990	1991	1992	1993	1994	1995	1996
IPP	0.306	0.373	0.427	0.421	0.448	0.95	1.223	1.266	1.428	1.566

Year	1997	1998	1999	2000	2001	2002	2003	2004	2005	2006
IPP	1.666	1.754	2.048	2.181	2.742	2.48	3.281	3.411	3.456	3.484

situation. For this, Han and Li (2005) took the effect of law enforcement into consideration and proposed a modified index of patent protection. The equation follows:

$$IPP(t) = L(t) * P^G(t)$$

where $L(t)$ denotes the effect of a country's law enforcement at time t, $P^G(t)$ denotes the patent protection index calculated with the Ginarte–Park method at time t, and $IPP(t)$ is the modified index of patent protection. With this method, Han and Li calculated China's index of patent protection during 1984–2002, part of which is presented in Table 8.2, together with the index of the following four years calculated in the same way.

Results

The time series in regressions should be stable otherwise we would get quasi-regression. The unit root test with ADF method shows that $\ln Erd$ and $\ln Gini$ are I (2) and other series are I (1). The Johansen cointegration test indicates four cointegrating equations at the 0.05 level; that is to say the unstable series in the model could be stable through some linear combination and therefore the causality reliable in the long run.

Both the demand and the technology state are expected to be a positive influence on R&D expenditure. The demand assumption is a contemporaneous effect while the technology state may have a lag influence. A regression trial was run which showed no difference between the contemporaneous and lagged $\ln Tech$ and also no accumulation influence. For this reason, further analyses were carried out using contemporaneous values.

The estimates resulting from model (15) with dependent variables R and Erd respectively are illustrated in Table 8.3. F-statistics of both functions are significant at the 1 per cent level, which means the null hypotheses that all the independent variables have no partial effect on R&D expenditure, R or Erd, could be rejected. T-statistics of most of the independent variables, except $\ln Tech$ in the function explaining R, are significant at the 1 per cent or 5 per cent level. Q-statistics of residual are not significant, which means the selection of independent variables is proper and the serial correlation does not exist. Further, the regressions show high explanation power with $\bar{R}^2$ 0.959 and 0.892 respectively. All the coefficients for both functions show the same direction (signs) with a

Table 8.3 Estimation results for the determinants of China's R&D

Dependent variable	*ln* R	*ln* Erd
ln *Gdp*	−4.289 (0.658)**	−6.776 (1.06)**
ln *Ex*	0.289 (0.09)**	0.702(0.145)**
ln *Gini*	8.377 (0.95)**	9.685 (1.531)**
ln *Tech*	0.521 (0.341)	1.961 (0.55)**
ln *IPP*	0.272 (0.111)*	0.456 (0.179)*
$\bar{R}^2$(s.e.e.)	0.959 (0.06)	0.892(0.096)
D.W. value	1.76	1.84
P-value (F-statistics)	0.000	0.000

Notes: Standard errors are in parentheses.
** and * indicate that the coefficient is significant at the 1 per cent and 5 per cent levels, respectively.

higher magnitude in the second one, suggesting that *Erd* seems to explain better the sensitivity to the factors. The analysis of the results is shown in Table 8.3.

First, the elasticity of *Gdp* with respect to R&D investment is significantly negative at the 1 per cent level and such negative influence of the domestic demand (national income) on Chinese enterprises' R&D investment is unexpected. A possible interpretation is that the large Chinese domestic market still leaves space for enterprises with relatively low technology level production capacity to satisfy needs. In other words, it appears that there is still plenty of room for enterprises to make profits even without innovation. Another possibility is the heterogeneity in the total needs of people in China. The purchasing power of the whole market, especially that of the majority low income group, is concentrated on basic needs instead of on high level products, which may lead to few incentives to R&D investment and innovation.

Second, for exports, *Ex*, a positive but limited influence on enterprises' R&D investment was found. This is expected since exports of Chinese goods are labour-intensive and low technology primarily processed, and enterprises can gain a market share in international markets through the advantages of low cost labour and natural resources inputs rather than through technology and innovation. It appears that there exists a partial effect of exports on R&D expenditure, which means exports are seen to spur R&D investment and innovation, especially those of enterprises, since the elasticity in *Erd* function is more than twice that of the other function.

Third, the income distribution, *Gini*, has a dominantly significant influence on enterprises' R&D investment, which tends to indicate that the innovation is concentrated on the wealthy. Income inequality shows a significant effect on enterprises' R&D investment through the expected profits from innovations and products selling at a high price, i.e. the demand pull for innovation amounts to pricing advantage on the higher income group.

All in all, the effective demand of the combined effect of national income, income distribution, and exports, appears to have a significantly positive influence on R&D expenditure with income distribution being the major incentive to enterprises' R&D investment and innovation.

Fourth, the positive elasticity of *Tech* with respect to R&D expenditure tends to indicate that the enhancement of China's technology state has reduced the innovation risk and also has induced further R&D investment to engage in superior and more profitable markets. This finding seems to suggest that the improvements in the technology state reduces the followers' innovation risk by standing on the shoulders of the pioneers, which in turn stimulates the enterprises' R&D investment and innovation. In addition, China's technology advances seem to have benefited, among other things, from spillovers which, with their own absorptive R&D efforts, have driven enterprises to invest more in R&D and compete with high-quality products for more profit.

Fifth, as expected, patent protection has a positive but limited influence on both China's R&D expenditure and the large and medium-sized industrial enterprises' expenditures on S&T.

In conclusion, both China's and the large and medium-sized industrial enterprises' R&D seem to be more sensitive to national income and income distribution than to the other three variables. This tends to suggest that domestic effective demand may be a major determinant of R&D investment. Also, enterprises' R&D investment appears to be more sensitive to the determinant factors since the estimates obtained in the second function are higher, especially those for exports, technology capacity and patent protection index.

Predictability checks

The analysis goes on to explore whether there are predictable trends in the effects of the discussed factors on R&D expenditure. For this purpose, regression (15) was run again keeping OLS constant over time but adopting a time-varying state space model to retest the dynamic effects of the independent variables on R&D expenditure. This is due to China's changing economic environment, such as deepening reforming policies and outside shocks.

There are two advantages in using the state space model. First, the time-varying effects of unobservable variables on explained variables can be embodied by state variables; second, the state space model can be estimated by a strong iterative algorithm, Kalman filter, which can filter out the effects of unobservable variables and best approximate state variables with the information provided by the pre-value of explained variable.

Based on model (15), the state space model with the dependent variable ln *Erd* follows:

Measure function:

$$\ln Erd = c(1) + \beta_1 * \ln Gdp + \beta_2 * \ln Ex + \beta_3 * \ln Gini + \beta_4 * \ln Tech + \beta_5 * \ln IPP \\ + [var = \exp(C(2))] \tag{16}$$

State function:

$$\beta_{it} = \omega\beta_{it-1} + \delta_{it} \quad i = 1,2,3,4 \quad t = 0,1,\cdots,T \tag{17}$$

With assumption

$$(u_t, \delta_t)' \sim N\left(\begin{pmatrix} 0 \\ 0 \end{pmatrix}, \begin{pmatrix} \alpha^2 & 0 \\ 0 & Q \end{pmatrix} \right) \tag{18}$$

β_{it} is time-varying to demonstrate the dynamics of elasticity of independent variables with respect to the dependent variable; u_t and δ_{it} are independent disturbances following N distribution with the expectation 0, variation σ^2 and co-variation Q.

Equations (16)–(18) are the state space model.[6] In the equations above, equation (16) is the measurement equation, denoting the common relationship of these variables and the R&D inputs. In this equation, parameters are state variables whose changes reflect the comprehensive effects of external factors like system on the relationship of effective market demand, technology state and enterprises' R&D inputs. Equation (17) is the state equation and it describes the creation procession of the state variable. The estimation value of variable parameters is obtained with the Kalman filter. The Kalman filter's iterative algorithm was estimated with Eviews 6.0.

The state space model can get the same regression as the OLS model with the one-step approach, and can also get the coefficients of every period with the Kalman filter. The dynamic effects of each independent variable are sequentially illustrated in Figure 8.1, showing their dynamic influences on enterprises' R&D expenditure respectively.

Figure 8.1 illustrates that the influences are complex. All the variables have fluctuated greatly until 2000 and reached individual's peaks or valleys around 1990–1996. In particular, the influence of domestic demand fluctuates but remains negative except in 1992–1996 with a sharp drop and increasing resistance after 1996; exports are also an obstacle with a severely fluctuating effect on R&D investment in the early stages but it remains positive after 1996 with a gradually strengthening tendency; income inequity is unexpectedly a barrier to expanding R&D investment before 1995 and turns out, inversely, to be the major incentive for R&D investment with a dramatically increasing effect during 1995–1996; technology capacity keeps a positive influence except during 1991–1997 with a valley in 1996; and patent protection always exerts a positive influence but the effect is always fluctuating with the weakest points in 1992 and 1993 and it is hard to get a predictable trend.

In general, it is possible to see that every variable has a fluctuated influence on enterprises' R&D expenditure with a significant change around 1990–1996, when China's reform was deepening and enterprises began to get more authority to run businesses and their investment strategies became more sensitive to market change. This can be explained by the fact that companies became more market-oriented during this period and therefore R&D investments, competition strategies, and adjustments to the market were widely seen. This seems to have had an important effect on R&D expenditure at the beginning of the 1990s.

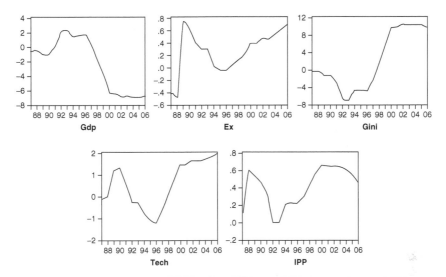

Figure 8.1 Dynamic effect of independent variables.

A final interesting point is the increasing influence of income distribution and technology capacity in contrast to the decreasing or non-significant influence of the other variables. This may indicate that the rich in China have earned more purchasing power for high level products and have exerted some dominant influence on enterprises' R&D investment and technology capacity; or that the appropriability of production is more important as an R&D strategy.

Conclusions

This chapter analysed, first, China's technology state through an index of technology distance in relation to advanced countries measured by the DEA Malmquist index. Second, it ran a dynamic analysis based on a time-varying state space model of effective demand and technology state influences. This second analysis is different to most previous works, which were based on static analysis.

The results show that not all the factors – gross consumption demand, technology capacity, the patent protection – have a positive influence on R&D investment and the innovation trajectory. In particular, national income (GDP) has a negative effect on China's R&D expenditure, while others exert a positive one, and it is the income distribution that makes the most significant contribution to R&D investment.

The evidence suggests that the dynamics of enterprises' R&D input in China tends to demonstrate a distinct rising tendency influenced mainly by the change of market demand and China's technology state.

Due to enterprises' limited production capacity and a large domestic market, companies have few incentives to compete through innovation; that is, lower income groups sustain the profit space and it is difficult to form demand diversity to spur R&D investment and innovation. In addition, the growth of China's GDP has not turned out to be an effective demand incentive to R&D input, probably due to the income inequity. But this income inequality seems to have a significant effect on enterprises' R&D investment via the expected profits from high-priced products resulting from innovations; that is, the demand pull for innovation amounts to a pricing advantage on the higher income group.

The overseas market shows a limited and even negative influence on enterprises' R&D investment, in line with previous studies. This makes sense since exports of Chinese goods are labour-intensive and in low technology and primary-processed grade compared to exports of developed countries which are mainly capital-intensive. Although China's international trade has made extraordinary progress, both in quantity and quality (in 2007, exports of Chinese primary goods were US$61.55 billion and manufactured goods were US$1,156.47 billion), the evidence tends to suggest that its effect is still negligible, implying that there are some unresolved issues in Chinese exports that weaken the effects of exports on R&D inputs.

The improvements in the technology state have reduced the followers' innovation risk, which, in turn, may stimulate the enterprises' R&D investment and innovation. Also, China's technology advances have benefited, among other things, from spillovers, with its own absorptive R&D efforts that have driven enterprises to invest more in R&D and to compete with high-quality products for higher profit. In addition, the patent application is significant for both China's R&D expenditure and the large and medium-sized industrial enterprises' expenditures on S&T, which justifies the positive effect of patent protection.

To conclude, and more broadly, the determinants of R&D investments in China present interesting routes for developing the literature on emerging markets. In this sense, Peng (2004) suggested that future studies need to have a focus on the factors affecting the success and failure of firms in international markets. From what this chapter has presented, it is possible to argue that the combination of factors affecting investments in R&D in a developing country context is affecting the performance of companies in markets overseas in ways which have yet to be understood.

Notes

1 See, for example, Romer (1990), Grossman and Helpman (1991), Aghion and Howitt (1998), Griliches (1979, 1980), Griliches and Mairesse (1990), Coe and Helpman (1995), and Keller (2002).
2 See OECD (2004), World Bank Institute (2005).
3 The data of China's expenditure on R&D as a share of GDP in the statistic annuals may not be a good proxy of s in the market-based framework, since it includes both the R&D expenditure of enterprises and that of scientific institutions which are reallocated from the central government and insensitive to market changes. Moreover, the statistics of enterprises' expenditure on R&D do not cover the expenditure on developing new products, which is not compatible with the term defined in this chapter.

4 This idea includes a technology continuum containing the technology level from the less efficient to the most efficient ones, and where a country's technological level can move from one position to another, generally from a low to a relatively higher one. This 'level' is the technology state. The technology state of one country depends on its technology opportunity, which involves the technological advances of that country and technology spillovers from other advanced economies.

5 The data for the United States, Japan and China are from the *International Monetary Fund Report, 2007*; GDP is measured in billion current international dollars (PPPs); and labour force measured in million persons, among which China's labour force is from the *China Statistical Yearbook, 2007* (National Bureau of Statistics 2007).

6 The state space model is the common form of variable parameter model which is composed by a group of measure function and state function. Many time series models such as the classical regression model and ARMA model are all the special form of state space model.

9 Concluding remarks and final reflections

John Saee

Throughout this research book, it is manifestly self-evident that China's economy, ever since the implementation of its 'open door' policy (*Gaige Kaifang* in Chinese) to international investment and trade in the late 1970s, has been growing exponentially; so much so that China is now the growth engine for the world economy, especially in recent years.

China, the fourth largest country in terms of size after Russia, Canada and the USA is now the world's second largest economy after the USA if adjusted for differences in cost of living (purchasing power parity differences) (Economy Watch, 2010). China also represents the world's biggest emerging economy, and has already become the number one world champion with respect to international trade (UNCTAD, 2010). China is globally the largest and the most important manufacturing centre in terms of economy of scale and economy of scope for enterprises worldwide.

China has in view of its open door policy attracted US$92.4 billion in 2008 in the form of foreign direct investment (FDI), which is an increase of 23.58 per cent annually (UNCTAD, 2010). Studies show that China's foreign exchange currency reserves also increased to about US$2.4 trillion in 2009, up by US$453 billion for the year (Samuelson, 2010).

What is also evidently clear is that China is increasingly becoming a formidable global power in driving the contemporary global economy. At the same time, China, having the largest credit reserves in the world has increasingly been acquiring tangible and intangible assets and hence influential role(s) in diverse markets of Asia, Europe, Africa, and North and South Americas. For the purposes of illustration, the USA, the richest nation and the only superpower in the world, has paradoxically in recent time received loans approaching a trillion US dollars from the Chinese Government in order to fund its ailing economy. This is clearly an indication of China's rising global economic power and has major political implications worldwide. A study from UNCTAD (UNCTAD, 2008) empirically supports the notion that China has increased its outward foreign direct investment since 2000 (i.e., from US$28 billion in 2000 to US$96 billion towards the end of 2007).

The global paradigm shift in economic dimension in favour of Asia, and China in particular, in the twenty-first century provides unfettered economic opportunities and enhanced prosperity for the Asian and Chinese peoples. This prosperity is also going to enrich strategically the global community as a whole, as long as there is free trade amongst nations predicated on the fair trade principle prevailing around the world. This is why this book has been written to illuminate various facets of China. These include the Chinese economic transformation (e.g. foreign direct investment, FDI; internationalization of Chinese investment) and the Chinese cultural and global mindset, as well as Chinese enterprise dimensions coupled with corporate governance and institutional responses in China. Thus, public policymakers and entrepreneurs alike around the world can further increase their insight into the Chinese economy and the Chinese global mindset that embraces international trade.

Chapter 1   This chapter broadly provides a contextual foundation for globalization, while witnessing a sea change in the world economy with far-reaching consequences on all aspects of human civilization. It is argued that the dramatic transformation due to globalization now taking place in the global economy and in China is unprecedented. The chapter maintains that increasing availability of global capital, and major breakthroughs in computing and communications technology, together with an increased reduction of barriers to international trade and investment in the form of eliminating protectionism around the world, has catalysed the momentous globalization of national economies worldwide.

Similarly, it is contended that globalization has been a major rationale for exponential growth of foreign direct investment (FDI) in contemporary society. Specifically, FDI flows to South, East and Southeast Asia, including China, rose to a new record level in 2007, reaching US$249 billion. Key variables contributing to this exponential growth in FDI included a favourable business sentiment about the region's economies, the significant rise in cross-border M&A sales and progress towards further regional economic integration and country-specific attributes. While East Asia continued to represent the lion's share of FDI to the region, flows to South and Southeast Asia also increased significantly. China, including Hong Kong, remained the largest FDI recipients in the region (UNCTAD, 2008).

With this in perspective, China, since the initiation of economic reforms in 1979, has become one of the world's fastest-growing economies. This has resulted in China becoming increasingly a major global player in the contemporary world economy, with an unfettered potential for economic development and business opportunities for MNEs and international entrepreneurs alike.

Notwithstanding these enormous business opportunities and prospects for FDI, as illustrated in this chapter, there are still several major challenges confronting foreign enterprises (MNEs) that could potentially hamper their sustained foreign direct investment strategically. The perceived obstacles and challenges, as identified in Chapter 1, represent weak corporate governance, prevalence of corruption, unsatisfactory foreign trade policy, lack of systematic enforcement of regulations, an unsatisfactory banking system and overly cumbersome application processes for FDI, together with inadequate systematic checks and balances as well as a lack of their systematic implementation based on the rule of law in a transparent manner in China.

Chapter 2 This chapter examines the role of the Chinese Government with respect to four major issues, namely: corporate governance; ownership; and the performance and role of how the government manages the entity. A comparison is drawn to evaluate national SOEs in China internationally.

The chapter contends that, although its economy is growing exponentially, China still experiences difficulty with regard to the SOEs that are not globally competitive. It cites there being about 300,000 state-owned enterprises in China; however, the real problem lies with those very large enterprises that need ongoing subsidies to survive. These SOEs employ in the region of over 75 million people, so if one formulates the economics and political cost-benefits, it is fair to state that it would not be viable to just close them down.

The chapter persuasively argues that the government cannot constantly inject funds to maintain its ineffective public enterprises, but it does do so due to social and political reasons. This is why it makes the state-owned enterprises less inclined to adopt major restructuring and undergo much needed transformations. The Chinese Government has apparently begun implementing reforms, including monitoring mechanisms, in order to come to grips with these formidable challenges associated with the operation of Chinese SOEs strategically. The chapter states, however, that it is clear that the current administration, though cautious about the pace of these reforms, is intent on implementing a more 'free market' version of capitalism, but they are not unaware of the risks involved.

Chapter 2 succinctly supports the thesis that organizational adaptation over time requires managers to alter their organizations' modus operandi based on environmental dynamics. For example, as competitive pressure escalates, it will become increasingly important that organizations make quick responses to the changing competitive landscape. Thus, it is imperative that managers recognize the strategic and organizational implications of (or requirements for) competing in changing environmental contexts (Slevin and Covin, 1997).

In China's case, the transformation of the economy was not an action but the result of reform. The transition has essentially opened the economy to the entrance and emergence of new business participants and opportunities. As a result, despite the turbulence and chaos in the environment, with sufficient time, firms have gradually transformed themselves and adopted a new set of strategic orientations.

The chapter concludes by arguing that the co-existence, competition and struggle between two competing systems have led to a transition process with unique 'Chinese characteristics'. And the economy continues to grow. With the reforms underway this also means that no organization will be given preferential treatment and that all will be treated the same under the national regulations.

Chapter 3 The view held in this chapter is that globalization of the world economy has had far-reaching implications for the existing organizational structures and hence their management practices around the world, and this includes management of enterprises in China. As a result, many organizations now recognize that they can increase their flexibility and responsiveness in globally competitive market environments through deployment of transnational project teams, powerful vehicles to develop innovation and change within their companies. Such teams consist of members with multiple nationalities, working on activities that transcend national borders.

The chapter outlines the need for project management that has arisen as a result of a number of emerging environmental forces in the contemporary global economy. Of the many emerging environmental forces involved, three feature more prominently:

- the growing demand for complex, sophisticated, customized goods and services;
- the exponential expansion of human knowledge; and
- intense competition among firms for profit maximization and provision of quality service fostered by globalization of the contemporary market economy.

In this chapter, an attempt has been made to understand the dynamics of project management, including international project management. Several challenges arising from project management by MNCs in China have also been identified. The chapter also discusses what strategies and best practice are to be adopted to render the project globally successful. It has been emphasized that the factors identified as crucial must be considered by management, in order to develop appropriate strategies to follow the best practice in international project management. China is no exception to this.

The chapter states that project management across professional, national, and cultural frontiers, including in China, is highly complex. The project manager's responsibility is to manage across these systems in order to meet specific business objectives within a finite timeline. The need to identify, distinguish and respond effectively to a distinct set of managerial requirements, thus becomes the foremost challenge facing international project managers. Consequently, in this chapter, various factors are identified that are crucial in the context of project management across cultures and must be considered in order to develop appropriate strategies to follow the best practice in international project management with reference to China. The conclusion that may be drawn is that in order for the firms to excel in international project management, they have to carefully consider and implement appropriate strategies relating to the following critical factors: conceptualization and initiation; project plan; communication; organization; organizational support; human subsystems; breaking the project into bite size chunks; client consultation and acceptance; education and training; and the product perspective.

Finally, most international projects often are identified by a weakness in either strategy or tactics that leads to different types of errors. Thus, the major challenge facing international project managers is to ensure that the tactics pursued in an international project are entirely complementary to the overall project management strategy. Furthermore, international project managers will greatly benefit by developing high-level intercultural communication competence, deemed an essential ingredient in managing successfully a culturally diverse project management team in China and globally.

Chapter 4   Here it is argued that, consistent with China's rising global economic power, the automobile industry generally has been recording massive growth rate recently. China, for the first time, surpassed the USA to take the global lead in car sales. Owing in large measure to anaemic sales growth in much of the developed world and targeted stimulus measures introduced in January 2009, China's automobile industry appears to have reached a critical milestone in its development and growth. Domestic industry dynamics notwithstanding, China's leading automobile companies have made little secret of their outward internationalization ambitions in recent years.

Outward internationalization is also being championed by the Chinese Government as a central pillar of a comprehensive and ambitious new automotive strategy. While confidence in successful near-term global expansion may well be premature, China's medium- to long-term impact on the global automobile industry will be as inevitable as it will be transformational. This chapter provided a contextual assessment of the motivations, prospects and challenges facing the Chinese automobile industry as it aims to shift gears and merge into the global automotive lanes.

This chapter also establishes that the Chinese automotive sector has been characterized by deep market fragmentation and cut-throat competition between state-owned and private automotive concerns, owing largely to a combination of bureaucratic means and market mechanisms on the one hand and de facto decentralization on the other hand (Richet and Ruet, 2008). By pushing for the consolidation of smaller car companies (Shirouzu, 2009c), the Chinese Government hopes to simultaneously pre-empt overcapacity risks and to nurture the development and growth of a small number of 'national champion' manufacturers with a strong potential to compete in the international arena.

At the same time, however, research study in this chapter has also acknowledged short- to medium-term competitive liabilities and disadvantages relative to global safety, quality control and emissions standards, and has been putting on the brakes by tightening export rules at a time when many of them appear poised to floor it (*China Daily*, 2007). In particular, the Chinese Government appears to have internalized the dangers of irrational market expansion, including ill-advised and counterproductive M&A deals (*China Daily*, 2009b; Xinhua, 2009) and potential costs and setback related to premature exports to the European and the US car markets, as evidenced by Japanese and South Korean car manufacturers' initial forays in the 1970s and 1980s, respectively. According to an industry analyst, much of the hype surrounding nascent international ambitions of Chinese carmakers appears at best premature, as '[T]hese export aspirations are a marketing tactic, not a real solid opportunity. But it's certainly a possibility in the future' (Associated Press, 2009).

The chapter concludes by arguing that in the near-term, the most immediately plausible impact of China on the global automotive industry will be in the form of foreign companies using the country as a lower-cost production base to serve the global car market. General Motors is said to have already expressed its intention to import cars from China to the USA, beginning in 2011. Hence, even if a Chinese 'economic tsunami' in the global automotive arena does not appear to be imminent, the question is not one of whether it will reach the shores of developed markets, but rather when it will do so. And once it does, the prospects of Chinese car manufacturers sweeping away Western car companies, or at the very least engendering a fundamental restructuring of the global automotive industry, will be all too real indeed.

Chapter 5 It is asserted in this chapter that the massive injection of foreign direct investment (FDI) into China has been followed by the phenomenal growth of China's outward FDI in recent years. The study in this chapter in citing data from UNCTAD (2008) shows that the volume of China's FDI outflow recorded an average annual growth of almost 55 per cent during the period 2002–2007.

While there has been an exponential growth of scholarly literature on FDI into China, an important issue, namely FDI location choice of Chinese firms, has not yet been empirically examined in the literature. The research study in this chapter was designed to address this theoretical gap.

With this mind, an investigation is made of the impact of economic factors and institutional forces on FDI location choice of Chinese multinational firms in the Asian region.

Meanwhile, a holistic conceptual framework is developed by synthesizing the two theoretical constructs of the eclectic paradigm and three dimensions (regulative, normative and cognitive) of institutions. This framework was empirically tested by using panel data of Chinese outward FDI in eight Asian economies covering the period from 1995 to 2007. The study in this chapter found that while both types of factors influence FDI location choice of Chinese investing firms in Asia, institutional factors demonstrated a higher level of complexity and diversity in determining FDI location choice in comparison with the impact from economic factors. The study argues that location choice of Chinese FDI is associated with relative differences in regulative and normative institutions between China and host economies, while the cognitive mindset that is proxied as the transaction intensity of Chinese exports exerts a significant impact. The study further reveals that location choices by Chinese firms have different patterns for different economy groups while demonstrating a dynamic change for different time frames.

The study in this chapter concludes that empirical results demonstrate the importance of factors from both the eclectic paradigm and institutional approach in explaining location choice by Chinese firms in the Asian region, as eight of the nine main variables tested in the study, except GDP growth, have been found significant to some extent in affecting the location choice of Chinese FDI.

Two implications can be drawn from the empirical findings regarding FDI location choice. First, empirical evidence from this study suggests that while traditional economic factors have a major role to play in affecting MNEs' decisions on FDI location, institutional factors may matter more and they demonstrate a higher level of complexity and diversity in determining FDI location choice. Further, a comparison of findings from the modelling analysis on the full sample and four subsamples reveals that generally speaking, the influence of traditional economic factors is more stable and seems to have a more fixed pattern, and that the impacts of institutional variables are more diversified and dynamic, while demonstrating more complex relationships between institutional factors and FDI location choice. Thus, it can be inferred that institutional variables play a more dynamic and also more significant role in the FDI location choices of Chinese firms.

In addition, the findings from this study suggests that while the mainstream FDI theories and frameworks regarding FDI location choice, which were generated mainly from studies on developed economies, are still applicable in the case for FDI outflows from China, some important theoretical modifications and extensions are needed in explaining FDI location choice by Chinese firms. Among the traditional variables, market size and potential have long been considered as the most important determinants for market-seeking FDI. Contrary to this, findings from this study reveal that absolute market size and market growth of the host economies did not affect or even negatively affect FDI location choices by Chinese MNEs.

On the whole, Chinese investors seek FDI involvements in economies with a higher level of market-oriented economic freedom. Chinese firms preferred locations where political and legal institutions resembled their home environment. Furthermore, the change of impacting direction from variable economic freedom indicates the dynamic evolution of institutional forces at home. These empirical findings provide strong support for the notion that distinctive and highly dynamic institutional forces at home contribute to the uniqueness of FDI location choices by Chinese firms.

The chapter also outlines a number of limitations arising from this study, including variables used in the study that may not accurately measure the institutional forces in play and the difficulty in measuring the behavioural pattern of investing firms using aggregate archival data. Finally, the research in this study recommends a bigger sample size of locations for FDI outflows from China and from a broad context of emerging economies, such as India, Brazil or Mexico.

Chapter 6   Here it has been advocated that China has spawned unprecedented and unfettered business opportunities for entrepreneurs and international firms due to increasing globalization of its economy. However, cultural differences coupled with a lack of intercultural competence have been the main reasons why many Western entrepreneurs and enterprises have been slow and in some case failed to achieve significant inroads into the Chinese market. In particular, the study in this chapter cites many barriers that are due to a lack of an understanding of cultural difference, including stereotypes and ethnocentrism, leading to prejudice resulting in mistrust and hostility.

Other impediments to effective intercultural interactions with the Chinese counterparts include fear of change, fear of the unknown, fear of threatened identity, fear of rejection, and/or fear of contradictions to a belief system. The study also reveals many outcomes of poor or ineffective intercultural communication with Chinese counterparts and the most notable one is the culture shock.

The mere shock of entering a different culture influences our abilities to communicate competently in those situations. For the participants, the results of poor intercultural communication seem obvious. These include incorrect assumptions, lack of understanding, prejudices, anger, and disrespect. One area of concern in intercultural communication is culture shock. Culture shock is a powerful result of poor intercultural communication skills. Culture shock is the emotional result of not being able to fulfil the basic need of understanding, controlling, and predicting others' behaviors.

(Furnham, 1987; Saee, 2005, 2006)

The study provides an examination of the Chinese cultural dimensions and their pervasive impact upon business practices that are prevalent in China, along with a scholarly examination of the various dimensions of intercultural communication competence, an understanding of which is a key indicator of intercultural competence.

The chapter concludes by stating that for entrepreneurs to successfully operate enterprises and business relationships in China, they may have to consider a number of issues. First, they are outsiders (lacking Guanxi) and thus they need to establish connections, and second, particularly for Westerners, there are huge cultural differences. These cultural differences can cause difficulty in aligning corporate and personal goals that may lead to differences in management style, and can lead to misunderstandings and mistrust. Consequently, it would take a great deal of developing cultural awareness and sensitivity on the part of the Western entrepreneurs so as to avoid such problems with Chinese business partners. Cultural adaptation to the Chinese cultural milieu on the part of the entrepreneurs and Western enterprises is recommended in terms of their corporate strategy and modus operandi. Developing globally intercultural competence can be of immense benefit to Western executives/firms in terms of promoting effectively international trade with China, one that is rapidly becoming a giant economic powerhouse in the twenty-first century.

Chapter 7   The research study in this chapter examines the effects of a proposed free trade agreement (FTA) between Australia and China with reference to the Australian textiles and service industries. The study also looks at various issues, including the free trade negotiations, the growing economic partnership between the countries and internationally, China's rapid economic growth and the history as well as the current state of the Australian textiles industry.

Theories that justify free trade between the two countries, which have considerable implications for mutual economic benefits, are also analysed.

At the other end of the spectrum, the negative consequences that arise from FTAs, are discussed with international reference and implications. The chapter concludes by citing numerous benefits arising from free trade agreements between the countries concerned.

In contrast to industry protectionism, the study strongly argues that the longer an industry remains under protective policies, the more uncompetitive it becomes.

The Australian Government in recognizing this, eliminated quota and tariff on textile related products that in turn rendered the Australian textile industry increasingly competitive. Consequently, the Australian firms can import from anywhere, as there are no longer quotas.

Given the controversial nature of the export of the Chinese textile products (i.e. being labelled by some analysts as social dumping), the study still argues that Australia, in this instance, cannot compete with China in regards to labour costs re the textile industry sector; however, the Australian TCF industry has demonstrated its resilience and technological innovations, thus becoming internationally competitive while generating a substantial amount of revenue and employment. The study in this chapter found that there has also been a focus on consumer responsiveness through innovations such as 'quick response'. Off shoring and outworkers have also been used to assist the industry. Glo-Weave was cited as an excellent example of how a textile company can adapt to the various aspects of global competition. They have reduced their workforce and saved costs by establishing offshore manufacturing bases. They have also become a niche company by focusing on quick stock delivery and on specialized textiles.

Chapter 8   This research study first of all, argues that R&D investment rate as a share of GDP is mainly determined by the market demand, technological capacity and the extent of patent protection. It examines the potential determinants of China's increasing R&D expenditure, which has jumped from 0.62 per cent in 1987 to 1.42 per cent in 2006. The research is justified by the fact that existing literature surrounding R&D addresses mainly productivity and growth issues but studies on R&D's determinants are scarce. Thus, this study addresses this gap by exploring the determinants of China's increasing R&D expenditure within a comprehensive framework. It also compares China's technology capacity against countries in the frontier, while attempting to identify potential determinants of China's expenditure on R&D. The findings show that the enhancement of technology capacity in China, benefiting mainly from technology transfers from advanced countries, could reduce the innovation risk and spur the host's R&D expenditure, whereas various factors of enlarged market demand would have a complex effect on enterprises' R&D investment: compared to the enterprises' production ability, such a large market, especially the demand of the lower income class on necessities, would impede China's further R&D investment and the major incentive for further R&D investment could arise from the advantage of serving the high-income group.

This research deduces that not all the factors – gross consumption demand, technology capacity, the patent protection – have a positive influence on R&D investment and innovation trajectory. In particular, national income (GDP) has a negative effect on China's R&D expenditure while others exert a positive one and it is the income distribution that makes the most significant contribution to R&D investment.

The evidence amassed in this study suggests that the dynamics of enterprises' R&D input in China tends to demonstrate a distinct rising tendency influenced mainly by the change of market demand and China's technology state.

Due to enterprises' limited production capacity and a large domestic market, companies have few incentives to compete through innovation; that is, lower income groups sustain the profit space and it is difficult to form demand diversity to spur R&D investment and innovation. In addition, the growth of China's GDP has not turned out to be an effective demand incentive to R&D input, probably due to the income inequity. But this income inequality seems to have a significant effect on enterprises' R&D investment via the expected profits from high-priced products resulting from innovations; that is, the demand pull for innovation amounts to the pricing advantage on the higher income group.

In the final analysis, an increasing prosperity for China, made possible through China's having adopted an open door policy to international trade and investment, is a great development for Chinese society and the world as a whole, since the mission of humanity ought to be eliminating poverty wherever it exists on earth so that peoples of different communities are liberated from their miserable existential needs.

With this in perspective, economic development ought to embrace comprehensive community development whereby public policies by different governments, including China, are made to achieve a number of objectives: provide access to free education to their peoples (no matter where and how remotely they live in their respective communities); provide them with equal opportunities to expanding labour markets; provide equal access to quality health care for their citizens; and eliminating corruption through the implementation and enforcement of a systematic regulatory framework that embraces thorough checks and balances based on a rule of law which is equally transparent and equitable to all.

Finally, economic development in China and elsewhere in the world will be incomplete and superficial without their citizens fully enjoying and hence exercising their innate and inalienable rights to be free.

In contrast to its past cultural revolutionary phase that caused enormous misery and suffering, including abject poverty to millions of Chinese citizens, China has ostensibly made enormous progress in the economic sphere. It has achieved this through its government adopting a wise economic open-door policy since 1979; this has lifted hundreds of millions of Chinese out of their poverty and thus it is a tribute to the Chinese leadership and the enterprising spirit of the Chinese people.

Reflecting strategically, China has even greater prospects on the horizon; however, the challenges still ahead for China are: eliminating the prevalence of corruption within the wider Chinese society; reducing huge disparity of incomes and living standards between rural and urban regions through diffusing prosperity to all regions in China based on economic and social development; a considerable reduction in environmental pollution; and concurrently opening up its society to greater freedom for its citizens while adhering and promoting comprehensively the universality and inalienability of human rights. This greater freedom involves the liberty of individuals with respect to their freedom of expression, freedom of the press, freedom of assembly and freedom of religion, coupled with an impartial rule of law applicable to all its citizens in a transparent manner.

All societies and their respective governments, which relentlessly pursue the foregoing strategic mission and objectives, have a greater chance to prosper sustainably and China is no exception to this.

Bibliography

Accenture (2005) 'China spreads its wings – Chinese companies go global', Accenture Policy and Corporate Affairs Group. Available at http://www.accenture.com/NR/rdonlyres/6A4C9C07-8C84-4287-9417-203DF3E6A3D1/0/Chinaspreadsitswings.pdf (accessed 13 December 2010).

Acemoglu, D. and Newman, A. (2002) 'The labor market and corporate structure', *European Economic Review*, 46: 1733–1756.

Adler, N. (1997) *International Dimensions of Organizational Behavior* (3rd edn), Cincinnati, OH: South-Western College Publishing.

Aghion, P. and Howitt, P. (1998) *Endogenous Growth Theory*, Cambridge, MA: MIT Press.

Aitken, B. and Harrison, A. (1999) 'Do domestic firms benefit from direct foreign investment? Evidence from Venezuela', *American Economic Review*, 89: 605–618.

Ali, S. and Guo, W. (2005) 'Determinants of FDI in China', *Journal of Global Business and Technology*, 1(2): 21–33.

Alibaba.com Corporation (2006) *Nantong YINGLAN Fashion Co., Ltd.* 2. Available at http://yinglan.en.alibaba.com/aboutus.html (accessed 15 June 2006).

Allen, S. and NZPA (2006) *Goff's Slow Boat to China*, in: bilaterals.org – everything that's not happening at the WTO releases 2006. Available at http://www.bilaterals.org/spip.php?article4070&lang=en (accessed 17 November 2010).

Alon, I., Fetscherin, M. and Sardy, M. (2008) 'Geely Motors: A Chinese automaker enters international markets', *International Journal of Chinese Culture and Management*, 1(4): 489–498.

Alvi, E., Mukherjee, D. and Eid, A. (2007) 'Do patent protection and technology transfer facilitate R&D in developed and emerging countries? A semiparametric study', *Atlantic Economic Journal*, 35: 217–231.

Amiti, M. and Smarzynska Javorcik, B. (2008) 'Trade costs and location of foreign firms in China', *Journal of Development Economics*, 85(1–2): 129–149.

Andreosso-O'Callaghan, B. and Wei, X. (2003) 'EU FDI in China: Locational determinants and its role in China's hinterland', in: *Proceedings of the 15th Annual Conference of the Association for Chinese Economics Studies* (ACESA), 2–3 October 2003, Melbourne, VIC. Available at http://mams.rmit.edu.au/6fe09elc6t8sz.pdf (accessed 5 January 2011).

Answers.com (2010) 'Free trade', in: Answers Corporation Random House Word Menu 2010. Available at http://www.answers.com/topic/free-trade (accessed 20 November 2010).

AP (Associated Press) (2009) 'GM looks to China to bolster US sales'. Available at http://www.msnbc.msn.com/id/30793097/ns/business-autos/ (accessed 16 December 2010).

Armstrong, C.E. and Shimuzu, K. (2007) 'A review of approaches to empirical research on the resource-based view of the firm', *Journal of Management*, 33(6): 959–986.

Ashton, K. and Ryan, S. (eds) (2000) 'Glo-Weave', Frances Burke Textile Resource Centre School of Fashion and Textiles, RMIT University, Melbourne, VIC.

AusIndustry (2003) *Expanded Overseas Assembly Provisions (EOAP) Scheme Guidelines*, AusIndustry – An Australian Government Initiative. Available at http://www.ausindustry.gov.au/library/EOAPGuidelinesDecember0320051103045047.pdf (accessed 18 June 2006).

Australian Science and Technology Heritage Centre (eds) (2000) 'Australian innovation in textile', in: *Technology in Australia 1788–1988*, Australian Science and Technology Heritage Centre Online Edition 2000, Melbourne, VIC. Available at http://www.austehc.unimelb.edu.au/tia/about.html (accessed 5 November 2010).

Automotive Business Review (2006) 'Chinese car exports may bypass mature markets', 2 February.

AutoWeb (2006) 'Intellectual property theft in the automotive industry: Scope, trends, and mitigating strategies'. Available at http://legacy.autoweb.net/web2006/pdf/ip%20theft.pdf (accessed 28 January 2010).

AWI, Australian Wool Innovation Ltd (2006) *China Free Trade Agreement*. Available at http://www.wool.com.au/LivePage.aspx?pageId=2130 (accessed 15 September 2006).

Babones, S. J. and Alvarez-Rivadulla, M.J. (2007) 'Standardized income inequality data for use in cross-national research', *Sociological Inquiry*, 77: 3–22.

Backhouse, R. (1985) *A History of Modern Economic Analysis*, New York: Basil Blackwell Ltd.

Baker, B.N., Murphy, D.C. and Fisher, D. (1983) 'Factors affecting project success', in: D.I Cleland and D.R. King (eds), *Project Management Handbook,* New York: Van Nostrand, pp. 669–685.

Baker, K. (2007) *Economic Tsunami: China's Car Industry Will Sweep Away Western Car Makers*, Dural, NSW: Rosenberg Publishing.

Baltagi, B. (2005) *Econometric Analysis of Panel Data*. New York: John Wiley & Sons.

Barney, J.B. (1991) 'Firm resources and sustained competitive advantage', *Journal of Management*, 17(1): 99–120.

Barrell, R. and Pain, N. (1997) 'Foreign direct investment, technological change and economic growth within Europe', *Economic Journal,* 107: 243–265.

Bartlett, C. and Ghoshal, S. (1997) 'The myth of a generic manager: New personal competencies for new management roles', *California Management Review,* 40(1): 92–116.

Beamish, P.W. (1993) 'The characteristics of joint ventures in the People's Republic of China', *Journal of International Marketing*, 1: 29–48.

Bebczuk, R.N. (2002) 'R&D expenditures and the role of government', *Estudios de Economía*, 29: 109–121.

Benn, R. (1996) 'Adult learning, cultural diversity and ethnoknowledge', paper presented at the Annual SCUTREA Conference, 2–4 July 1996, University of Leeds.

Berger, C.R. (1979) 'Beyond initial interactions', in: H. Giles and R. St Clair (eds), *Language and Social Psychology*, London: Edward Arnold, pp. 122–144.

Berger, C.R. and Calabrese, R. (1975) 'Some explorations in initial interactions and beyond', *Human Communication Research*, 5: 99–112.

Bettis, R.A. and Hitt, M.A. (1995) 'The new competitive landscape', *Strategic Management Journal*, 16 (Special issue): 7–19.

Bevan, A. and Estrin, S. (2004) 'The determinants of foreign direct investment into European transition economies', *Journal of Comparative Economics,* 32(4): 775–787.

Bevan, A., Estrin, S. and Meyer, K. (2004) 'Foreign investment location and institutional development in transition economies', *International Business Review,* 13: 43–64.

Bhardwaj, A., Diets, J. and Beamish, P. (2007) 'Host country culture influences on foreign direct investment', *Management International Review,* 47(1): 29–50.

bilaterals.org (2005) *China, Australia Inch Closer to FTA Talks,* in: bilaterals. org – everything that's not happening at the WTO releases 2005. Available at http://www.bilaterals.org/spip.php?article1517&lang=en (accessed 29 November 2010).

bilaterals.org (2006a) *China Established Nine FTAs in Past Five Years,* in: bilaterals. org – everything that's not happening at the WTO releases 2006. Available at http://www.bilaterals.org/spip.php?article3779&lang=en (accessed 7 December 2010).

bilaterals.org (2006b) *US FTAs,* in: bilaterals.org 2006 – everything that's not happening at the WTO releases 2006. Available at http://www.bilaterals.org/rubrique.php3?id_rubrique=55&var_recherche=US (accessed 20 April 2006).

Bo, Z. (2000) 'Economic development and corruption: Beijing beyond "Beijing"', *Journal of Contemporary China,* 9(25): 467–487.

Bolduc, D.A. (2006) 'Brilliance faces safety issues – Chinese brand promises quick fix for failed side-impact test', *Automotive News Europe,* 11(25): 6.

Bolman, L.G. and Deal, E.D. (1997) *Reframing Organisations* (2nd edn), San Francisco, CA: Jossey-Bass Inc.

Bowerman, B., O'Connel, R. and Koehler, A. (2005) *Forecasting, Time Series, and Regression.* Cole, CA: Thomas Brooks.

Bown, C.P. (2009) 'U.S.–China trade conflicts and the future of the WTO', *Fletcher Forum of World Affairs Journal,* 33(1): 27–48.

Braendle, U.C., Gasser, T. and Noll, J. (2005) 'Corporate governance in China – Is economic growth potential hindered by Guanxi?', *Business & Society Review,* 110(4): 389–405.

Braunerhjelm, P. and Svenson, R. (1996) 'Host country characteristics and agglomeration in foreign direct investment', *Applied Economics,* 28: 833–840.

Briggs, C. and Dodyk, P. (2006) 'Understanding the project management process in China', Study #04-9369. Available at www.pmi.org/Knowledge-Center/~/media/PDF/Surveys/pp_dodyk.ashx (accessed 17 December, 2010).

Brown, O. (2005) *AUSTRALIA WATCH: Long March for Australia, China FTA,* in: bilaterals.org – everything that's not happening at the WTO. Available at http://www.bilaterals.org/spip.php?article1718&lang=en (accessed 1 December 2010).

Brown, S.L. and, Eisenhardt, K.M. (1997) 'The art of continuous change: Linking complexity theory and time-paced evolution in relentlessly shifting organizations', *Administrative Science Quarterly,* 42(1): 1–34.

Bruton, G.D., Lau, C.M., Lu, Y. and Rubanik, Y. (2004) 'The impact of institutional differences: Strategic orientation differences between two emerging markets', in: *Conference Proceedings of Asia Academy of Management Conference,* Shanghai, China, May 2004.

Buckley, P.J. and Casson, M. (1976) *The Future of Multinational Enterprises,* Macmillan: London.

Buckley, P.J., Clegg, L.J., Cross, A.R., Liu, X., Voss, H. and Zheng, P. (2007) 'The determinants of Chinese outward foreign direct investment', *Journal of International Business Studies,* 38: 499–518.

Buckley, P.J., Cross, A.R., Tan, H., Liu, X. and Voss, H. (2008) 'Historical and emergent trends in Chinese outward direct investment', *Management International Review,* 48(6): 715–748.

Burgess, V. (2004) 'Players await procurement rules', Factiva, 12 November, Document AFNR000020041111e0bc0005g. Available at http://global.factiva.com.ezproxy.lib.swin.edu. au/en/eSrch/ss_hl.asp (accessed 12 November 2004).

Business Monitor International (2010) *China Business Forecast Report Q2 2010*, (AN 48001771), London: BIM, p7-7.

Cai, K.G. (1999) 'Outward foreign direct: A novel dimension of China's integration into the regional and global economy', *The China Quarterly,* 160: 856–880.

Callick, R. (2005) 'China trade deal far from free', *Australian Financial Review*, 18 March, John Fairfax Holdings Limited, Document AFNR000020050317e13i0003r, viewed 1 June 2006.

Caselli, F. and Wilson, D.J. (2004) 'Importing technology', *Journal of Monetary Economics*, 51: 1–32.

CEDA, Committee for Economic Development of Australia (2005) *China's Future in Australia*, Melbourne, VIC: CEDA,

CEDA, Committee for Economic Development of Australia (2010) *Growth 55: China in Australia's Future*, CEDA. Available at http://www.ceda.com.au/research/previous-topics/research/2009/11/growth-report/growth55.aspx (accessed 2 November 2010).

Chadee, D.D., Qui, F. and Rose, E.L. (2003) 'FDI location at the subnational level: A study of EJVs in China', *Journal of Business Research*, 56: 835–845.

Charnes, A., Cooper, W. and Rhodes, E. (1978) 'Measuring the efficiency of decision and making units', *European Journal of Operational Research*, 2: 429–444.

Chen, H.M. and Chen, T.J. (1998) 'Network linkages and location choice in foreign direct investment', *Journal of International Business Studies,* 29: 445–467.

Chen, M. (1994) 'Guanxi and the Chinese art of network building', *New Asia Review,* Summer: 40–43.

Chen, M. (1995) *Asian Management Systems,* London: Routledge.

Chen, M. and MacMillan, I.C. (1992) 'Nonresponse and delayed response to competitive moves: The roles of competitor dependence and action irreversibility', *Academy of Management Journal*, 35: 539–570.

Chen, M.J. and Miller, D. (1994) 'Competitive attack, retaliation and performance: An expectancy-valence framework', *Strategic Management Journal*, 15: 85–102.

Chen, Y. and Puttitanum, T. (2005) 'Intellectual property rights and innovation in developing countries', *Journal of Development Economics*, 78: 474–493.

Cheng, L.K. and Kwan, Y.K. (2000) 'What are the determinants of the location of foreign direct investment: The Chinese experience', *Journal of International Economics,* 51(2): 379–400.

Cheng, S. and Stough, R.R. (2007) 'The pattern and magnitude of China's outward FDI in Asia', in: R.S. Rajan, R. Kumar and N.Virgill (eds), *New Dimensions of Economic Globalization: Surge of Outward Foreign Direct Investment from Asia*, London: Imperial College Press.

Child, J. and Rodrigues, S.B. (2005) 'The internationalisation of Chinese firms: A case for theoretical extension?', *Management and Organisation Review,* 1(3): 381–410.

Child, J. and Tsai, D. (2005) 'The dynamic between firms' environmental strategies and institutional constraints in emerging economies: Evidence from China and Taiwan', *Journal of Management Studies*, 42: 95–125.

China Daily (2005) 'China's car makers ready to go global?' 17 April. Available at http://www.chinadaily.com.cn/english/doc/2005-04/17/content_434882.htm (accessed 21 February 2010).

China Daily (2007) 'China plans stricter auto export rules', 2 January. Available at http://www.chinadaily.com.cn/china/2007-01/02/content_773224.htm (accessed 21 February 2010).

China Daily (2009a) 'China's automobiles struggling to enter EU market', 12 December. Available at http://www.chinadaily.com.cn/bizchina/2009-12/08/content_9140762.htm (accessed 21 February 2010).

China Daily (2009b) 'China's car companies "must learn" GM lesson', 29 June. Available at http://www.chinadaily.com.cn/cndy/2009-06/29/content_8331466.htm (accessed 21 February 2010).

China Daily Information Company (2004) *China Presses EU on Market Economy Status*. Available at http://www.chinadaily.com.cn/english/doc/2004-06/29/content_343941. htm (accessed 15 October 2010).

China Daily Information Company (2006) 'EU could start 'dumping' investigations'*, China Daily News*, 10 May 2006, Factiva, Document BDU0000020060510e25a00011 (accessed 15 April 2006).

China Internet Information Center (2006a) *Year 2001: Results on Measuring China's Market Economy and the Comparison on Domestic and Overseas Researches*. Available at http://www.china.org.cn/english/2003chinamarket/79436.htm (accessed 5 January 2010).

China Internet Information Center (2006b) *EU: Market Economy Status Underway*. Available at http://www.china.org.cn/english/BAT/170844.htm (accessed 16 November 2010).

Chung, C.H., Fung, H.G. and Kwan, F.Y. (2005) 'Corporate governance and reforms', *China & World Economy*, 13(5): 28–42.

Churchill, G.A. (1991) *Marketing Research: Methodological Foundation*, (5th edn), Chicago, IL: The Dryden Press.

CIA, Central Intelligence Agency (2006) 'China 2006', in: *CIA – The World Factbook*. Available at https://www.cia.gov/library/publications/the-world-factbook/geos/ch.html (accessed 15 February 2006).

Clarke, A. (1999) 'A practice use of key success factors to improve the effectiveness of project', *International Journal of Project Management*, 17: 139–145.

Clutterbuck, D. (1989) 'Breaking through the cultural barriers', *International Management*, December: 41–42.

Coe, D.T. and Helpman, E. (1995) 'International R&D spillovers', *European Economic Review*, 39: 859–887.

Coe, D.T., Helpman, E. and Hoffmaister, A.W. (1997) 'North–South R&D spillovers', *Economic Journal*, 107: 134–149.

Cohen,W.M. and Levinthal, D.A. (1989) 'Innovation and learning: The two faces of R&D,' *The Economic Journal*, 99: 569–596

Cohen, W.M., Nelson, R.R. and Walsh, J. (2000) 'Protecting their intellectual assets: Appropriability conditions and why U.S. manufacturing firms patent (or not)', NBER Working Paper No. W7552. Available at http://www.nber.org/papers/w7552.

Commonwealth of Australia (2003) *Review of TCF Assistance 31 July 2003*, Inquiry Report, No. 26. Available at http://www.pc.ov.au/__data/assets/pdf_file/0020/26822/tcf. pdf (accessed 7 December 2010).

Corporate Financing Week (2009) 'Ups and downs: China's erratic path to auto superpower'. Available at http://www.corporatefinancingweek.com/file/84238/ups-and-downs-chinas-erratic-path-to-auto-superpower.html (accessed 10 January 2010).

Cotton Australia (2010a) *Fact Sheet Booklet*. Available at http://www.cottonaustralia.com. au/media/Fact_Sheet_Booklet.183.pdf (accessed 2 December 2010).

Cotton Australia (2010b) *Facts and Figures - Research and Technology*. Available at http:// www.cottonaustralia.com.au/facts/factsandfigures.aspx?id=13 (accessed 18 December 2010).

Coughlin, C.C., Terva, V. and Arromdee, V. (1991) 'State characteristics and the location of foreign direct investment within the United States', *The Review of Economics and Statistics*, 73: 675–683.

Cui, L. and Jiang, F. (2009) 'FDI entry mode choice of Chinese MNCs: A strategic behaviour perspective', *The Journal of World Business*, 44: 434–444.

Culem, C.G. (1988) 'The location determinants of direct investment among industrialized countries', *European Economic Review*, 32: 885–904.

Cullen, J.B. (1999) *Multinational Management: A Strategic Approach*, Cincinnati, OH: South-Western College Publishing.

D'Andrade, R.G. (1984) 'Culture meaning system', in: R.A. Shweder and R.A. LeVine (eds), *Culture Theory: Essays on Mind, Self and Emotion*, Cambridge: Cambridge University Press, pp. 88–119.

Darwar, N. and Frost, T. (1999) 'Competing with giants – Survival strategy for local companies in emerging markets', *Harvard Business Review*, 77(2): 119–129.

Daude, C. and Stein, E. (2007) 'The quality of institutions and foreign direct investment', *Economics and Politics*, 19(3): 317–344.

De Oliveria, P.S., Bolduc, D.A. and Webb, A. (2006) 'Despite obstacles, Chinese carmakers are keen to come to Europe', *Automotive News Europe*, 11(25): 24.

Deng, P. (2001) 'WFOEs: The most popular entry mode into China', *Business Horizons*, 44(4): 63–72.

Deng, P. (2004) 'Outward investment by Chinese MNCs: Motivations and implications', *Business Horizons*, 47(3): 8–16.

Deng, P. (2007) 'Investing for strategic resources and its rational: The case of outward FDI from Chinese companies', *Business Horizons*, 50(1): 71–81.

Deng, P. (2009) 'Why do Chinese firms tend to acquire strategic assets in international expansion?', *Journal of World Business*, 44: 74-84.

Department of Commerce Hubei Province (2006) *Acquisition of Wuhan Yudahua Group Co., Ltd.* Available at http://english.hbdofcom.gov.cn/file/2006/1-18/113722.html (accessed 15 June 2006).

DFAT, Department of Foreign Affairs and Trade, Australian Government (1997) *Background Guide to the Australia New Zealand Economic Relationship*. Available at http://www.dfat.gov.au/geo/new_zealand/anz_cer/cer.pdf (accessed 10 November 2010).

DFAT, Department of Foreign Affairs and Trade, Australian Government (2001a) *'Australia's Trade: Influences into the New Millennium*. Available at http://www.dfat.gov.au/publications/newmillennium/australia_trade.pdf (accessed 15 December 2010).

DFAT, Department of Foreign Affairs and Trade, Australian Government (2001b) *An Australia–USA Free Trade Agreement: Issues and Implications*. Available at http://www.dfat.gov.au/publications/aus_us_fta_mon/aus_us_fta_mon.pdf (accessed 15 December 2010).

DFAT, Department of Foreign Affairs and Trade, Australian Government (2005a) *Australia–China Free Trade Agreement Joint Feasibility Study*. Available at http://www.dfat.gov.au/fta/china/feasibility_full.pdf (accessed 29 December 2010).

DFAT, Department of Foreign Affairs and Trade, Australian Government (2005b) *The AUSTA: Facts at a Glance*. Available at http://www.dfat.gov.au/trade/negotiations/us_fta/fact_sheets/ausfta_at_a_glance.pdf (accessed 10 March 2006).

DFAT, Department of Foreign Affairs and Trade, Australian Government (2005c) *Accessing the World's Largest Procurement Market*. Available at http://www.dfat.gov.au/trade/negotiations/us_fta/fact_sheets/Government_Procurement.pdf (accessed 1 May 2005).

DFAT, Department of Foreign Affairs and Trade, Australian Government (2005d) *China: Market Economy Status*. Available at http://www.dfat.gov.au/geo/china/fta/market_economy_status.html (accessed 7 December 2010).

DFAT, Department of Foreign Affairs and Trade, Australian Government (2006a) *Fact Sheet: Australia's Free Trade Agreements: An Essential Guide*. Available at http://www.dfat.gov.au/trade/fs_fta_essential_guide.html (accessed 14 August 2006).

DFAT, Department of Foreign Affairs and Trade, Australian Government (2006b) *Australia–China FTA negotiations – Fifth Round of Negotiations*, Subscriber update, June 2006. Available at http://www.dfat.gov.au/fta/china/060601_subscriber_update.html (accessed 17 December 2010).

DFAT, Department of Foreign Affairs and Trade, Australian Government (2006c) *Singapore–Australia Free Trade Agreement (SAFTA)*. Available at http://www.dfat.gov.au/trade/negotiations/australia_singapore_agreement.html (accessed 10 September 2006).

DFAT, Department of Foreign Affairs and Trade, Australian Government (2006d) *Thailand–Australia Free Trade Agreement (TAFTA)*. Available at http://www.dfat.gov.au/trade/negotiations/aust-thai/index.html (accessed 10 August 2006).

DFAT, Department of Foreign Affairs and Trade, Australian Government (2006e) *The Australia–United States Free Trade Agreement (AUSFTA) Advancing Australia's Non-Agricultural Exports*. Available at http://www.dfat.gov.au/trade/negotiations/us_fta/fact_sheets/Non_Ag.pdf (accessed 10 March 2006).

DFAT, Department of Foreign Affairs and Trade, Australian Government (2006f) *APEC Progress on Tariffs: Implications for a New Agenda*. Available at http://www.dfat.gov.au/apec/reports/tariffs.pdf (accessed 17 September 2006).

DFAT, Department of Foreign Affairs and Trade, Australian Government (2010a) *Australia–China Free Trade Agreement Negotiations*. Available at http://www.dfat.gov.au/fta/china/index.html (accessed 3 November 2010).

DFAT, Department of Foreign Affairs and Trade, Australian Government (2010b) *Potential Benefits – Overview*. Available at http://www.dfat.gov.au/geo/china/fta/facts/overview.html (accessed 5 September 2010).

DFAT, Department of Foreign Affairs and Trade, Australian Government (2010c) *China – Fact Sheet*. Available at http://www.dfat.gov.au/geo/fs/chin.pdf (accessed 30 December 2010).

DFAT, Department of Foreign Affairs and Trade, Australian Government (2010d) *Australia–United States Free Trade Agreement*. Available at http://www.dfat.gov.au/trade/negotiations/us_fta/final-text/chapter_4.html (accessed 10 December 2010).

DFAT, Department of Foreign Affairs and Trade, Australian Government (2010e) *ASEAN–Australia–New Zealand Free Trade Agreement*. Available at http://www.dfat.gov.au/fta/aanzfta/index.html (accessed 10 December 2010).

DFAT, Department of Foreign Affairs and Trade, Australian Government (2010f) *Agreement Establishing the ASEAN–Australia–New Zealand Free Trade Area (AANZFTA) – Making Use of AANZFTA to Export or Import Goods*. Available at http://www.dfat.gov.au/fta/aanzfta/making_use_of_aanzfta.pdf (accessed 11 December 2010).

DFAT, Department of Foreign Affairs and Trade, Australian Government (2010g) *Australia–Chile Free Trade Agreement*. Available at http://www.dfat.gov.au/fta/aclfta/index.html (accessed 11 December 2010).

DFAT, Department of Foreign Affairs and Trade, Australian Government (2010h) *Australia–Chile Free Trade Agreement – Facts at a Glance*. Available at http://www.dfat.gov.au/fta/aclfta/facts_at_a_glance.html (accessed 12 December 2010).

DFAT, Department of Foreign Affairs and Trade, Australian Government (2010i) *Asia-Pacific Economic Cooperation (APEC)*. Available at http://www.dfat.gov.au/apec (accessed 10 December 2010).

DFAT, Department of Foreign Affairs and Trade, Australian Government (2010j) *Free Trade Agreements under Negotiation* Available at http://www.dfat.gov.au/fta/index.html (accessed 12 December 2010).

DIIRD, Department of Innovation, Industry and Regional Development, Australian Government (2006) *VicStart – Inform, Develop, Connect – Technology Commercialisation Initiative*. Available at http://www.business.vic.gov.au/busvicwr/_assets/main/lib60031/vicstart%20brochure%20aug06.pdf (accessed 29 December 2010).

DIISR, Department of Innovation, Industry, Science and Research, Australian Government (2010) *Textile, Clothing and Footwear Industries*. Available at http://www.innovation.gov.au/INDUSTRY/TEXTILESCLOTHINGANDFOOTWEAR/TCFINDUSTRIES/Pages/default.aspx (accessed 11 November 2010).

DiMaggio, P.L. and Powell, W.W. (1983) 'The iron cage revisited: Institutional isomorphism and collective rationality in organisational fields', *American Sociological Review*, 48: 147–160.

Dinsmore, C.P. (ed.) (1993) *The AMA Handbook of Project Management*, New York: American Management Association.

Disdier, A. and Mayer, T. (2004) 'How different is Europe? Structure and determinants of location choice by French firms in Eastern and Western Europe', *Journal of Comparative Economics*, 32(2): 280–296.

Dodd, C. (1998) *Dynamics of Intercultural Communication*, New York: McGraw Hill.

Dosi, G. (1982) 'Technological paradigms and technological trajectories', *Research Policy*, 11: 147–162.

Dosi, G. (1988) 'Sources, procedures and microeconomic effects of innovation', *Journal of Economic Literature*, 26: 1120–1171.

Dunfee, T.W. and Warren, D.E. (2001) 'Is Guanxi ethical? A normative analysis of doing business in China', *Journal of Business Ethics*, 32(3): 191–204.

Dunne, T. (2007) 'China's car exports scale up big time', *Bloomberg BusinessWeek*, 4 June. Available at http://www.businessweek.com/globalbiz/content/jun2007/gb20070604_816866.htm (accessed 15 January 2010).

Dunning, J.H. (1993) *Multinational Enterprises and the Global Economy*, Wokingham: Addison-Wesley.

Dunning, J.H. (1998) 'Location and multinational enterprises: A neglected factor?', *Journal of International Business Studies*, 29(1): 45–67.

Dunning, J.H. (2001) 'The eclectic (OLI) paradigm of international production: Past, present and future', *International Journal of the Economics of Business*, 8(2): 163–190.

Dunning, J.H. (2006) 'Towards a new paradigm of development: Implications for the developments of international business', *Transnational Corporation*, 15(1): 173–227.

Dunning, J.H. and Lundan, S. (2008) 'Institutions and the OLI paradigm of the multinational enterprise', *Asia Pacific Journal of Management*, 25(4): 573–593.

Eakeley, D. (1997) 'China is showing an interest in the rule of law', *The National Law Journal*, November 10, p. A23.

Eaton, J., and Kortum, S. (1999) 'International technology diffusion, theory and measurement', *International Economic Review*, 40:537–570.

Economy Watch (2010) 'Global economy China', in: *Economy Watch*, Economy, Investment and Finance Reports. Available at www.economywatch.com/world_economy/

world-economic-indicators/global-economy/global-economy-china.html (accessed 3 May 2010).

Eisenhardt, K.M. and Martin, J.A. (2000) 'Dynamic capabilities: what are they?', *Strategic Management Journal*, 21: 1105–1121.

EUbusiness Ltd. (2006) 'Mandelson talks IPR, as China clamours for "market economy status"'. Available at http://www.eubusiness.com/Trade/060607064719.qfia8wdr (accessed 15 November 2006).

Falk, M. (2006) 'What drives business R&D intensity across OECD countries?', *Applied Economics*, 38:533–547.

Fan, Y. (2002) 'Questioning guanxi: Definition, classification and implications', *International Business Review*, 11(5): 543–561.

Fare, R., Grosskopf, S. and Roos, P. (1995) 'Productivity and quality in Swedish pharmacies', *International Journal of Production Economics*, 39: 137–147.

Farrell, D., Gersch U. A. and Stephenson, E. (2006) 'The value of China's emerging middle class', *McKinsey Quarterly* (Special Edition): 60–69.

Ferdinand, J., Graca. M, Antonacopoulou, E. and Easterby-Smith, M. (2005) 'Dynamic capability: Tracking the development of a concept', EBK Working Paper 2005/09, Swindon: ESRC.

Fishman, T. (2005) *China, Inc.: How the Rise of the Next Superpower Challenges America and the World,* New York: Scribner.

FreeRepublic (1997) *The Case for Free Trade (Milton Friedman).* Available at http://www.freerepublic.com/focus/f-news/1154295/posts (accessed 25 October 2010).

Frisbie, J. (2006) *US-China Economic Relations Revisited,* Statement to the Senate Committee on Finance, 29 March 2006, US-China Business Council. Available at http://www.uschina.org/public/documents/2006/04/finance-committee-testimony.pdf (accessed 17 December 2010).

Furnham, A. (1987) 'The adjustment of sojourners', in: Y.Y. Kim and W.B. Gudykunst (eds), *Cross-cultural Adaptation*, Vol. XI of the International and Intercultural Communication Annual, Newbury Park, CA: Sage, p. 4261.

GAFTT, Global Alliance for Fair Textile Trade (2006) *The Istanbul Declaration*, GAFTT Report. Available at http://www.fairtextiletrade.org/istanbul/declaration.html (accessed 10 April 2006).

Gallini, N. (2002) 'The economics of patents: Lessons from recent U.S. patent reform', *Journal of Economic Perspectives*, 16: 131–154.

Gan, L. (2008) 'R&D plights of Chery in mid-grade and high-grade cars'. Available at http://www.waseda.jp/gsaps/gp/project2008/pdf/workshop2008_4.pdf (accessed 10 January 2010).

Gao, T. (2003) 'Ethic Chinese networks and international investment: Evidence from inward FDI in China', *Journal of Asian Economics,* 14: 611–629.

Gare, S. (1995) 'Slaves to fashion', *The Australian*, 13 May 1995.

Garnaut, R. (1996) *Open Regionalism and Trade Liberalization,* Singapore: Institute of Southeast Asian Studies.

Ginarte, J.C. and Park, W.G. (1997) 'Determinants of patent rights: A cross-national study', *Research Policy*, 26: 283–301.

Gleick, J. (1987) *Chaos: Making a New Science*, New York: Penguin Books.

Green, S. (2004) *China's Quest for Market Economy Status,* Royal Institute of International Affairs. Available at http://www.chathamhouse.org.uk/files/3168_bnmay04.pdf (accessed 10 December 2010).

Greenwood, J. and Mukoyama, E. (2001) 'The effect of income distribution on the timing of new product introduction', mimeo, University of Rochester, Rochester, NY.

Griffith, R., Redding, S. and van Reenen, J. (2004) 'Mapping the two faces of R&D: Productivity growth in a panel of OECD industries', *The Review of Economics and Statistics*, 86: 883–895.

Griliches, Z. (1979) 'Issues in assessing the contribution of research and development to productivity growth', *The Bell Journal of Economics*, 10: 92–116.

Griliches, Z. (1980) 'R&D and the productivity slowdown', *The American Economic Review*, 70: 343–348.

Griliches, Z. and Mairesse, J. (1990) 'R&D and productivity growth: Comparing Japanese and U.S. manufacturing firms', in: Charles R. Hulten (ed.), *National Bureau of Economic Research Studies in Income and Wealth* (Vol. 53), Chicago, IL: University of Chicago Press.

Grimm, C. and Smith, K. (1997) *Strategy as Action: Industry rivalry and coordination*, Cincinnati, OH, South-Western College Publishing.

Grosse, R. and Trevino, L. J. (1996) 'Foreign direct investment in the United States: An analysis by country of origin', *Journal of International Business Studies*, 27(1): 139–155.

Grosse, R. and Trevino, L. J. (2005) 'New institutional economics and FDI location in Central and Eastern Europe', *Management International Review*, 45(2): 123–145.

Grossman, G. M. and Helpman, E. (1991) *Innovation and Growth in the Global Economy*, Cambridge, MA: MIT Press.

Gudykunst, W.B. (1991) *Bridging Differences*, Newbury Park, CA: Sage.

Gudykunst, W.B. (1993) 'Toward a theory of effective interpersonal and intergroup communication: An anxiety/uncertainty management (AUM) perspective', in: R. Wiseman, R. and I. Koester (eds), *Intercultural Communication Competence*, Newbury Park, CA: Sage, pp. 33–71.

Gudykunst, W.B. and Hammer, M.R. (1983) 'Basic training design: Approaches to intercultural training', in: R.W. Brislin and D. Landis (eds), *Handbook of Intercultural Training* (Vol. 1), New York: Pergamon, pp. 118–154.

Gudykunst, W.B. and Kim, Y.Y. (1997) *Communicating with Strangers* (3rd edn), Boston, MA: McGraw Hill.

Gudykunst, W.B., Wiseman, R. and Hammer, M. (1977) 'Determinants of a sojourner's attitudinal satisfaction', in: B. Ruben (ed.), *Communication Yearbook 1*, New Brunswick, NJ: Transaction.

Guirdham, M. (1999) *Communicating across Cultures*. London: Macmillan Press.

Gupta, A. K. and Wang, H. (2009) 'Beijing Auto: Lucky to lose Opel', *Bloomberg BusinessWeek*. Available at http://www.businessweek.com/globalbiz/content/aug2009/gb2009089_714329.htm(accessed 15 December 2009).

Haley, G.T., Tan, C.T. and Haley, U.C. (1998) *New Asian Emperors, The Overseas Chinese, Their Strategies and Competitive Advantages*, Oxford: Butterworth-Heineman.

Hall, E. T. (1976) *Beyond Culture*, New York: Anchor Press.

Hameri, A.P. (1997) 'Project management in a long-term and global one-of a kind projects', *International Journal of Project Management*, 15: 251–257.

Hamilton, C. (2001) 'The case for fair trade', *Journal of Australian Political Economy*, 48: 61–72.

Han, Yu-xiong and Li, Huai-zu (2005) 'Quantitative analysis for intellectual property protection level of China', *Studies in Science of Science*, 3: 377–382.

Harris, P.R. and Moran, T.R. (1995) *Managing Cultural Differences*, Houston, TX: Gulf Publishing.

He, W. and Lyles, M. (2008) 'China's outward foreign direct investment', *Business Horizons*, 51: 485–491.

Helfat C.E. (2000) 'Guest editor's introduction to the special issue: The evolution of firm capabilities', *Strategic Management Journal*, 21(10–11): 955–960.

Helfat, C.E. and Peteraf, M.A. (2003) 'The dynamic resource-based view: Capability lifecycles', *Strategic Management Journal*, 24(10): 997–1010.

Heller, M. and Eisenberg, R. (1998) 'Can patents deter innovation? The anticommons in biomedical research', *Science*, 28: 698–701.

Heritage Foundation (2008) *Index of Economic Freedom 1995–2007*, Washington, DC: Heritage Foundation.

Hewstone, M. and Giles, H. (1986) 'Social groups and social stereotypes in inter-group communication: Review and model of intergroup communication breakdown', in: W. Gudykunst (ed.), *Intergroup Communication*, London: Edward Arnold.

Hill, C. (ed.) (2003) *International Business: Competing in the Global Marketplace* (4th edn), Boston, MA: McGraw-Hill Irwin.

Hirst, P. and Thompson, G. (1996) *Globalization in Question*, Cambridge: Polity Press.

Hitt, M.A., Tyler, B.B., Hardee, C. and Park, D. (1995) 'Understanding strategic intent in the global marketplace,' *The Academy of Management Executive*, 9(2): 12–19.

Hitt, M.A., Bierman, L., Shimizu, K. and Kochhar, R. (2001) 'Direct and moderating effects on human capital on strategy and performance in professional firms: A resource-based perspective', *Academy of Management Journal*, 44(1): 13–28.

Ho, Simon S.M. (2003) *Corporate Governance in China: Key Problems and Prospects*, Hong Kong: The Chinese University Press.

Hodgetts, R.M. and Luthans, F. (2000) *International Management*, New York: McGraw-Hill Inc.

Hofstede, G. (1983) 'The cultural relativity of organisational practices and theories', *Journal of International Business Studies*, 14(2): 75–89.

Hofstede, G. (1991) *Cultures and Organisations: Software of the mind*, London: McGraw-Hill.

Hofstede, G. (2001) *Cultural Consequences: Comparing Values, Behaviours, Institutions and Organisations across Nations*. Beverly Hills, CA: Sage.

Hofstede, G. (2005) *Cultures and Organisations: Software of the Mind* (2nd edn), New York: McGraw-Hill.

Hong, E. and Sun, L. (2006) 'Dynamics of internationalisation and outward investment: Chinese corporations' strategies', *The China Quarterly*, 187: 610–634.

Hoogvelt, A. (2001) *Globalization and the Postcolonial World – The New Political Economy of Development Second Edition*, London: Palgrave.

Horstmann, I., Macdonald, J. and Slivinski, A. (1985) 'Patents as information transfer mechanisms: To patent or (maybe) not to patent', *Journal of Political Economy*, 93(5): 837–858.

Hoskisson, R., Eden, L., Lau, C.M. and Wright, M. (2000) 'Strategies in emerging economies', *Academy of Management Journal*, 43(3): 249–269.

Hsiao, C. (2003) *Analysis of Panel Data* (2nd edn), New York: Cambridge University Press.

Hua, C. (2005) *China, Chile warm to FTA*, in: bilaterals.org – everything that's not happening at the WTO releases 2005. Available at http://www.bilaterals.org/spip.php?article1973&lang=en (accessed 8 October 2010).

Huang, H.E. and Orr, G. (2007) 'China's stated owned enterprises: Board governance and the Communist Party', *Mckinsey Quarterly*, February: 108–111.

Hughes-Wiener, G. (1986) 'The "learning how to learn" approach to intercultural orientation', *International Journal of Intercultural Relations*, 10: 485–505.

Hung, Y. (1997) 'Response to risks in the property investment in China', *Proc., Int. Symp. on Marketization of Land and Housing in Socialist China*, Hong Kong: Hong Kong Baptist University, pp. 1–6.

Hunt, R.M. (2006) 'When do patents reduce R&D?', *American Economic Review, Papers and Proceedings*, 96: 87–91.

IAMAW, International Association of Machinists and Aerospace Workers (2005) 'China dolls', *IAM Journal*, 11(1): 8–23.

IFBWW, International Federation of Building and Wood Workers (2001) *The International Federation of Building and Wood Workers (IFBWW)*. Available at http://home.iprolink.ch/fitbb/index.html (accessed 20 March 2006).

Iles, P.H. and Paromjit K. (1997) 'Managing diversity in transnational project teams', *Journal of Managerial Psychology*, 12(2): 95–117.

IMD International and World Economic Forum (1995–2007) *IMD World Competitiveness Yearbooks, 1995–2007,* Geneva: The Foundation, various volumes.

IMF, International Monetary Fund (2000) *Globalization: Threat or Opportunity?,* IMF issues brief 00/01. Available at http://www.imf.org/external/np/exr/ib/2000/041200to.htm (accessed 21 October 2010).

Industry Commission (1997) *The Textiles, Clothing and Footwear Industries*, Industry Commission Report No. 59, Industry Commission, Commonwealth of Australia, September 1997. Available at http://www.pc.gov.au/ic/inquiry/59tcf/inquiry_documents/finalreport/59tcf1.pdf (accessed 20 December 2010).

Ingrassia, P. (2010) *Crash Course: The American Automobile Industry's Road from Glory to Disaster*, New York: Random House.

Interfax Information Service (2005) 'Iron ore price negotiations mired by Chinese government involvement'. Available at http://www.interfax.cn/showfeature.asp?aid=11305&slug=IRON%20ORE (accessed 1 June 2006).

International Labour Organisation (2008) *Labour Statistics Database 2008*. Available at http://www1.unece.org/stat/platform/display/DISA/1.2+Labour+%28ILO%29 (accessed 17 June 2009).

International Monetary Fund Report (2007) *IMF World Economic Outlook Database October 2007* Available at http://www.imf.org/external/pubs/ft/weo/2007/02/weodata/index.aspx

J. D. Power and Associates (2010) 'China Automotive Monthly: Market Trends' (January), unpublished report.

Jackson, S.E. (1992) 'Team composition in organizational settings: Issues in managing an increasingly diverse workforce', in: S. Worchel, W. Wood And J.A. Simpson (eds), *Group Process and Productivity*, Newbury Park, CA: Sage, pp. 138–176.

Jackson, T. (1993) *Organizational Behavior in International Management,* London: Butterworth Heinemann.

Jaffe, A. (1988) 'Technological opportunity and spillovers of R&D: Evidence from firms' patents, profits, and market value', *American Economic Review*, 76: 984–1001.

Jaffe, A. (2000) 'The U.S. patent system in transition: Policy innovation and the innovation process', *Research Policy*, 29: 531–558.

Jakob B.M. and Damania, R. (2001) 'Labour demand and wage-induced innovation: Evidence from the OECD countries', *International Review of Applied Economics*, 15: 323–334.

Jiang D.C. (2004) 'Transnational Corporation's influences on R&D ability of Chinese enterprises: A model analysis', *Nankai Economic Studies*, 4: 62–66.

Jiang, F. (2006) 'The determinants of the effectiveness of foreign direct investment in China: An empirical study of joint and sole ventures', *International Journal of Management*, 23(4): 891–908.

Johanson, J. and Vahlne, J.E. (1977) 'The internationalization process of the firm – A model of knowledge development and increasing foreign market commitments', *Journal of International Business Studies*, 8(1): 23–32.

Johanson, J. and Wiedersheim-Paul, F. (1975) 'The internationalization of the firm: Four Swedish cases', *Journal of Management Studies*, 12(3): 305–322.

Johns, T.G. (1999a) 'Managing the behavior of people working in teams: Applying the project management method', *International Journal of Project Management,* 13(1): 33–38.

Johns, T.G. (1999b) 'On creating organizational support for the project management method', *International Journal of Project Management,* 17: 47–53.

Jones, C.I. (1995) *R&D-Based Models of Economic Growth*, Chicago, IL: University of Chicago Press.

Judd, K. (1985) 'On the performance of patents', *Econometrica*, 53: 567–585.

Kahn, W.A. (1993) 'Facilitating and undermining organizational change: A case study', *Journal of Applied Behavioral Science*, 29(1): 32–55.

Kan-Softek Solutions Pvt. Ltd (2005) 'CHINA: China grabs 74 per cent of EU import market'. Available at http://www.bharattextile.com/newsitems/1999303 (accessed 10 April 2006).

Kanwar, S. and Evenson, R.E. (2003) 'Does intellectual property protection spur technological change?', *Oxford Economic Papers*, 55: 235–264.

Kealey, D.J. and Ruben, B.D. (1983) 'Cross-cultural personnel selection: Criteria, issues and methods', in: D. Landis and R. Brislin (eds), *Handbook of Intercultural Training* (Vol. 1), New York: Pergamon, pp. 155–175.

Keller, W. (2002) 'Trade and the transmission technology', *Journal of Economic Growth*, 7: 5–24.

Kerzner, H. (1998) *Project Management: A Systems Approach to Planning, Scheduling and Controlling*, New York: John Wiley and Sons.

Khanna, P. (2009) *The Second World: How Emerging Powers are Redefining Global Competition in the Twenty-First Century*, New York: Random House.

Kiley, D. (2007) 'Hyundai still gets no respect', *BusinessWeek*, 21 May: 68–70.

Kindleberger, C. (1969) *American Business Abroad,* New Haven, CT: Yale University Press.

Kogut, B. and Singh, H. (1988) 'The effects of national culture on the choice of entry mode', *Journal of International Business Studies,* 19(3): 411–432.

Kostova, T. and Zaheer, S. (1999) 'Organisational legitimacy under conditions of complexity: The case of the multinational enterprise', *Academy of Management Review,* 24(1): 64–81.

Learned, E.P., Christensen, C.R., Andrews, K. and Guth, W.D. (1965) *Business Policy*, Homewood, IL: Irwin.

Lederman, D. and Maloney, W.F. (2003) 'R&D and development', World Bank Policy Research Working Paper 3024.

Lee, C., Fujimoto, T. and Chen, J. (2002) 'The impact of globalization on the Chinese automobile industry: Policy assessments and typology of strategies', *Actes du GERPISA* (Groupe d' Etudes et de Recherches Permanent sur l'Industrie et les Salariés de l'Automobile), No. 34 (October): 89–97. Available at http://www.gerpisa.univ-evry.fr/ (accessed 20 January 2010).

Lee, C.Y. (2003) 'Firm density and industry R&D intensity: Theory and evidence', *Review of Industrial Organization*, 22: 139–158.

Lerner, J. (2002) 'Patent protection and innovation over 150 years', National Bureau of Economic Research (NBER) Working Paper W8977.

Lewis, R. (1996) 'Take the 'big' out of big projects: Break them into manageable chunks', *Infoworld,* 18(20): 24.

Li, P. (2006) 'The path and pattern of international technology transfer', *Journal of World Economy,* 29: 85–93.

Li, S. (2005) 'Why a poor governance environment does not deter foreign direct investment: The case of China and its implications for investment protection', *Business Horizons,* 48(2): 297–302.

Li, S. and Filer, L. (2004) 'Governance environment and mode of investment', paper presented at the Academy of International Business Annual Meeting, July 10–13, Stockholm, Sweden.

Li, Y., Sun, Y.-F. and Liu, Y. (2006) 'An empirical study of SOEs' market orientation in transitional China', *Asia Pacific Journal of Management,* 23(1): 93–113.

Lianfa Textile Co., Ltd (2010) *Brief Introduction of Jiangsu Lianfa Textiles Co.Ltd,* Jiangsu Lianfa Textile Co., Ltd. Available at http://www.js-lianfa.com/en/gywm. aspx?id=2 (accessed 17 December 2010).

Lim, D.S. and Mohamed, M.Z. (1999) 'Criteria of project success: An exploratory re-examination', *International Journal of Project Management,* 17(4): 243–248.

Lin, C. (2001) 'Corporatisation and corporate governance in China's economic transition', *Economics of Planning,* 34: 5–35.

Lin, J.Y. (2003) *Economic Theory and Economic Reform in China: Neo-Classical Economics vs. Neo-Socialist Economics?* Los Angeles, CA: UCLA International Institute.

Lin, J.Y., Tao, R. and Liu, M. (2006) 'Decentralization and local governance in China's economic transition', in: Pranab Bardhan and Dilip Mookherjee (eds), *Decentralization and Local Governance in Developing Countries: A Comparative Perspective,* Cambridge, MA: MIT Press, pp. 305–328.

Lin, Y. (2001) *Between Politics and Markets: Firms, Competition, and Institutional Change in Post-Mao China,* New York: Cambridge University Press.

Liu, H. and Li, K. (2002) 'Strategic implications of emerging Chinese multinationals: The Haier case study', *European Management Journal,* 20(6): 699–706.

Liu, H., Buck, T. and Shu, C. (2005) 'Chinese economic development, the next stage: Outward FDI?', *International Business Review,* 14(1): 97–115.

Liu, Q. (2006) *Corporate Governance in China: Current Practices, Economic Effects and Institutional Determinants,* CESifo Economic Studies Advance Access published April 24, pp. 1–39.

Liu, X.M., Romilly, P., Song, H.Y. and Wei, Y.Q. (1997) 'Country characteristics and foreign direct investment in China: A panel data analysis', *Weltwirtschaftliches Archiv,* 133(2): 313–329.

Luo, Y. (1995) 'Business strategy, market structure, and performance of international joint ventures: The case of joint ventures in China', *Management International Review,* 35(3): 241–265.

Luo, Y. and O'Connor, N. (1998) 'Structural change to foreign direct investment in China: An evolutionary perspective', *Journal of Applied Management Studies,* 7(1): 95–109.

Luo, Y. and Tung, R.L. (2007) 'International expansion of emerging market enterprises: A springboard perspective', *Journal of International Business Studies,* 38: 481–498.

Lustig, M. and Koester, I. (1993) *Intercultural Competence: Interpersonal Communication Across Cultures.* New York: Harper Collins.

Lysgaard, S. (1955)'Adjustment in a foreign society', *International Social Science,* 7(1): 45–51.

Ma, R., Wu, X. and Zheng, S. (2006) 'The evolution of technological capabilities at Chery Automobile: A dynamic resource-based analysis', paper presented at International Conference on Management Science and Engineering (ICMSE). Conference Proceedings, pp. 1761–1766. Available at http://ieeexplore.ieee.org/xpl/mostRecentIssue.jsp?punumber=4094461 (accessed 20 January 2010).

McCarthy, D. and Puffer, S. (1995) '"Diamonds and rust" on Russia's road to privatization', *Columbia Journal of World Business*, Fall: 56–69.

Mahbubani, K. (2008) *The New Asian Hemisphere: The Irresistible Shift of Global Power to the East*, New York: Public Affairs.

Mallin, C.A. (2004) *Corporate Governance*, Oxford: Oxford University Press.

Maloney, W.F. and Rodriguez-Clare, A. (2007) 'Innovation shortfalls', *Review of Development Economics*, 11: 665–684.

Markusen, J.R. (1983) 'Factor movements and commodity trade as complements', *Journal of International Economics*, 13: 341–356.

Martin, J. and Nakayma, T. (1999) 'Thinking dialectically about culture and communication', *Communication Theory*, 9(1): 1–25.

Mercer Management Consulting (2005) 'Chinese automotive market 2010'. Available at http://www.altassets.net/private-equity-knowledge-bank/industry-focus/article/nz6592.html (accessed 23 January 2010).

Meredith, D. and Dyster, B. (1999) *Australia in the Global Economy: Continuity and Change*, Cambridge: Cambridge University Press.

Meredith, J. and Mantel, S.J. (2006) *Project Management: A Managerial approach* (6th edn), New York: Wiley & Sons.

Meyer, K., Estrin, S., Bhaumik, S. and Peng, M.W. (2009) 'Institutions, resources and new strategies in emerging economies', *Strategic Management Journal*, 30: 61–80.

Midler, P. (2009) *Poorly Made in China: An Insider's Account of the Tactics Behind China's Production Game*, Hoboken, NJ: Wiley.

Miller, J. (2007) 'Africa's new car dealer: China', *The Wall Street Journal*, 28 August, pp. B1–B2.

Moder, J.J. (1988) 'Network techniques in project management', in: D.I. Cleland and W.R. King (eds), *Project Management Handbook*, New York: Van Nostrand Reinhold, pp. 324–373.

MOFCOM, Ministry of Commerce (1996–2003) *Almanac of China's Foreign Economic Relations and Trade*, Beijing: Ministry of Commerce, People's Republic of China.

MOFCOM, Ministry of Commerce (2004–2008). *China Commercial Yearbook*, Beijing: Ministry of Commerce, People's Republic of China.

Moore, M. (2003) *'A World Without Walls – Freedom, Development, Free Trade and Global Governance'*, New York: Cambridge University Press.

Morck, R., Yeung, B. and Zhao, M. (2008) 'Perspectives on China's outward foreign direct investment', *Journal of International Business Studies*, 39(3): 337–350.

Morris, C. (1996) *Quantitative Approaches in Business Studies* (4th edn), London: Pitman Publishing.

Morrison, W.M. (2008) 'China's economic conditions', *Key Workplace Documents*, No. 499, New York: Cornell University.

Mukoyama, T. (2003) 'Innovation, imitation, and growth with cumulative technology', *Journal of Monetary Economics*, 50: 361–380.

Mundell, R.A. (1957) 'International trade and factor mobility', *American Economic Review*, 47(3): 321–336.

Murphy, K., Shelifer, A. and Vishny, R. (1989) 'Income distribution, market size and industrialization', *Quarterly Journal of Economics*, 104: 537–564.

Murray, J.Y., Gao, G.Y., Kotabe, M. and Zhou, N. (2007) 'Assessing measurement invariance of export market orientation: A study of Chinese and non-Chinese firms in China', *Journal of International Marketing,* 15: 41–62.

Muzychenko, O. and Saee, J. (2004) 'Cross-cultural professional competence in higher education', *Journal of Management Systems*, 16(4): 1–20.

N.N. (2010) *Textile and Clothing Industry Cluster.* Available at http://jpkc.tjpu.edu.cn/2007/gjmysw/ckwx/Textile%20and%20Clothing%20Industry%20Cluster.pdf (accessed 15 December 2010).

National Bureau of Statistics (1996) *China Regional Economy: A Profile of Seventeen Years of Reform and Opening-Up*, Beijing: China Statistical Press.

National Bureau of Statistics (2007) *China Statistical Yearbook 2007*, Beijing: China Statistical Press.

Newbert, S.L. (2007) 'Empirical research on the resource-based view of the firm: An assessment and suggestions for future research', *Strategic Management Journal*, 28(2): 121–146.

Newman, K. (2000) 'Organizational transformation during institutional upheaval', *Academy of Management Review*, 25: 602–619.

Ng, L.F. and Tuan, C. (2002) 'Building a favourable investment environment: Evidence for the facilitation of FDI in China', *The World Economy,* 25(8): 1095–1114.

Nonaka, I. and Takeuchi, H. (1995) *The Knowledge-Creating Company*, New York: Oxford University Press.

North, D.C. (1990) *Institutions, Institutional Change and Economic Performance*, New York: Cambridge University Press.

NZMFAT, New Zealand's Ministry of Foreign Affairs and Trade (2010) *The Agreement.* Available at http://www.chinafta.govt.nz/1-The-agreement/index.php (accessed 29 December 2010).

Oberg, K. (1960) 'Cultural shock: Adjustments to new cultural environments', *Practical Anthropology*, 7: 177–182.

OECD (2004) *Science and Technology Statistical Compendium 2004,* Paris: OECD, p. 16.

Oliver, C. (1996) 'The institutional embeddedness of economic activity', in: J.A. Banm and J.E. Dutton (eds), *Advances in Strategic Management* (Vol. 13), Greenwich, CT: JAI Press, pp. 162–186.

Osborn, A. (2007) 'Crash course in quality for Chinese cars – Chery's hot-selling Amulet crumples in a Russian test, raising broad safety issue', *The Wall Street Journal*, 8 August, p. B1.

PACIA, Plastics and Chemicals Industries Association (2004) *Feasibility Study on an Australia China Free Trade Agreement – China – Market Economy Status – Implications for Anti-Dumping Remedies*, Supplementary Submission to the Department of Foreign Affairs & Trade. Available at http://www.pacia.org.au/_uploaditems/docs/10.china_fta_sup.pdf (accessed 14 May 2006).

Pajunen, K. (2008) 'Institutions and inflows of foreign direct investment: A fuzzy-set analysis', *Journal of International Business Studies,* 39: 652–669.

Papageorgiou, C. (2003) 'Imitation in non-scale R&D growth model', *Economics Letters*, 80: 287–294.

Pardu, W. (1996) 'Managing change in a project environment', *CMA Magazine*, May.

Park, W.G. and Ginarte, J.C. (1997) 'Intellectual property rights and economic growth', *Contemporary Economic Policy*, 15: 51–61.

Parry, S. (1998) 'Just what is a competency?', *Training,* (June): 58–64.

Pavitt, Keith L.R. (2001) 'Public policies to support basic research: What can the Rest of the World learn from US theory and practice? (And what they should learn)', *Industrial and Corporate Change*, 10: 761–779.

Pearce, W.P. and Kang, K. (1987) 'Conceptual migrations, understanding "Travelers Tales" for crosscultural adaptation', in: Y.Y. Kim and W.B. Gudykunst (eds), *Cross-Cultural Adaptation,* Vol. XI of the International and Intercultural Communication Annual, Newbury Park, CA: Sage, pp. 20–41.

Pei, M. (2007) 'Corruption threatens China's future', Carnegie Endowment for International Peace, 55: 1–8. Available at http://www.carnegieendowment.org/files/pb55_pei_china_corruption_final.pdf (accessed 4 February 2009).

Peng, M.W. (2004) 'Identifying the big question in international business research', *Journal of International Business Studies*, 35(2): 99–108.

Peng, M.W. and Delios, A. (2006) 'What determines the scope of the firm over time and around the world?', *Asia-Pacific Journal of Management*, 24: 385–405.

Peng, M.W., Wang, D.Y.L. and Jiang, Y. (2008) 'An institution-based view of international business strategy: A focus on emerging economies', *Journal of International Business Studies*, 39(5): 920–936.

People's Daily Online (2006) 'Investment into China records 8% rise'. Available at http://english.people.com.cn/200603/14/eng20060314_250433.html (accessed 5 November 2010).

Perez-Sebastian, F. (1999) 'Transitional dynamics in an R&D-based growth model with imitation: Comparing its predictions to the data', *Journal of Monetary Economics*, 45: 437–461.

Perkowski, J. (2006) 'The coming China car boom', *Far Eastern Economic Review* (April): 23–26.

Pestana, B. (1996). *Textiles & Apparel of Australia*, Morescope Publishing Pty Ltd, Victoria.

Peters, T. (1994) *The Tom Peter Seminar*, New York: Random House.

Pfeiffer, J. (1994) *Competitive Advantage through People,* Boston, MA: Harvard Business School Press.

Pinto, J.K. and Slevin, D.P. (1987) 'Critical success factors in successful project implementation', *IEEE Transactions on Engineering Management*, 3(1): 22–28.

Poon, L. (n.d.) *The People's Republic of China,* History of China. Available at http://www-chaos.umd.edu/history/prc.html#prc (accessed 21 November 2010).

Poston, D., Mao, M.X. and Yu, M. (1994) 'The global distribution of the overseas Chinese around 1990', *Population and Development Review,* 20(3): 631–645.

Prestowitz, C.V. (2005) *Three Billion New Capitalists: The Great Shift of Wealth and Power to the East*, New York: Basic Books.

Productivity Commission, Australian Government (2008) *Modelling Economy-wide Effects of Future TCF Assistance*, Productivity Commission Research Report. Available at http://www.pc.gov.au/__data/assets/pdf_file/0003/81777/tcf-assistance-modelling.pdf (accessed 17 December 2010).

Qian, G., Li, L., Li, J. and Qian, Z. (2008) 'Regional diversification and firm performance', *Journal of International Business Studies,* 39: 197–214.

Rauch, J. and Trindade, V. (2002) 'Ethnic Chinese networks in international trade', *The Review of Economics and Statistics,* 84(1): 116–130.

Reinthaler, V. and Wolff, G.B. (2004) 'The effectiveness of subsidies revisited: Accounting for wage and employment effects in business R&D', ZEI Working Paper, No. B21, Center for European Integration Studies, University of Bonn.

Reto F. and Zweimuller, J. (2006) 'Income distribution and demand-induced innovations', *Review of Economic Studies*, 73: 941–960.

Richet, X. and Ruet, J. (2008) 'The Chinese and Indian automobile industry in perspective: Technology appropriation, catching-up and development', *Transition Studies Review*, 15(3): 447–465.

Richter, F.-J. (1999) *Business Networks in Asia, Promises, Doubts, and Perspectives*, Westport CT: Quorum Books.

Roberts, H.M. (2007) *Project Management Book*. Available at http://www.hraconsulting-ltd.co.uk/project-management-book-0101.htm (accessed July 20, 2009).

Robinson, R.D. (1978) *International Business Management: A Guide to decision* (2nd edn), Hinsdale, IL: The Dryden Press.

Romer, P.M. (1990) 'Endogenous technological change', *Journal of Political Economy*, 98: 71–102.

Rosenau, M.D., Jr. (1984) *Project Management for Engineers*, New York: Van Nostrand Reinhold.

Rosenberg, N. (1974) 'Science, invention and economic growth', *Economic Journal*, 3: 51–77.

Ruben, B.D. and Kealey, D.J. (1979) 'Behavioral assessment of communication competency and the prediction of crosscultural adaptation', *International Journal of Intercultural Relations*, 3: 15–47.

Rugman, A.M. (2005) *The Regional Multinationals,* Cambridge: Cambridge University Press.

Rugman, A.M. and Li, J. (2007) 'Will China's multinationals succeed globally or regionally?', *European Management Journal,* 25(5): 333–343.

Rui, H. and Yip, G. S. (2008) 'Foreign acquisitions by Chinese firms: A strategic intent perspective', *Journal of World Business* 43(2): 213–226.

Rumelt, R.P., Schendel, D. and Teece, D.J. (1994) *Fundamental Issues in Strategy: A Research Agenda*, Boston, MA: Harvard Business School Press.

Russo, W. (2009) *The Path to Globalization of China's Automotive Industry*. Available at http://www.glgroup.com/News/The-Path-to-Globalization-of-Chinas-Automotive-Industry-39128.html (accessed 7 January, 2011).

Saee, J. (2005) *Managing Organizations in a Global Economy*, Mason, OH: Thomson South-Western.

Saee, J. (2006) *Managerial Competence within the Hospitality and Tourism Service Industries: Global Contextual Analysis*, New York: Routledge.

Saee, J. (2007) *Contemporary Corporate Strategy: Global Perspectives,* New York: Routledge.

Samovar, L.A. and Porter, R.E. (eds) (1994*) Intercultural Communication: A Reader* (7th edn), Belmont, CA: Wadsworth.

Samuelson, R.J. (2010) 'China's $2.4 trillion grip on the global economy', *Washington Post*, 25 January.

Sanford, J. (2005) 'Beat China on costs', *Canadian Business*, 78(22): 51–59.

Satya, J.G. (1998) *Restructuring State-owned Enterprises in China*. Available at http://www.mtholyoke.edu/courses/sgabriel/soe.htm (accessed 12 December 2010).

Scherer, F.M. (1982) 'Demand-pull and technological invention: Schmookler revisited', *Journal of Industrial Economics*, 30: 225–237.

Schmookler, J. (1966) *Invention and Economic Growth*, Cambridge, MA: Harvard University Press.

Scott, W.R. (2001) *Institution and Organisation* (2nd edn), London: Sage Publications.

Sebenius J.K. and Qian, C. (2008) 'Cultural notes on Chinese negotiating behavior', Working Paper -09-076, Harvard Business School.

Sethi, D., Guisinger, S.E., Phelan, S.E. and Berg, D.M. (2003) 'Trends in foreign direct investment flows: A theoretical and empirical analysis', *Journal of International Business Studies*, 34: 315–326.

Sethi, D., Guisinger, S., Ford, D.L. and Phelan, S.E. (2002) 'Seeking greener pastures: A theoretical and empirical investigation into the changing trend of foreign direct investment flows in response to institutional and strategic factors', *International Business Review,* 11: 685–705.

Shapiro, C. (2000) 'Navigating the patent thicket: Cross licenses, patent pools, and standard setting', in: A. Jaffe, J. Lerner and S. Stern (eds), *Innovation Policy and the Economy* (Vol. 1), Cambridge, MA: National Bureau of Economic Research and MIT Press.

Shen L.Y., Wu, G.W.C. and Ng, C.S.K. (2001) 'Risk assessment for construction joint ventures in China', *Journal of Construction Engineering and Management*, (January/February): 76–81.

Sheth, J.N. and Sisodia, R.S. (2006) *Tectonic Shift: The Geoeconomic Realignment of Globalizing Markets*, Thousand Oaks, CA: Response Books.

Shirouzu, N. (2009a) 'Hollywood beckons China's BYD', *The Wall Street Journal Asia*, 10 December, p. 19.

Shirouzu, N. (2009b) 'BYD of China aims to sell electric car in U.S. next year', *The Wall Street Journal Europe*, 24 August, p. 7.

Shirouzu, N. (2009c) 'China's auto industry to consolidate', *The Wall Street Journal*, 5 February, p. B1.

Shirouzu, N. (2010) 'Car makers face cooldown in China market', *The Wall Street Journal*, 6 January, p. B1.

SIMIC, Shanghai International Maritime Information Center, 上海国际海事信息与文献网) (2007) '中国汽车出口情况简析,' 12 January. Available at http://www.simic.net.cn/news/detail.jsp?id=7537 (accessed 27 January 2010).

Simpfendorfer, B. (2009) *The New Silk Road: How a Rising Arab World is Turning Away from the West and Rediscovering China*, New York: Palgrave Macmillan.

Simpkins, J. (2009) 'Financial crisis gives Chinese car companies a chance to get up to speed', *Money Morning*, 24 September. Available at http://moneymorning.com/2009/09/24/chinese-car-companies/ (accessed on 28 January 2010).

Slack, N., Chambers, S. and Johnston, R. (2001) *Operations Management* (3rd edn), Harlow: UK Pearson Education Limited.

Slevin, D.P. and Covin, J.G. (1997) 'Time, growth, complexity, and transitions: Entrepreneurial challenges for the future', *Journal of Entrepreneurship: Theory and Practice*, 22(2): 43–68.

Smith, K.G., Grimm, C.M., Chen, M.J. and Gannon, M.J. (1989) 'Predictors of competitive strategic actions: Theory and preliminary evidence', *Journal of Business Research*, 18: 245–258.

Smith, K.G., Grimm, C.M., Gannon, M.J. and Chen, M.-J. (1991) 'Organizational information processing, competitive responses and performance in the U.S. domestic airline industry', *Academy of Management Journal*, 34: 60–85.

Smith, K.G., Grimm, C.M. and Gannon, M.J. (1992) *Dynamics of Competitive Strategy*, Newsbury Park: CA: Sage Publications.

Smith, L.A. and Haar, J. (1993) 'Managing international projects', in: P.C. Dinsmore (ed), *AMA Handbook of Project Management*, New York: American Management Association, pp. 441–448.

Snell, S.A., Davison, S.C., Hamrick, D.C. and Snow, C.C. (1993) 'Human resource challenges in the development of transnational teams', Working Paper, International Consortium for Executive Development Research, Lexington, MA.

Snow, C.C., Davison, S.C., Snell, S.A. and Hambrick, D.C. (1996) 'Use transnational teams to globalize your company', *Organizational Dynamics*, 24(4): 50–67.

Solow R. (1956) 'A contribution to the theory of economic growth', *Quarterly Journal of Economics*, 70: 65–94.

South Africa Good News (2009) 'Chinese car company to invest R660m in SA', 14 July. Available at http://www.sagoodnews.co.za/index2.php?option=com_content&do_pdf=1&id =2522 (accessed 30 January 2010).

SPC, State Planning Commission (1997) 'Regulation on the management of tax and fee items for the development of construction projects', Beijing: Beijing Real Estate No. 1, pp. 18–19.

Spitzberg, B. and Cupach, W. (1984) *Interpersonal Communication Competence,* Beverly Hills, CA: Sage.

SSBC, State Statistical Bureau of China (1996–2008) *China Statistical Yearbook 1996-2008.* Beijing: China Statistical Press.

Standifird, S. and Marshall, R. (2000) 'The transaction cost advantage of *guanxi*-based business practices', *Journal of World Business,* 35(1): 21–42.

Stark, J. (1992) *Engineering Information Management System: Beyond CAD/CAM to Concurrent Engineering*, New York: Van Nostrand Reinhold.

Stephan, W. and Stephan, C. (1996) *Intergroup Relations,* Boulder, CO: Westview Press.

Stewart, H. (2006) 'US-China trade war looms', Guardian Unlimited, 26 March. Available at http://observer.guardian.co.uk/business/story/0,,1739428,00.html (accessed 25 October 2010).

Stinchcombe, A.L. (1997) 'On the virtues of the old institution', *Annual Review of Sociology,* 23: 1–18.

Stoian, C. and Filippaios, F. (2008) 'Dunning's eclectic paradigm: A holistic, yet context specific framework for analysing the determinants of outward FDI evidence from international Greek investments', *International Business Review,* 17: 349–367.

Stoler, A. (2004) *Market Economy Status for China: Implications for Antidumping Protection in Australia*, Institute for International Business, Economics & Law Australia–China Business Council of South Australia. Available at http://www.iibel. adelaide.edu.au/speech/ACBCSA2809042.pdf (accessed 16 December 2010).

Suchman, M.C. (1995) 'Managing legitimacy: Strategic and institutional approaches', *Academy of Management Review,* 20: 571–610.

Sun, J. (2006) 'China: The next global auto power?', *Far Eastern Economic Review*, (March): 37–41.

Suranovic, S. (2004) *International Trade Theory and Policy – Overview.* Available at http://internationalecon.com/Trade/Tch40/T40-4.php (accessed 29 November 2010).

Sutex Co., Ltd (2010) *Brief Introduction (SUTEX Profile)*, Jiangsu Textile Industry (Group) Import & Export Co., Ltd (Sutex). Available at http://www.sutex.net.cn/en/ jianjie/ei.asp (accessed 17 November 2010).

Svetličič, M. (2003) 'Theoretical context of outward foreign direct investment from transition economies', in: M. Svetličič and M. Rojec (eds), *Facilitating Transition by Internationalization: Outward Direct Investment from European Economies in Transition*, Aldershot: Ashgate, pp. 3–28.

Swain, N.J. and Wang, Z. (1997) 'Determinants of inflow of foreign direct investment in Hungary and China: Time-series approach', *Journal of International Development*, 9(5): 695–726.

Switzer, P. (2004) 'Big gains for little firms in US deal' (ABXAUS0020041206e0c700032), 7 December, Factiva. Available at http://global.factiva.com.ezproxy.lib.swin.edu.au/en/ eSrch/ss_hl.asp (accessed 26 April 2005).

Tam, O.K. (2002) 'Ethical issues in the evolution of corporate governance in China', *Journal of Business Ethics,* 37(3): 303–320.

Taylor, A. (2010) 'Hyundai smokes the competition', *Fortune*, 18 January, pp. 62–71.

TCFUA, Textile, Clothing and Footwear Union of Australia (2005) *Why the TCFUA Opposes an Australian–China Free Trade Agreement*, Working Document, TCFUA National Council, 10–12 May. Available at http://www.tcfvic.org.au/China%20Free%20 Trade%20Agreement.pdf (accessed 18 December 2010).

Teece, D.J., Pisano, G. and Shuen, A. (1997) 'Dynamic capabilities and strategic management', *Strategic Management Journal*, 18: 509–533.

TFIA, The Council of Textile and Fashion Industries of Australia (2005a) *TFIA Newsletter*, May.

TFIA, The Council of Textile and Fashion Industries of Australia (2005b) *TFIA Newsletter*, October.

The Canberra Times (2004) *The Canberra Times News*. Available at http://global.factiva. com.ezproxy.lib.swin.edu.au/en/eSrch/ss_hl.asp (accessed 1 May 2005).

The Economist (2004) 'A new knot in textile trade', The Economist print edition, 16 December. Available at http://www.economist.com/finance/displaystory.cfm?story_ id=E1_PVDPRSP&CFID=90934486&CFTOKEN=4acb778-f9cdb4c2-6f7b-49b0- 9ac1-4f34d9c0a814 (accessed 19 December 2010).

The Economist (2005a) 'The great stitch-up', The Economist print edition, 26 May. Available at http://www.economist.com/business/displaystory.cfm?story_id=E1_QDTTDNP (accessed 19 December 2010).

The Economist (2005b) 'A knotty problem', The Economist print edition, 2 June. Available at http://www.economist.com/node/4034069?story_id=4034069 (accessed 19 November 2010).

The Economist (2006) 'Material fitness – Italian textiles and China', The Economist Newspaper, 23 February. Available at http://www.economist.com/node/5545480 (accessed 10 December 2010).

The Heritage Foundation (2010a) *Index of Economic Freedom 2010.* Available at http:// www.heritage.org/index/ (accessed 7 December 2010).

The Heritage Foundation (2010b) *Ranking the Countries.* Available at http://www.heritage.org/index/Ranking (accessed 7 December 2010).

The Istanbul Declaration Coalition (2005) *Global Alliance Praises U.S.–China Textile Bilateral Deal Will Save Millions of Jobs Worldwide*, The Istanbul Declaration Coalition – Trade Groups from more than 50 countries supporting fair trade for textiles and clothing, press statement. Available at http://www.itkibusa.org/ Geneva-November2005/GAFTT--US%20China%20Bilateral%20Nov8%20London-- PressStatement--nov10.pdf (accessed 25 November 2010).

Thom, W. (2009) *The Corporate Advantages of a Project Management Process*. Available at http://www.pmhut.com/the-corporateadvantages-of-a-project-management-process (accessed 20 July 2009).

Timm, P.R. (1989) *Managerial Communication*, Englewood Cliffs, NJ: Prentice-Hall.

Treadstone (2010) *TCF Strategic Investment Scheme (SIP) Post 2005*, Treadstone–Government Grants & Business Development. available at http://www.treadstone.com.au/tcf-strategic- investment-scheme-sip-post-2005/ (accessed 15 December 2010).

Trevino, L. Thomas, D. and Cullen, J. (2008) 'The three pillars of institutional theory and FDI in Latin America: An institutionalisation process', *International Business Review*, 17: 118–133.

Triandis, H.C. (1994) *Culture and Social Behavior*, New York: McGraw-Hill.

Tubbs, S.L. and Moss, S. (1987) *Human Communication*, New York: Random House.

UNCTAD, United Nations Conference on Trade and Development (2001) *World Investment Report 2001: Promoting Linkages*. Available at http://www.unctad.org/en/docs/ wir2001_en.pdf (accessed 16 December 2006).

UNCTAD, United Nations Conference on Trade and Development (2004) *World Investment Report 2004: The Shift towards Services*. Available at http://www.unctad.org/en/docs/wir2004_en.pdf (accessed 26 November 2010).

UNCTAD, United Nations Conference on Trade and Development (2005) *World Investment Report 2005: Transnational Corporations and the Internationalization of R&D*, Country Factsheet: China. Available at http://www.unctad.org/sections/dite_dir/docs/wir05_fs_cn_en.pdf (accessed 5 December 2010).

UNCTAD, United Nations Conference on Trade and Development (2006) *World Investment Report 2006: FDI from Developing and Transition Economies: Implications for Development*. Available at http://www.unctad.org/en/docs/wir2006_en.pdf (accessed 2 December 2010).

UNCTAD, United Nations Conference on Trade and Development (2008) *World Investment Report 2008: Multinational Corporations and the Infrastructure Challenge*. Available at http://www.unctad.org/en/docs/wir2008_en.pdf (accessed 5 February 2009).

UNCTAD, United Nations Conference on Trade and Development (2010) *World Investment Report 2010: Investing in a Low-Carbon Economy*. Available at http://www.unctad.org/en/docs/wir2010_en.pdf (accessed 3 December 2010).

Urata, S. (2002) 'Globalization and the growth in free trade agreements', *Asia-Pacific Review*, 9(1): 20–32. Available at http://unpan1.un.org/intradoc/groups/public/documents/APCITY/UNPAN014344.pdf (accessed 12 December 2010).

van Pottelsberghe de la Potterie, B. and Lichtenberg, F. (2001) 'Does foreign direct investment transfer technology across borders?', *Review of Economics and Statistics*, 83: 490–497.

Vaughan, H. (2008) 'Project management in China', *PM World Today*, February, X(II).

Venables, A.J. (1999) 'Fragmentation and multinational production', *European Economic Review*, 43: 935–945.

Vernon, R. (1966) 'International investment and international trade in the Product Cycle', *Quarterly Journal of Economics*, 80: 190–207.

von Zedtwitz, M. (2006) 'International R&D strategies in companies from developing countries: the case of China', in: UNCTAD (ed.), *Globalization of R&D and Developing Countries*, New York and Geneva: United Nations, pp. 117–140.

Webber, M. and Waller, S. (2001) *Refashioning the Rag Trade*, Sydney: UNSW Press, Sydney.

Wei, G. and Geng, M. (2008) 'Ownership structure and corporate governance in China: Some current issues', *Managerial Finance*, 34(12): 934–952.

Wei, Y. (2003) *Comparative Corporate Governance: A Chinese Perspective*, The Netherlands: Kluwer Law International.

Wei, Y. and Liu, X. (2001) *Foreign Direct Investment in China: Determinants and Impact*, Cheltenham: Edward Elgar.

Weiss, J.W. and Wysocki, R.K. (1992) *Five-Phase Project Management: A Practical Planning and Implementation Guide*, Reading, MA: Addison-Wesley.

Weldon, E. and Vanhonacker, W. (1999) 'Operating a foreign-invested enterprise in China: Challenges for managers and management researchers', *Journal of World Business*, 34(1): 94–107.

Wernerfelt, B. (1984) 'A resource-based view of the firm', *Strategic Management Journal*, 5(April–June): 171–180.

Whitley, R. and Czaban, L. (1998) 'Institutional transformation and enterprise change in an emergent capitalist economy: The case of Hungary', *Organization Studies*, 19(2): 259–280.

Wilhelm A.D. (1994) *The Chinese Negotiating Table*, Washington, DC: National Defense University Press.

Winter, S.G. (2003) 'Understanding dynamic capabilities', *Strategic Management Journal*, 24(10): 991–995.

Wolf, M. (2004) *Why Globalization Works*, New Haven, CT:Yale University Press.

World Bank (2008) *World Development Indicator 2008 (WDI)*, World Bank Database, December, Business & Economics Information Service (BEIS), University of Auckland.

World Bank Institute (2005) *Knowledge Assessment Methodology*. Available at http://info.worldbank.org/etools/kam2005/.

World Economic Forum (2010) *Global Competitiveness Report 2010–2011*. Available at http://www3.weforum.org/docs/WEF_GlobalCompetitivenessReport_2010-11.pdf (accessed 29 December 2010).

World Intellectual Property Organisation (2008) *Statistics on Patents*, December, Business & Economics Information Service (BEIS), University of Auckland.

WTO, World Trade Organization (2001) 'WTO successfully concludes negotiations on China's entry', press releases, No. 243. Available at http://www.wto.org/english/news_e/pres01_e/pr243_e.htm (accessed 19 December 2010).

WTO, World Trade Organization (2010a) *Tariffs*, World Trade Organization Report. Available at http://www.wto.org/english/tratop_e/tariffs_e/tariffs_e.htm (accessed 18 December 2010).

WTO, World Trade Organization (2010b) Press releases (Press/598) International Trade Statistics. Available at http://www.wto.org/english/news_e/pres10_e/pr598_e.htm (accessed 3 May 2011).

Wu, H.L. and Chen, C.H. (2001) 'An assessment of outward foreign direct investment from China's transitional economy', *Europe–Asia Studies*, 53(8): 1235–1254.

Wu, X. (2005) 'Corporate governance and corruption: A cross-country analysis', *Journal of Policy, Administration, and Institutions*, 18: 151–170.

Wu, X. and Ding, W. (2009) 'Chinese firms' internationalization paths by strategic asset-seeking outward foreign direct investment', paper presented at the Portland International Conference on Management of Engineering & Technology (PICMET), Conference Proceedings, pp. 173–179. Available at http://ieeexplore.ieee.org/xpl/mostRecentIssue.jsp?punumber=5230479 (accessed 21 January 2010).

Xie, K., Du J. and Peng H. (2008) 'Perspectives to independent innovation in Chinese automobile companies', paper presented at the 5th International Conference on Innovation and Management (ICIM 2008), Maastricht, the Netherlands, December 10–11.

Xinhua (2007a) 'Chinese cars win increasing buyers in M.E., N. Africa markets', 26 December. Cited in *The Financial Express*. Available at http://www.thefinancialexpress-bd.com/more.php?news_id=20918 (accessed 28 January 2010).

Xinhua (2007b) 'Great potential for Chinese cars in Egypt, North Africa', 16 December. Cited by the Ministry of Commerce, People's Republic of China. Available at http://hzs2.mofcom.gov.cn/aarticle/workaffair/200712/20071205287057.html (accessed 28 January 2010).

Xinhua (2009) 'China's car makers urged to learn from U.S. crisis by "thinking small"', 3 January. Available at http://news.stonebtb.com/Global_Trade/15570-China-s-car-makers-urged-to-learn-from-U-S-crisis-by-thinking-small-.shtml (accessed 28 January 2010).

Yang, X., Jiang, Y., Kang, R. and Ke, Y. (2009) 'A comparative analysis of the internationalization of Chinese and Japanese firms', *Asia Pacific Journal of Management*, 26(1): 141–162.

Yasin, M.M. (2000) 'An empirical investigation of international project management practices: The role of international experience', *Project Management Journal*, 31(2): 20–30.

Yeung, H.W.-C. (1999) 'The internationalisation of ethics Chinese business firms from Southeast Asia: Strategies, processes and competitive advantages', *International Journal of Urban and Regional Research,* 23(1): 88–102.

Yeung, M.Y.I. and Tung, L.R. (1996) 'Achieving business success in Confucianism societies: The importance of guanxi (connections)', *Organizational Dynamics*, 25(2): 54–66.

Yi, Z., Zigang, Z., Xiaobo, M. and Shengjie, H. (2004) 'Determinants of structural change to sequential foreign direct investment across China: A synthesised approach', *Singapore Management Review*, 26(1): 63–80.

Yiu, D. and Makino, S. (2002) 'The choice between joint venture and wholly owned subsidiary: An institutional perspective', *Organisation Science,* 13(6): 667–683.

Youngor Group Co., Ltd (2008) *Group Overview*, Youngor Group Co, Ltd. Available at http://en.youngor.com/about.do?cid=200811070246144574 (accessed 18 December 2010).

YuLun Group Co., Ltd (2010) *About us*, Jiangsu YuLun Textile Group Co., Ltd. Available at http://www.chinayarn.com/mart/prod/corp_en.asp?id=1561 (accessed 17 December 2010).

Yunshi, M. and Jing, Y. (2005) 'Overseas investment trends change with times', *China Daily*, 11 October.

Zachariadis, M. (2004) 'R&D-induced growth in the OECD?', *Review of Development Economics*, 8: 423–439.

Zaheer, S. (1995) 'Overcoming the liability of foreignness', *Academy of Management Journal*, 38(2): 341–363.

Zajac, E. (1995) 'SMJ 1994 best paper prize to Birger Wernerfelt', *Strategic Management Journal*, 16: 169–170.

Zakaria, F. (2008) *The Post-American World*, New York: W.W. Norton.

Zeng, M. and Williamson, P.J. (2007) *Dragons at Your Door: How Chinese Cost Innovation Is Disrupting Global Competition*, Boston, MA: Harvard Business School Press.

Zhang, K.H. (2000) 'Why is U.S. direct investment in China so small?', *Contemporary Economic Policy*, 18(1): 82–94.

Zhang, K.H. (2001) 'How does foreign direct investment affect economic growth in China?', *Economics of Transition*, 9(3): 679–693.

Zhang, K.H. (2002) 'Why does China receive so much foreign direct investment?', *China & World Economy*, 3: 49–57.

Zhang, K.H. (2006) 'Does international investment help poverty reduction in China?', *The Chinese Economy*, 39(3): 79–90.

Zhang, K.H. and Song, S. (2000) 'Promoting exports: The role of inward FDI in China', *China Economic Review*, 11(4): 385–496.

Zhang, Y. (2003) *China's Emerging Global Businesses: Political Economy and Institutional Investigations*, New York: Palgrave Macmillan, p. 222.

Zheng, Y. (2007) *De Facto Federalism in China: Reforms and Dynamics of Central-Local Relations*, Hackensack, NJ: World Scientific.

Zhou, K.Z., Poppo, L. and Yang, Z. (2008) 'Relational ties or customised contracts? An examination of alternative governance choice in China', *Journal of International Business Studies,* 39: 526–534.

Zhou, L., Wu, W.-P. and Luo, X. (2007) 'Internationalization and the performance of born-global SMEs: The mediating role of social networks', *Journal of International Business Studies,* 38: 673–690.

Zhu, Q. (2008) 'Reorientation and prospect of China's combat against corruption', *Crime Law and Social Change*, 49(2): 81–95.

Zukin, S. and DiMaggio, P. (1990) *Structures of Capital: The Social Organisation of the Economy*, Cambridge: Cambridge University Press.

Zweimuller, J. (2000) 'Schumpetererian entrepreneurs meet Engel's Law: The impact of inequality on innovation driven growth', *Journal of Economic Growth*, 5: 185–206.

Index